RELOCATING IDENTITIES
IN LATIN AMERICAN CULTURES

RELOCATING
identities IN LATIN AMERICAN CULTURES

edited by Elizabeth Montes Garcés

This book is part of the
Turning Points: Occasional Papers
in Latin America Studies Series.
ISSN 1716-9429

UNIVERSITY OF
CALGARY
PRESS

© 2007 Elizabeth Montes Garcés
Published by the University of Calgary Press
2500 University Drive NW
Calgary, Alberta, Canada T2N 1N4
www.uofcpress.com

Library and Archives Canada Cataloguing in Publication

Relocating identities in Latin American cultures / edited by Elizabeth Montes Garcés.

(Turning points : occasional papers in Latin American studies ; v. 2)
Includes bibliographical references and index.

ISBN 978-1-55238-209-7

1. Latin American literature—20th century—History and criticism.
2. Identity (Psychology) in literature. 3. Identity (Psychology)—Latin America. 4. Social change in literature. 5. Social change—Latin America.

I. Montes Garcés, Elizabeth, 1962- II. Series.

PQ7081.A1R316 2007   860.9'358098   C2006-906588-8

We acknowledge the financial support of the Government of Canada, through the Book Publishing Industry Development Program (BPIDP), and the Alberta Foundation for the Arts for our publishing activities. We acknowledge the support of the Canada Council for the Arts for our publishing program.

Printed and bound in Canada by AGMV Marquis
∞ This book is printed on 60 lb. Rolland Enviro 100 natural text
Cover design, page design and typesetting by Mieka West

Table of Contents

Acknowledgments

This volume represents the collective effort of eleven scholars who contributed articles and ideas to make this project possible. Originally the book was going to contain the proceedings of the *Negotiating Identities in Latin American Cultures* conference held at the University of Calgary on 30 and 31 January 2004. However, only two of the articles read at the conference are part of this volume. In the process of editing, I realized that the main focal points in which all contributors are interested are the impact of space and time on the re/definition of identities in Latin America. Therefore, the title was changed to *Relocating Identities in Latin America*, which captures not only the space/time factor, but also the spirit of the changes in identity construction in our globalized world.

I would like to express my deepest gratitude to Dr. Stephen Randall, the dean of Social Sciences at the University of Calgary, for his continuous support. I am also grateful to Dr. Jane Kelley for her guidance in the completion of the project. I am also indebted to the many reviewers that patiently revised the articles and provided their invaluable suggestions that helped us improve our manuscripts. I would like to especially acknowledge the contribution of my colleagues and friends Myriam Osorio and Elsy Cardona for their insightful comments.

In addition, I would like to thank my former students Blanka Bracic and Isabel Cascante for the technical support and thoughtful suggestions they offered, as well as Dr. Luis Torres, the head of the Department of French, Italian and Spanish, for his support. For a DVD of the film *Miroslava*, and the copyright permission to reprint pictures from the film, I am indebted to the director Alejandro Pelayo, the producer Alma Rossbach, the photographer Emmanuel Lubezki, and Dora Moreno at IMCINE. Finally, I would like to thank my colleague and friend, Dr. Hendrik Kraay, for his generosity, enthusiasm, and professionalism in the completion of this project.

1 INTRODUCTION

Elizabeth Montes Garcés, University of Calgary

This volume explores the ever-changing process of the de/construction of identities in Latin-American literatures and cultures. Responding to a number of phenomena such as migration, globalization, and gender, the eleven articles contained in this book engage the questions of location, time, and place. Three of the articles are revised versions of papers presented at the *Negotiating Identities in Latin American Cultures* conference held at the University of Calgary on 30 and 31 January 2004. However, the process of preparing the manuscript for publication revealed that *Relocating Identities* was a more appropriate title for the collection, since considerations of space and time are crucial in the analysis of all of the cultural and literary products (novels, short stories, essays, plays, poems, and films) included in this publication. The theoretical approaches used to study the topic are quite eclectic and they range from close readings to textual analyses based on feminism, deconstruction, postcolonial theory, and cultural studies.

Latin American theorists such as Santiago Castro Gómez and Jesús Martín Barbero[1] address in their studies the importance of change in the conceptions of time and space. According to Barbero (1993, 373), globalization, with its emphasis on mass communication, accentuates the split between the local and the global. While the corporate elite occupies global cyberspace to handle their financial transactions and hold economic power, Latin American countries prevail in the dislocated time/space of their local cultures. In other words, the technical revolution has promoted the revival of identitary movements all over Latin America. In order to counteract the power exercised by transnational corporations and mass media, Latin

Americans take refuge in the reaffirmation of their localities and the reinvention of their own sense of identity.

The revival of identitary movements and the growing importance of localities can be also associated with the changes in the conceptions of time and space in the transition from modernity to postmodernity. Drawing on several studies by geographers like David Harvey and Eduard Soja, Caren Kaplan[2] argues that in modernity, time was a privileged category over space because it allowed for the possibility of progress, a concept so dear to the strengthening of capitalism. On the other hand, postmodernity reasserts the power of space over time. The reassertion of space brings about a tendency to privilege localities because, as Harvey maintains, "place becomes the locus of social identity" (Kaplan 1996, 151).

In contrast with the assessments of Barbero and Kaplan regarding the bolstering of local identities, Gwen Kirkpatrick (2003, 79) argues that movement is the key factor in defining identities in the American hemisphere. The continuous displacement of peoples has had a profound effect on the constitution of identities. Therefore, identities are no longer tied to class, race, gender, or nationality because those categories are continually negotiated as individuals move from place to place in search of better and safer living conditions. The new globalized order promotes the exacerbated flux not only of information, goods, and services, but also of peoples who see in the centres of power the answers to their various problems and hope for a better future; thus the impetus to migrate. Several articles in this volume explore not only the impact of immigration on the de/construction of national identities, but also the creative ways in which immigrants negotiate restrictions imposed on them to find spaces in which to rebuild a new sense of identity.

Due to repressive governments, civil war, political persecution, civil unrest, and precarious economic conditions, thousands of Latin Americans have been forced into exile and displacement over the past two centuries. As a result of that tragedy, new subjectivities are being constructed in the process of reclaiming localities in order to establish a new sense of community. Another more recent factor changing the conception of time and space has to do with the speed of communication in the age of globalization. Information technologies have reduced time and distances dramatically; so much so that virtual spaces are created as individuals find new ways to gather, relate to one another, and identify themselves. Despite these modalities of human contact, access to communication, now more than ever, has promoted exclusionary practices based on gender, as men and women strive to find spaces for self-realization and self-expression.

The process of inquiry into the question of identities in Latin America is framed within two key periods of massive migration, consolidation, and widespread questioning of the boundaries of nation states: the turn of the twentieth century and the current shift into the twenty-first century. From the beginning of the twentieth century, continuing through the First World War, the Spanish Civil War, and the Second World War, Latin America experienced a massive influx of people coming from Europe and the Middle East (Spain, Italy, Great Britain, France, Lebanon, and Turkey). Most settled in Mexico, Argentina, Chile, Uruguay, Brazil, Colombia, and Venezuela.

Thomas E. Skidmore and Peter H. Smith (2001, 71) argue that immigration played a crucial role in the making of Argentina. According to these two authors, "between 1857 and 1930 Argentina received a net immigration (immigrants minus emigrants) of 3.5 million, meaning that about 60 percent of the total population increase could be attributed to immigration." While an influx of capital came mostly from British investors, the labour force was provided by the masses of immigrants that arrived at the port of Buenos Aires. These people came not only from Italy and Spain, but also from the impoverished *pampas* (Argentina's prairies). In the midst of the economic boom, two very distinct and often opposing social classes emerged: the privileged landed elite, and the underprivileged *gauchos* (Argentina's cowboys) and waged labourers.

In the first section of this book, Norman Cheadle and Richard Young study closely the effects of massive migration in the construction of an Argentinean identity in the port city of Buenos Aires at the turn of the twentieth century. Cheadle analyzes the attempts made by Raúl Scalabrini Ortiz and Leopoldo Marechal to define the "man-in-the-street" through an intertextual dialogue between Scalabrini's essay *El hombre que está solo y espera* (1931) and Marechal's *Adán Buenosayres* (1948). In spite of their seemingly opposing ideological views, Cheadle demonstrates that Marechal and Scalabrini promoted a more broadly encompassing and democratic identity for Argentineans, especially in comparison with the narrow light in which they are seen in the contemporary neo-liberal context.

However, it is clear that the role of women in creating Argentina's national identity was greatly underappreciated in the male-dominated cultural discourse of the early twentieth century. It was not until the last decades of the twentieth century that the issue underwent a thorough scrutiny in Argentina's cultural scene. Examples of that process have included the publication of novels such as Alicia Dujovne Ortiz's *Mireya*. Published in 1998, the novel narrates the story of a Parisian prostitute who was both Henri de Toulouse-Lautrec's (1864–1901) lover, and the model for his famous painting *Salon de la rue de Moulins*. She was also Carlos Gardel's (1890–1936) mistress and source of inspiration for his tango songs in Buenos Aires. In his contribution to this collection, Richard Young argues that "The age is, so to speak, embodied in [Mireille/Mireya], not just through her life, but in the traces of her body that remain in the cultural artefacts of the time, in painting and tango in particular." Alternating between the redhead Mireille and the blond Mireya, she manages to cross the boundaries of time and space to bridge two cities (Buenos Aires and Paris) and two cultures in her search for identity.

As seen in Marechal, Scalabrini and, more recently, in Dujovne Ortiz, the exile and displacement of peoples is one of the key elements that character-izes not only the experience lived by millions of Latin Americans, but also the prevailing factor that articulates the notion of identity in literature, film, and other forms of cultural expression. While an enormous exodus of people from Europe and the Middle East immigrated into Latin America in the 1880s and 1890s, a continuous flow of Latin American emigrants and refugees driven by political persecution or economic crisis landed in North America and southwestern Europe during the 1980s and 1990s. Moreover, declared or undeclared civil wars and natural disasters have forced millions of individuals into migration and displacement within the boundaries of their own nations. In their respective articles, the creative writer Luis Torres and the literary critic and translator Mercedes Rowinsky-Guerts take on the task of studying the devastating effects of political exile on the lives and poetics of several Latin American writers.

In "Exile and Community," Luis Torres analyzes not only his own poetry, but also the written works of several Canadian and Latino-Canadian writers including Jorge Etcheverry, Julio Torres Recinos, Carmen Rodríguez, Ann Ireland, Nela Rio, and José Leandro Urbina. He argues that poetry not only allows artists to express the pain caused by the trauma of exile, but also that it provides the tools to search for a new sense of community. In a very poignant analysis of the metaphors that have been associated with exile, Torres combines Levinas's ethics, Homi Bhabha's cultural studies theory, and Liisa Malkki's remarks on displacement to survey the way in which creative writers and critics have characterized space and locality. The struggle to overcome the pain of exile produces the knowledge necessary to rebuild what Torres calls, after Malkki (1997, 92), "communities of memory." As a result, most of the literary works by exiled writers encompass not only testimonies of pain and devastation, but also the resources to recreate spaces and reinvent their own sense of identity in a newly adopted land such as Canada.

In the same vein, Mercedes Rowinsky-Guerts studies how, in Cristina Peri Rossi's latest book of poetry, *Estado de exilio* [*State of Exile*] (2003), the poetic voice is able to bridge two cultures: that of the beloved Uruguayan homeland she was forced to leave, and that of Spain, her new adopted country. As Rowinsky-Guerts notes in her essay, exile forced Peri Rossi to leave behind all the "things that matter[ed]" in her life, namely the space in which she once lived, the objects she considered familiar, and the people she cared for. As a poet, she was threatened with silence because she was denied access to her audience when her books were banned from all bookstores in Uruguay. She had to make great efforts to regain the voice that was so suddenly silenced. It is through her contact with the "other," namely the Catalonian writer Ana María Moix and her poetry, that Peri Rossi manages to regain balance in her life. In *Estado de exilio* the use of images associated with the figure of the mother and the motherland allows Peri Rossi to find a new existence and a new sense of self.

The mother figure is an image that in Peri Rossi´s case allows the poet to regain a sense of identity that was lost due to exile. However, Myriam Osorio demonstrates how, in Albalucía Angel´s *Las Andariegas* (1984), a group of women travelers regain that sense of identity by casting doubt over their origins and the place that has been assigned to them in canonical literature. In classical texts such as the Greek tragedies, the mother-daughter relationship is a conflictive one. Angel re-enacts in her novel the confrontation between Electra and her mother Clytemnestra. This is done to make the reader aware that Electra's excessive identification with her father Agamemnon and the symbolic order was responsible for her promoting the destruction of her mother (the semiotic), cancelling out any possibility of finding a space in which to construct an identity. According to Osorio's analysis in this collection, "[Electra] must reject in herself what she despises in her mother and as a result she perpetuates the patriarchal symbolic order."

The search for women's genealogies takes the travelers to two other places (the Garden of Eden and the Valley of Anáhuac) where they encounter two key figures crucial in the constitution of women's identities in Latin American cultures: Eve and Moctezuma's daughter. Based on the feminist theory of Luce Irigaray and Julia Kristeva, Osorio demonstrates how Albalucía Angel manages to counteract the pervasiveness of the image of Eve as a suffering mother in favour of a powerful and sensual woman endowed with the ability to create and procreate. On the other hand, Osorio argues that Angel rewrites the story of Malinche, Mexico's raped indigenous mother figure. In Angel's retelling of the story of Tecuichpo, Moctezuma´s daughter is portrayed not as a victim but as a hero for her nation; her defiant gestures towards Hernán Cortés become the first rebellious act against the power of the Spanish oppressor.

Rewriting the Malinche story is an important step towards redefining the social identity of Mexican women. This is not only true of Albalucía Angel's *Las Andariegas,* but also of Elena Garro's 1962 short story, "La culpa es de los Tlaxcaltecas." Malinche's canonical story of betrayal and guilt is completely undermined by Garro through comparing the decisive role played by women in Aztec society with the passive behaviour expected of an upper middle-class wife in contemporary Mexico City. Laura Aldama, the protagonist of "La culpa es de los Tlaxcaltecas," overcomes the constraints of time and returns to ancient Tenochtitlan where she is reunited with her former Indian husband. While there she discovers that according to Aztec tradition, she has the power to endow rulership. When she returns to the present, this knowledge enables her to redefine the culturally assigned gender roles of contemporary Mexican society.

If Laura Aldama succeeds in reclaiming a new space for the reinvention of gendered identities, Miroslava Stern is not that lucky in recreating a "room of her own." According to Nayibe Bermúdez, while in Guadalupe Loaeza's short story "Miroslava" (*Primero las damas,* 1989) the focalization allows readers to have access to the actress' inner thoughts and Miroslava is given the chance to find a place in Mexican society, in Alejandro Pelayo's film *Miroslava* (1992), the director's decisions in the adaptation of the short story do not allow the protagonist the opportunity to reinvent herself as a Mexican woman. Miroslava occupies the liminal space between her native Czech Republic and her adopted country of Mexico. However, the strict rules that govern heteronormativity in Mexican society during the fifties became the most difficult hurdles that the movie star has to overcome while adapting to her adopted land. In contrast with those who successfully take advantage of their position in the interstitial hinge between cultures and genres such as Mireya in Alicia Dujovne Ortiz's novel, or Laura Aldama in "La culpa es de los Tlaxcaltecas," Miroslava's attempt to negotiate a space for self-definition fails dramatically in Alejandro Pelayo's film.

In Catherine Den Tandt's analysis of *Sirena Selena vestida de pena* (2000), the first novel by the Puerto Rican writer Mayra Santos Febres, the critic shows yet another facet of the search for new identities. The novel dramatically undermines the metaphors of hybridity, indeterminacy, and *créolité* that were used to describe Caribbean identities in seminal studies such as Antonio Benítez Rojo's *La isla que se repite: El Caribe y la perspectiva posmoderna* (1989), and *Le discours antillais* (1981) by Edouard Glissant. Santos Febres is not concerned with the re/construction of national projects that was so important for Puerto Rican writers (Luis

Rafael Sánchez, Rosario Ferré, and Ana Lydia Vega) of the seventies and eighties. Instead, Santos Febres's novel focuses on the total deconstruction of gendered identities through the use of performance. For the protagonist of the novel, a young boy/girl, the stage is a privileged space in which to display the weaknesses and sensual, appealing gestures of a female singer. Den Tandt argues that his hybridity and marginalization are not identitary markers, but simply a strategy that allows common individuals to survive in a contemporary society highly influenced by globalization where gender, ethnicity, and nationality are interchangeable.

Is literature simply another commodity in the age of globalization? Following Brett Levinson's claims in his book *The Ends of Literature: The Latin American "Boom" in the Neoliberal Marketplace*, Den Tandt argues that literature has lost its privileged position as a valuable discourse on identities due to the increased importance of mass culture; however, the critic also acknowledges the contribution of Mayra Santos Febres. According to Den Tandt, Santos Febres makes creative use of mass media marketing strategies not only to promote her novels, but also to represent the inner workings of the globalized economy in a literary text.

Survival seems to be the name of the game, and the possibility to change one's life in a minute is a very attractive proposition for a society stimulated by the pursuit of money. In Claudine Potvin's comparative analysis of Fyodor Dostoyevsky's *The Gambler* (1866), Cristina Peri Rossi's *La última noche de Dostoievski* (1992), Martin Scorsese's *Casino* (1995), and Fabián Bielinsky's *Nueve reinas* (2000), the critic discusses how all identities are ephemeral, as the categories of ethnicity, nationality, gender, or language lose their meaning as identitary markers in gaming practices. Potvin goes further, suggesting that "gambling represents to a degree the ultimate challenge of relocating identities, as every player bets on displacement." Gamblers are always on the edge of achieving their dreams to become somebody else and, in their frenzy to achieve that goal, the question of identity is continually deferred in favour of the persistence of the game itself.

The Colombian social scientist Santiago Castro Gómez claims that culture in the age of globalization is controlled by the repertoire of symbols and signs that are technically devised by corporations in order to guarantee the production and reproduction of capital. For Paola Hernández, the theatre of Teatro da Vertigem is a means to confront audiences with the pervasive effects of globalization in Brazilian society. By staging their plays in many parts of São Paulo (prisons, hospitals, churches, and streets) and parodying biblical texts such as Revelations, Teatro da Vertigem manages not only to undermine mass media representations of Brazilian identities, but also to give voice to the marginalized groups left out by globalization.

What is the role of the intellectual in globalization? Rita De Grandis attempts to answer this question by comparing César Fernández Moreno's *América Latina en su literatura* (1972) and Néstor García Canclini's *Latinoamericanos buscando lugar en este siglo* (2002). According to De Grandis, while the first one is highly influenced by Adorno's distinction between high and low culture, García Canclini gives tremendous importance to the rise of popular culture. Moreover, identities can no longer be tied to national boundaries in a globalized society, so they have to be found in a decentred cultural space. Therefore, while intellectuals like César Fernández Moreno take an elitist position regarding the phenomenon of identities in Latin America, Néstor García Canclini becomes, in De Grandis's words, a sort of "cultural broker" who acknowledges the struggle of marginalized groups.

Santiago Castro Gómez points out the changes that have occurred in the social sciences and the humanities and, consequently, to the role of artists and scholars in the globalized world. The growth of the field of cultural studies has shifted the object of study from texts, art pieces, myths, values, and traditions to the production, distribution, and reception of those cultural artefacts. This shift in the object of study can probably explain why the role of the intellectual has also been transformed in the context of globalization. Debra Castillo and Edmundo Paz Soldán have thoroughly investigated the impact of mass media in Latin American literature. This process started at the turn of the twentieth century with the fascination that Latin American writers experienced with cinematography, and with the strong influence that radio broadcasting had on the political and cultural scene. In their book, *Latin American Literature and Mass Media*, Castillo and Paz Soldán demonstrate that the very technology that has made globalization possible has also been an extremely useful tool in the hands of several generations of Latin American writers and artists who have borrowed their techniques to communicate their message more effectively.

While the ideas and opinions of thinkers, intellectuals, and artists have had a strong influence over the cultural milieus of the past, nowadays their power to control any cultural scene has been quite diminished. It is instead the big corporations who exercise control over the images and representations that guarantee the production and reproduction of capital. However, the search for the aesthetic is not lost in the age of globalization. Most of the articles in this collection, from Richard Young's study on Alicia Dujovne Ortiz's *Mireya* to Catherine Den Tandt's article on *Sirena Selena vestida de pena*, demonstrate that novelists, playwrights, poets, filmmakers, and essay writers have devised new ways to create identity. Curiously enough, it is through fiction and language that writers in Latin America set the stage on which identities are played out, and where markers of identity such as race, class, gender, language, and national origin are de/constructed. Literature and the arts are the means that allow audiences to see the manipulation behind the images and representations controlled by economic emporiums. Fully aware of the inner workings of globalization, Latin American writers have taken advantage of mass media techniques not only to sell their books, but also to make audiences aware of the impact of such tactics in the reification and consolidation of images or representations of women and men in contemporary Latin American society.[3]

Some Latin-American intellectuals like Jesús Martin Barbero or Carlos Monsiváis have a rather pessimistic view regarding the potential of Latin American societies to counteract the effects of globalization. Carlos Monsiváis (2003, 421) warns us that globalization has eroded the quality of artistic venues such as literature to the point where the creative use of language has significantly diminished. On the other hand, Barbero (1993, 373) not only signals the fracture between the global and the local, but also claims that the idea of the individual as an imaginary unity has also been broken due to the proliferation of referents with which subjects identify themselves nowadays. He also warns us that, while mobility and deterritorialization paradoxically favour the validation of local identities, they have also turned into the easy targets of marketing strategists for promoting consumerism.

However, in this volume, all the specialists demonstrate that the tension between the local and the global has not necessarily rendered a negative effect on the construction of Latin American identities. Fiction writers, poets, filmmakers, and playwrights have devised a language to show the crisis faced by individuals in the confrontation with the repertoire of images and representations with which Latin American subjects have been identified. Only by discerning and fully contesting those representations would it be possible to regain a sense of self and create a new imaginary community.

Works Cited

Ángel, Albalucía. 1984. *Las andariegas*. Barcelona: Argos Vergara.

Barbero, Jesús Martín. 1993. Communication, Culture and Hegemony: from the Media to Mediations. Trans. Elizabeth Fox and Robert E. White. London: Sage.

———. 2003. Identidad, tecnicidad, alteridad: apuntes para re-trazar el mapa nocturno de nuestras culturas. *Revista Iberoamericana* 69 (203): 367–87.

Benítez-Rojo, Antonio. 1989. *La isla que se repite: El Caribe y la perspectiva posmoderna*. Hanover, NH: Ediciones del Norte

Blayer, Irene María F., and Mark Cronlund Anderson. 2004. *Latin American Narratives and Cultural Identity*. New York: Peter Lang.

Castillo, Debra, and Edmundo Paz Soldán. 2001. *Latin American Literature and Mass Media*. New York: Garland.

Castro Gómez, Santiago. 2003. Apogeo y decadencia de la teoría tradicional: Una visión desde los intersticios. *Revista Iberoamericana* 69 (203): 343–53.

Dostoyevsky, Fyodor. 1966. *The Gambler Bobok: A Nasty Story*. London: Penguin.

Dujovne Ortiz, Alicia. 1998. *Mireya*. Buenos Aires: Alfaguara.

Durán-Cogan, Mercedes F., and Antonio Gómez Moriana. 2001. *National Identities and Sociopolitical Changes in Latin America*. New York: Routledge.

Fernández Moreno, César (coord.). 1972. *América Latina en su literatura*. México: Siglo XXI.

García Canclini, Néstor. 2002. *Latinoamericanos buscando lugar en este siglo*. Buenos Aires: Paidós.

Garro, Elena. 1994. La culpa es de los tlaxcaltecas. In *Cuentos mexicanos inolvidables*, ed. Edmundo Valadés, 87–108. Mexico: Asociación Nacional de Libreros. Originally published in 1962.

Glissant, Edouard. 1981. *Le discours antillais*. Paris: du Seuil.

Kaplan, Caren. 1996. *Questions of Travel: Postmodern Discourses of Displacement*. Durham: Duke Univ. Press.

Kirkpatrick, Gwen. 2003. Nómadas o nativos, abejas o arañas: Literatura en movimiento en América Latina. *Revista de Crítica Literaria Latinoamericana* 58: 79–89.

Levinson, Brett. 2001. *The Ends of Literature: The Latin American "Boom" in the Neoliberal Marketplace*. Palo Alto, CA: Stanford Univ. Press.

Malkki, Liisa H. 1997. News and Culture: Transitory Phenomena and the Fieldwork Tradition. In *Anthropological Locations: Boundaries and Grounds of a Field Science*, ed. Akhil Gupta and James Ferguson, 86–101. Berkeley: Univ. of California Press.

Marechal, Leopoldo. 1992. *Adán Buenosayres*. 14th ed. Buenos Aires: Sudamericana, 1992.

Monsiváis, Carlos. 2003. De cómo vinieron los estudios culturales y a lo mejor se quedan. *Revista Iberoamericana* 69 (203): 417–24.

Peri Rossi, Cristina. 2003. *Estado de exilio*. Madrid: Visor.

———. 1992. *La última noche de Dostoievsky*. Madrid: Grijalbo.

Santos Febres, Mayra. 2000. *Selena sirena vestida de pena*. Madrid: Mondadori.

Sarlo, Beatriz. 1988. *Una modernidad periférica: Buenos Aires 1920 y 1930*. Buenos Aires: Nueva Visión.

Scalabrini Ortiz, Raúl. 1931. *El hombre que está solo y espera*. 11th ed. Buenos Aires: Plus Ultra, 1971.

Skidmore, Thomas E. and Peter H. Smith. 2001. Argentina: Prosperity, Deadlock, and Change. In *Modern Latin America*, 68–106. 5th ed. New York: Oxford Univ. Press.

Torres, Luis A. 2002. *El exilio y las ruinas*. Santiago, Chile: RIL.

Film

Miroslava. Directed by Alejandro Pelayo, Instituto Mexicano de Cinematografía, 1992.

Notes

1   Santiago Castro Gómez is a Colombian social scientist who works for Instituto Pensar, a research institute at Universidad Javeriana in Bogotá. He has written extensively on the implications of using postcolonial and cultural studies theories to study Latin American reality. Jesús Martín Barbero is Colombian scholar. He is currently a professor

and researcher in communication and culture at the Universidad Javeriana in Bogotá, Colombia. In several of his works he analyzes the impact of globalization on Latin American societies.

2   Caren Kaplan is perhaps one of the few critics to address in her works the shortfalls of feminist theories in light of the influence exercised by globalization in contemporary society. In her book *Questions of Travel: Postmodern Discourses of Displacement*, Kaplan warns us that, "The local appears as the primary site of resistance to globalization through the construction of temporalized narratives of identity (new histories, rediscovered genealogies, imagined geographies, etc.), yet that very site prepares the ground for appropriation, nativism and exclusions" (1996, 160). Paradoxically, Euro-American feminist theories of subjectivity have fluctuated between mobility and location as ways to assert gendered identities. However, these tendencies imply the homogenization of differences or the overlooking of transnational alliances. Those tendencies are also present in the Latin American context, where feminist studies have followed the Euro-American trends revealing the urgent need to develop theoretical approaches to analyze displacement and the construction of gendered identities from the Latin American perspective.

3   The process of incorporating mass media techniques in fiction writing can be traced very early in the development of Latin American literature, from the use of technical words borrowed from the natural sciences in César Vallejo's poetry, to the influence of film in novels by Guillermo Cabrera Infante and Manuel Puig. Many contemporary female writers (Fanny Buitrago, Angeles Mastreta, Isabel Allende, Laura Esquivel, and Ana Teresa Torres) have borrowed techniques such as the language or structure of soap operas and romance novels to question representations of men and women in contemporary Latin American societies. However, many scholars like Carlos Monsiváis have been highly critical of their accomplishments, underscoring that their fiction could be labeled as "light literature." Perhaps such scholars have failed to see the literary craft beyond the telling of the story and have been completely seduced by the tale itself.

2 CITIES AND IDENTITIES AT THE TURN OF THE TWENTIETH CENTURY

Twentieth-Century *homo bonaerense*: The Buenos Aires "Man-in-the-Street" in Raúl Scalabrini Ortiz and Leopoldo Marechal

Norman Cheadle, Laurentian University

The following essay has grown around two texts: *El hombre que está solo y espera* (1931), by Raúl Scalabrini Ortiz, and *Adán Buenosayres* (1948), by Leopoldo Marechal. On the one hand, Scalabrini's cultural essay was an instant popular and critical success, and its importance has endured.[1] Marechal's novel, on the other hand, was received with hostility by the liberal literary establishment and, though its importance is widely recognized, it has remained somewhat marginal in the Argentine canon to this day. Symptomatic of this is that Beatriz Sarlo, the dominant intellectual in Argentine cultural and literary studies, has scarcely touched it in her enormous critical production.[2] In fact, the only truly major critic to take it seriously has been Angel Rama (1926–83), who has been called Sarlo's silenced interlocutor.[3] The work of both Sarlo and Rama informs my article, which at one level puts these two thinkers into dialogue with one another. However, the dialogue I wish to foreground is the one sustained textually between Scalabrini Ortiz and Marechal about what it means to be Argentine in the first half of the twentieth century. If Marechal's is the dominant voice, it is because he reinscribes Scalabrini's essay into his own totalizing novel. Extratextually, however, the last word goes to Scalabrini.

Shortly after the first Perón government fell in 1955, the two met on the street in Buenos Aires. "He looked into my eyes and said with anger and bitterness: 'We'll have to start again from scratch. All over again...'"[4] Scalabrini's lament, echoed even more darkly by Sarlo a half-century later, stands as his comment on one of the political crises that outwardly mark the struggle for cultural hegemony and for the right to define Argentine identity.

It also marks the beginning of the end of an era, which we may say began with the Centenary Generation of writers, Ricardo Rojas and Leopoldo Lugones in particular. Alarmed by the changes wrought by massive foreign immigration, they both endeavoured to forge an archetype of national identity. Rojas proposed the denizen of "Eurindia," a harmonious hybrid formed from *criollos* and the (conveniently extinct) aboriginals, in order to distinguish native Argentines from European immigrants. Lugones resignified the similarly defunct *gaucho*, symbol of barbarism in the nineteenth century, as the mythical incarnation of true Argentine identity. The *martinfierrista* generation was satisfied with neither of these. Jorge Luis Borges mythified the *compadrito*, the suburban descendent of the *gaucho*, as yet another cultural line of defense against the undesirable foreigner. But Scalabrini Ortiz and Leopoldo Marechal were having none of this xenophobic mythification. In *Adán Buenosayres*, Marechal hilariously sends up the whole lineage of telluric archetypes, as well as the cult of the *compadrito*. For his part, Scalabrini invents the *Hombre de Corrientes y Esmeralda*, the regular guy at the downtown street corner of Buenos Aires, a type who has been called "Adán Buenos Aires" by José María Rosa (1971, 11–14).[5] That this Peronist and revisionist historian should identify the two has obvious political significance. The literary connection, and its cultural significance, between Scalabrini's lower- to middle-class man-in-the-street and Marechal's protagonist is what I shall be exploring below.

> Context: Looking back from 2001 (B.
> Sarlo) and from 1976 (A. Rama)

Shortly before the crisis that shook Argentina in December 2001, when Argentines of all social backgrounds took to the streets in protest and forced the entire government to resign, Beatriz Sarlo wrote a piece in the August 2001 issue of *Punto de Vista* entitled "Ya nada será igual" ["Nothing will be the same anymore"]. Aware that the impending crisis was not only economic (the ravages of neo-liberalism), social (the corruption of public institutions), and political (the erosion of public confidence in government that reached a breaking point two months later), Sarlo affirmed that it was impossible to think about the problem without taking into account "la dimensión cultural donde juegan los factores activos de la identidad" (2001b, 5a) ["the cultural dimension where the active factors of identity are at play"]. What did it mean, Sarlo asks, to be Argentine in the first sixty years of the twentieth century? She reckons that, in spite of everything, a sense of national identification was possible because of near-universal literacy, political enfranchisement, and relatively secure employment (5b). This favourable situation began to erode in the late 1950s when Juan Domingo Perón's authoritarian populist regime was forcibly terminated by the liberal "Revolución Libertadora," a military coup that set off the downward spiral that reached its nadir with the genocidal military dictatorship of 1976–82. By century's end, according to Sarlo, the triangular support of literacy/citizenship/employment sustaining national cultural identity had been definitively broken, leaving an atomized, postmodern society and "two nations" – the haves and the have-nots – separated by abysmal economic and cultural differences (11c).

When Sarlo asks, in the past tense, "What did it mean to be Argentine?" she is echoing – forlornly – a question that was continually on the lips of Argentine intellectuals during the first decades of the twentieth century. However, back then it was posed in a present tense opening expectantly on the future: What is *argentinidad*?[6] Who are we Argentines becoming? The question was tinged by identitary angst, but also filled with confidence, even defiant bravado. Whereas Sarlo speaks in 2001 of *desesperación* and *desesperanza* (2001b, 11c), ["desperation and lack of hope"], the verb *esperar* [to expect, to hope]) and its noun form *esperanza* constituted a key ideologeme in the public intellectual discourse of the 1920s. The young Jorge Luis Borges wrote his culturally programmatic 1926 essay *El tamaño de mi esperanza* [*The Enormity of my Hope*] in that same time period. Raúl Scalabrini Ortiz sketched the Buenos Aires man-in-the-street as *El hombre que está solo y espera* [*The Man Who is Alone and Waits/Hopes*] (1931). And the eponymous protagonist of Leopoldo Marechal's *Adán Buenosayres*, set in the 1920s, defines himself as an *"argentino en esperanza"* (1948, 166) ["an Argentine in a state of hopeful expectancy"] Borges later abjured of his youthful nationalist-populist enthusiasm, becoming sceptical and politically conservative, while both Scalabrini and Marechal, in their different ways, persisted in their pursuit of a new definition of Argentineness, one that embraced the vast demographic and political changes that swept Argentina in the first half of the twentieth century.[7]

Sarlo's contention that there was such a thing as a unifying sense of Argentine identity, sustainable over six decades or so, in spite of all class and cultural conflict, is a notion open to debate. As Tulio Halperín Donghi has shown, the thesis of the "two nations" with two parallel historiographical traditions had been circulating at least since the 1930s, when the historian Julio Irazusta published his revisionist works *La Argentina y el imperialismo británico* (1934) and *Ensayo sobre Rosas, en el centenario de la suma del poder (1835–1935)* (1935). Halperín Donghi makes it clear that "[e]l marco político y cultural es entonces decisivo para entender el nacimiento del revisionismo" (qtd. in Rama 1983, 204) ["the political and cultural frame is, then, decisive in order to understand the birth of revisionism"], implying that revisionism arose from an already existing political and cultural schism. Thus it is not surprising that this fracture should subsequently be theorized as a field of cultural production. By 1965 Noé Jitrik could speak of "la bipolaridad en la historia de la literatura argentina" (qtd. in Rama 1983, 206). ["the bipolarity of the history of Argentine literature"]. In the "culture wars" that polarized Argentina from the 1930s onward, Borges defended the liberal tradition on one side of the barricade, while Scalabrini Ortiz and Marechal placed themselves squarely on the opposite side.

One of the most lucid commentaries on this development is Angel Rama's seminal article in Argentine cultural studies entitled "Rodolfo Walsh: La narrativa en el conflicto de las culturas," written in 1974 and revised in 1976. The moment of writing is crucial to understanding the article's tone: Argentina was virtually in a state of civil war, living within the frame of a chiaroscuro vision opposing Official Argentina to its economically, socially, and culturally repressed Other. The apocalyptic atmosphere of that period fostered the sense of an irresistible teleological thrust towards either impending catastrophe, as in Ernesto Sabato's novel *Abaddón, el exterminador* (1973), or the inevitable triumph of the emerging culture. Unlike Sarlo, who in 2001 looked back on four decades of gradual erosion of a previously cohesive Argentine identity, Rama (1983, 197) saw "dos formaciones culturales enfrentadas" ["two cultural formations in confrontation"], which in turn stem from

dos proposiciones encontradas fundamentales.... Están por un lado los intereses de una poderosa y sofisticada oligarquía.... Por otro lado se registran las tercas e insistentes demandas de una baja clase media, un proletariado que ha crecido poderosamente con respecto al de otros países hispanoamericanos y un vasto sector marginalizado en su mayoría de procedencia rural pero de reciente urbanización (196), [así como] los inmigrantes europeos que se pusieron en contacto con las aportaciones culturales de esos sectores criollos de la sociedad. (200)

[two fundamental propositions at odds with one another…. On one side are the interests of a powerful and sophisticated oligarchy…. On the other side are the stubborn and insistent demands of a lower middle class, a proletariat that has mightily increased, compared to that of other Spanish American countries, and a vast marginalized sector, mainly of rural origin but recently urbanized(196), [as well as] the European immigrants who have come into contact with the cultural contributions of those *criollo* sectors of society. (200)]

Rama admits that his dual scheme simplifies the plurality of social strata and cultural tendencies (197), but he stands by the veracity of the overall pattern of dominant culture versus a dominated culture or set of cultures, the latter emerging slowly but surely.[8]

It is reasonable to expect, Rama says, that literature should register this whole process "like a faithful seismograph" (204). Alongside the official pantheon of venerated writers – Domingo Faustino Sarmiento, Bartolomé Mitre, Leopoldo Lugones, and Borges (203) – arises an alternative canon formed with Juan Bautista Alberdi, Eugenio Cambaceres, José Hernández, Armando Discépolo, Roberto Arlt, Raúl Scalabrini Ortiz, Leopoldo Marechal, "etcétera" (205). This "etcétera" continues with Julio Cortázar and finally Rodolfo Walsh, for whom the article is named. Rama's thesis is that Marechal (b. 1900), Cortázar (b. 1914), and Rodolfo Walsh (b. 1927) represent three succeeding generations in a progressive movement toward "building a bridge" (230) from the representations of high culture to those of the popular subculture. Marechal takes the step of parodically deploying classical forms to express popular contents; Cortázar moves further to efface the formal support of high culture; Walsh embraces the popular forms of journalism, detective novels, and *testimonio*.

What interests us here is not Rama's generational theory, but the particular importance he places on Marechal's *Adán Buenosayres*, echoing Cortázar's assertion, in his 1949 review of the novel, that it was "un acontecimiento extraordinario en las letras nacionales" (Cortázar 1966, 23) ["an extraordinary event in our national literature"]. Indeed, he devotes a good deal more attention to Marechal's novel than to either Cortázar or Walsh.[9]

Rama highlights Marechal's discovery of Peronism, implying that this "conversion" in 1945 enabled Marechal to complete the novel begun in the 1930s.[10] But more important is the cultural *reconversión*, or restructuring, of cultural sensibilities evidenced in the writing of *Adán Buenosayres*.[11] Marechal takes his eponymous poet protagonist, steeped in the codes of classical and religious literature proper to the dominant culture, and immerses him in the concrete, sensible reality of popular urban and suburban Buenos Aires. The Neoplatonic poet reads this reality as an instantiation or incarnation of the eternal forms or archetypes of Western culture. This sets up a parodic game of double-coding: the codes of high culture meet and clash with those of popular culture, generating two simultaneous readings, which demand the "*lector cómplice*" ["the accomplice reader"] theorized by Cortázar to realize a third reading. However, as Rama (1983, 216) points out, "[t]odo estilo paródico ... corresponde a un cierto derrumbamiento, todavía inicial, de las pautas estéticas vigentes y por ende de las doctrinas filosóficas que sostienen una determinada comunidad" ["every parodic style ... corresponds to a certain collapse of reigning aesthetic norms and therefore of the philosophical doctrines that sustain a given community"]. If Rama's position has a fault, it is that he does not push this insight far enough. In my reading of the novel, the entire metaphysical superstructure, a form of Christian Neoplatonism that sustains Adán's view of the world, comes tumbling down, which is how one may explain his symbolic death announced at the beginning of the novel. Nevertheless, Rama's seminal contribution is to read Marechal's movement in its cultural/historical context as a key moment of transition; if the line he proposes from Marechal to Cortázar to Walsh is debatable, there can nevertheless be no doubt that Marechal's scriptural move paves the way for later generations of writers – Ricardo Piglia and César Aira, to mention two very different examples.

In terms of cultural identity, the very title of Marechal's novel implies a claim that the text will give us a rendering of *homo bonaerense* or "Buenos Aires Man." As we shall see, the rhetorical move of making Buenos Aires a metonym of the nation had already been (problematically) accomplished by Raúl Scalabrini Ortiz. (In reality, this identitary claim can be challenged, as it continually has been) Marechal's character, read as a rhetorical construction of *homo bonaerense*, is riven by the cultural fissure between universalist high culture and the concrete *porteño* culture in which he participates: he reads the world with classical and "metaphysical" codes, but socially, as a school teacher, he lives in the concrete reality of Scalabrini's man at the corner of Corrientes and Esmeralda. This is most poignantly illustrated by the stubbornness with which he projects onto Solveig Amundsen, the female object of his desire, the Neoplatonic duality of *Madonna Intelligenza* informing a material girl. When he loses in the game of love, he reads his loss as the death of the individual girl and the reassertion of the eternal Platonic archetype, whereas it is much more plausible that it is his own symbolic construction of the world which proves inadequate (Cheadle 2000, 6, 31–35, 58–63). This inadequacy, on Rama's reading, would reflect the profound cultural shift that he observes: the aesthetic and philosophical norms of the dominant culture are collapsing. Adán Buenosayres figures, then, as a fractured sense of *argentinidad*, or national identity. In Rama's optimistic reading, this fracture is a dialectical moment of a transitional process in which the repressed subculture emerges to displace the dominant one, effecting this transition by reappropriating the codes of the latter in the service of the former. (Sarlo, perhaps in dialectical counterpoint, reads the crisis of 2001 as the death knell sealing the failure of this historical process.)

Rama glosses over Marechal's own subsequent position as outlined in "Claves de Adán Buenosayres." In this essay, Marechal reaffirms the Neoplatonic, metaphysical codes as the keys to reading the novel correctly; he comes down definitively in favour of the paradigms of traditional "high" culture to the detriment of the concrete, sensible world rendered in popular language that gives the novel its vitality and cultural relevance. It is important to consider the context of Marechal's apparent retreat into spiritual elitism. The essay was written after the fall of Perón's government in 1955 during a period when Marechal, a committed Peronist, found himself proscribed from the literary and cultural scene. Marginalized from concrete world of history, he took refuge in the same eternal order of traditional metaphysics and religion from which his protagonist was being weaned. In Marechal's words: "De todo laberinto se sale por arriba" ["The way out of every labyrinth is upward"].[12] Instead of moving forward from the impasse in which Adán Buenosayres found himself, he regressed. As he put it: "soy un retrógrado pero no un oscurantista" (Marechal 1966, 22) ["I am retrograde but not obscurantist"]. This avowal is to be understood in terms of a spatial metaphor: he goes back (against the downhill flow of history) and upwards towards the light of the sun/source, which shines down from heaven to illuminate the world. Implicit here is the traditionalist authoritarian metaphysics that justifies hierarchical order: truth flows from above to below. True, the "higher order" in which Marechal takes refuge is quite divorced from any form of power here on earth – the Argentine society from which he is marginalized, for example. Nevertheless, the metaphysical construct persists as a stubborn symptom of the same authoritarianism bequeathed by the premodern Spanish colonial order both to the subculture repressed by the liberal project of modernity, and to Argentine liberalism itself, "el primer patriciado moderno" ["the first modern patrician order"], in Angel Rama's (1983, 196) formulation, which imposes its dominance "con áspero exclusivismo" ["with harsh exclusiveness"].). It is symptomatic in the sense that it remains the virtual fallback position of the Leopoldo Marechal who, in the 1930s, before his "conversion" to Peronism, signed a manifesto, published in the reactionary Catholic magazine *Crisol*, in support of General Franco in the Spanish Civil War (Bianchi 2001, 44).

This brings us to a problem that Rama passes over, that of Catholicism and the role of the Church in the political and social developments between General José F. Uriburu's conservative military coup in 1930 through the rise and fall of Peronism in the 1940s and 1950s. This is the dark side of Peronism that leftist partisans of the movement prefer to downplay. Nevertheless, the Argentine Catholic Church is inextricably involved in the struggle between the "two nations" for cultural hegemony. From the Church's viewpoint, "el liberalismo se presenta como una filosofía peligrosa en lo religioso, científico y metafísico" (Altamirano 2001, 45) ["liberalism is a dangerous philosophy with respect to religion, science, and metaphysics"]. This is so, because "[e]l liberalismo es una visión global que compite con la otra única visión global que es la de la Iglesia" (Altamirano 2001, 45) ["liberalismo is a global vision that competes with the only other global vision, which is that of the Church"]. In the 1930s and 1940s, liberation theology was still far in the future. At that time, the Church had little sympathy for leftism; godless socialism and communism were unfortunate consequences of the drift away from Catholic values. Gustavo J. Franceschi, writing in the mainstream Catholic publication *Criterio*, gladly received the military coup of June 1943 that initiated Perón's rise to power: "Dios es criollo: en otras palabras, la Divina Providencia cuida de nosotros mucho más de lo que merecemos. El ejército salvó positivamente la situación: la revolución militar impidió la revolución social" (qtd. in Bianchi 2001, 13) ["God is Creole: in other words, Divine Providence looks after us much better than we deserve. The army salvaged the situation in a positive way: the military revolution prevented social revolution"]. In her study of the complicated relations between Catholicism and Peronism, Susana Bianchi shows that the Church hierarchy's expectations included not only the generally shared hopes for an end to political corruption and social injustice, but also "que el ejército llevara a cabo las inconclusas tareas" (16) ["that the army carry out the unfinished business"] of Uriburu's coup of 1930. She concludes that the Church aspired to establish "un Estado autoritario de corte corporativo con base en la identificación entre el catolicismo y la nacionalidad" (16) ["a corporate-style, authoritarian state based on the identification of Catholicism and nationality"]. *Dios es criollo* means, among other things, *Dios es argentino*: in terms of national identity, *argentinidad* is Catholic, not liberal.

This right-wing Catholicism, dominant in the 1930s and early 1940s, is what Bianchi calls *integrista* or fundamentalist. However, there was a broad range of positions within the Catholic community, including a minority group of *católicos democráticos*.[13] Inspired by the French priest Jacques Maritain's *Humanisme intégral* (1939), the democractic Catholics – pejoratively called *católicos liberales* by their right-wing, fundamentalist adversaries – aimed at a reconciliation of Catholic and liberal values. By the end of World War II, democratic Catholics, whose organ of expression was the revue *Orden Cristiano*, were gaining in influence. Politically, the most divisive issue between fundamentalist and democratic Catholics was their position vis-à-vis the Second World War; the former was openly pro-Axis, the latter pro-Allied. Culturally, the fundamentalists – influenced by the reactionary Spaniard Ramiro de Maetzú, Franco's ambassador to Argentina – were deeply Hispanicist, identifying with a reactionary *españolidad* nostalgic for the Golden Age of Spanish Empire, when Carlos V was the champion of orthodox Catholicism against the heterodoxy of the Protestant Reformation. They were also unabashedly anti-Semitic. The democratic Catholics, on the other hand, favoured a more universalist and less Hispanicist cultural identification; and they deplored anti-Semitism.

Marechal's position as a Catholic in this spectrum is difficult to determine. He has spoken favorably of Maritain.[14] Leonardo Senkman (1992, 10) acknowledged Marechal's links to pro-Francoist, anti-liberal Catholic circles, but was careful not to include Marechal in the ilk of rabid anti-Semites.[15] In any case, as David Viñas has complained: "El escritor de clase media goza de ese ambiguo privilegio: convertirse en reaccionario u optar por la revolución.... En este aspecto Marechal pudo ser cualquier cosa" (1971, 104) ["The middle-class writer enjoys this dubious privilege: to turn into a reactionary or choose the revolution.... In this respect Marechal could be anything"]. It is quite a stretch from his collaboration in right-wing Catholic publications such as *Convivio* and *Sol y Luna* (the latter, particularly pro-Hispanic) in the 1930s, to explicit and enthusiastic endorsement of the Cuban Revolution in 1967 (Viñas 1971, 104). It would seem that, though always Catholic and anti-liberal, Marechal's politics moved to the left over time.

This complicates one's reading of *Adán Buenosayres*, since the novel is explicitly set in the 1920s, was begun in the early 1930s, but was largely written after 1945. The text is rife with passages expressing right-wing Catholic ideology, but due to the parodic narrative technique and Marechal's relentless irony, it is possible and even probable that such views – anti-Semitism, for example – are being satirized rather than endorsed. Many are the inversions that we are invited to read into the ethos, or the actual pragmatic intention, not only of specific textual passages, but also of the novel a whole.[16] The most egregious inversion concerns the identity of the narrator, as will be discussed below.

El Hombre de Corrientes y Esmeralda
and Adán Buenosayres

From a larger historical perspective, this struggle between cosmovisions (to use Rama's term), traditionalist Catholicism versus modernizing liberalism, reflects the geopolitical history of Latin America. As Walter Mignolo (1995, 29) has observed in the context of postcolonial studies, the Spanish colonization of America constitutes the first wave of Westernization, which in turn was succeeded by the northern European capitalist imperialism. In Argentina, the chief player in this second wave was England; the liberal modernization project was heavily dependent on the English capital that financed the infrastructure, the railways in particular, and made possible the export beef business that enriched the Argentine oligarchy.

It was against this English neocolonialism that Raúl Scalabrini Ortiz rebelled so vehemently, beginning with his essay *Política británica en el Río de la Plata* (1936) and continuing with several books denouncing foreign ownership of the railways. His anti-imperialist nationalism and high profile as writer led him to become the chief theoretician of the democratic nationalist Fuerza de Orientación Radical de la Joven Argentina [Force for the Radical Orientation of Young Argentina] , or FORJA, though he never formally joined the association (Galasso 1998, 113). However, the book that made him famous predates this highly politicized period of his life and belongs, as Adolfo Prieto (1969, 59) maintains, to the 1920s.[17] *El hombre que está solo y espera* is a cultural essay belonging to his "artiste" period, as Beatriz Sarlo (1988, 215) somewhat snidely put it, when Scalabrini frequented the avant-garde writers of the Martín Fierro generation. The essay is characterized by a sympathetic attitude to the middle-class *porteño* male – his speech, his behaviour, and his foibles.

In terms of content, Scalabrini offers a new take on the "problem" of immigration. His theory is that the vast numbers of foreign men without women have produced a "tragedia sexual" (1931, 49) ["sexual tragedy"] in Buenos Aires. The lower-class hordes have frightened *porteños* into cloistering their women in the home, away from public space, and the city has retreated into an unhealthy prudishness. However, around 1925, there is a social and cultural sea change: sexual mores begin to loosen up somewhat. This change is generational; the sons of immigrants are coming into their own to produce the type Scalabrini calls, with a capital H, "el Hombre de Corrientes y Esmeralda" (hereafter, the Hombre C&E), quite different from their fathers. Having grown into adulthood with scant possibility of a relationship with a woman, they develop a peculiar psychology divorced from their European background and informed by "el espíritu de la tierra" ["the spirit of the land"]: the Hombre C&E is a new incarnation of the man of the Argentine pampas (51). Alone, with no concrete social insertion via family, "[s]e quedó inmóvil, hundido en apatía inerte, esperando" (50) ["he was left immobile, sunk in inert apathy, waiting/hoping"]. He is quite sceptical about the ideals and institutions received from Europe: "La Tradición, el Progreso, la Humanidad, la Familia, la Honra ya son pamplinas" (99) ["Tradition, Progress, Humanity, Family, Honour are now nonsense"]. Nor do religion and the Church mean anything to him: "ve que la iglesia no es lo que ha sido, que la escolástica es sillería de falsedad" (117) ["he sees that the church is not what it once was, that scholasticism is so much fake masonry"]. A "místico sin Dios" (57) ["mystic without God"], he invests his hope and faith in the future of the city and the country. His anti-intellectualism is directed not against the new poets of the avant-garde, whom he appreciates (82), but against insecure Argentine replicas of European academicians.

Scalabrini's essay, abounding in strained logic and even contradictions, is not entirely convincing as an intellectual argument.[18] Its staying power as a canonical text is due to its extraordinary rhetorical efficacy. One especially effective strategy is "double hyperbole," according to David William Foster (1986, 54); a disjunctive proposition is made – of the type "Not this, but that" – and then the distinguishing characteristics of both sides are exaggerated. The prime example is the generational division between European immigrants and their native-born sons. The former are characterized hyperbolically, from the prejudiced viewpoint of their Creole hosts:

Los intrusos formaban hordas de la más pésima calaña, de la estofa más vil. Eran refugos [*sic*] de razas que se atropellaban en su codicia sin freno, catervas desbocadas por una ilusión de fortuna, que traían consigo, acrecentados, todos los defectos de su sociedad, y no sus virtudes. Eran seres mezquinos de miras, atenaceados por una gula insatisfecha. Seres sensuales y procelosos, sin continencia, que gustaban del estrépito, de la música, de la danza, de la jarana. (Scalabrini 1931, 45)

[The intruders formed hordes of the very worst ilk, of the vilest sort. They were fugitives of races that pushed and shoved each other in their unbridled greed, herds stampeding after the dream of fortune, who brought with them, magnified, all the defects of their society, and not their virtues. They were beings of sordid view, in the grip of unsatisfied gluttony. Sensual and tempestuous beings, without continence, who relished noise, music, dance, revelry.]

In the next generation, by contrast, the Hombre C&E is "ocioso, taciturno, sufrido y altanero" (51) ["idle, taciturn, long-suffering, and haughty"]. Ideologically, this allows Scalabrini to drive a wedge between the culture of Europe and that of Argentina: "la continuidad de la sangre se quebró ... tampoco es el hijo del europeo urbano el hijo de su progenitor, es hijo de la ciudad" (49) ["the continuity of the blood line was broken ... nor was the son of the urban European the son of his progenitor, he is the son of the city"]. Or, in another formulation, "es el hijo primero de nadie que tiene que prologarlo todo" (40) ["he is the first son of no one, who has to prologue everything"]. Son of the city of Buenos Aires, son of no one: the Hombre C&E is Adam starting from scratch, with no blueprint to follow, and his task is enormous, both daunting and inspiring: "[c]onstruir, construirlo todo ... hasta la misma realidad" (23) ["to build, to construct everything... even reality itself"]. In a spirit both avant-garde and populist, Scalabrini is repeating the gesture of American utopianism, declaring *tabula rasa* in order to build a new world.

The rhetorical strategy of (double) hyperbole must be seen in light of Scalabrini's overarching rhetorical *ethos*, the ethical pact that he establishes with the reader. His text begins thus:

LECTOR: No catalogue de vacío de sentido a lo que en el interior de este libro llamo "espíritu de la tierra." Si por ingenuidad de fantasía le es enfadoso concebirlo, ayúdeme usted y suponga que "el espíritu de la tierra" es un hombre gigantesco.... Es un arquetipo enorme que se nutrió y creció con el aporte inmigratorio, devorando y asimilando millones de españoles, de italianos, de ingleses, de franceses, sin dejar de ser nunca idéntico a sí mismo. (Scalabrini 1931, 19)

> [READER: Do not classify as void of meaning what I call inside this book "spirit of the earth." If you are not given to fantasizing and you find the conceit annoying, help me out and suppose that "the spirit of the earth" is a gigantic man.... It is an enormous archetype that has fed upon and has grown with the influx of immigration, devouring and assimilating millions of Spaniards, Italians, Englishmen, and Frenchmen, without ever ceasing to be identical to itself.]

This plea for the "spirit of the earth" may look like just another version of the telluric topos whose chief exponent was Ricardo Rojas, as discussed by Adolfo Prieto (1969, 61ff.). The difference, however, is in the rhetorical presentation, the relation established between writer and reader. In his *Eurindia* (1924, 8), Rojas presents himself as the privileged priestly conduit who receives the sacred word of the future *indianista* utopia: "Yo no sé si esta palabra llegó a mis oídos en la voz del mar, o si la hallé en el viento de la noche ... o si subió de los propios abismos del alma" ["I know not whether this word came to my ears on the voice of the sea, or if I found it in the night wind ... or if it arose from the very depths of my soul"]. In sharp contrast to this self-aggrandizing, romantic mystification, Scalabrini treats his reader as an equal from the beginning, and the "spirit of the earth" is proposed as a heuristic device with which to experiment. It's as though he were saying: "Look, I know you weren't born yesterday, you aren't fooled by pretty phrases, but I'm inviting you to help me in this project of identitary construction, to invent who we are – and let's think big!" This pact is reaffirmed throughout the essay:

Usted, lector ... que ya debe ser mi amigo, puesto que llegó hasta aquí.... Durante todo el trayecto [de este ensayo] fue y será el lector, el experimentador y el juez simultáneamente de mi veracidad. Usted sólo [*sic*] rastreaba la humanidad de estas páginas. ¡Ojalá hayamos acertado entre los dos! (Scalabrini 1931, 96–97)

> [You, reader ... who must be my friend by now, since you've come this far with me.... Throughout the entire trajectory [of this essay] you were and will be the reader, the one who experiences, and the judge simultaneously of my veracity. You alone tracked down the humanity of these pages. Let's hope that between the two of us we have got it right!]

Scalabrini's rhetoric establishes a relationship of sincere, cordial respect between writer and reader, an ethical pact that will permit an inclusive, democratic construction of the *Hombre de Corrientes y Esmeralda*, to be invented collectively out of the volatile demographic flux of 1920s Buenos Aires.[19]

In Marechal's *Adán Buenosayres* (1948), Raúl Scalabrini Ortiz is caricatured in the *petizo* ["pipsqueak"] Bernini, one of seven mock heroes parodically modeled on the *martinfierristas*.[20] Two notions in particular from Scalabrini are satirically sent up in the novel. The first is Scalabrini's "sexual tragedy" theory, which comes in for especially ferocious treatment; Bernini ends up in the Circle of Lust in the mock inferno of Cacodelphia (Marechal 1948, 506). This is hardly surprising: the Catholic Marechal cannot tolerate open discussion of sexuality, much less accept that it could be such an important factor in social and cultural formation. The second object of satire is the topos "spirit of the earth," and it is here that I would like to focus attention for a moment.

In Book Three of *Adán Buenosayres*, the seven "heroes" make an expedition through Saavedra, a suburban no man's land. The journey serves as a transparent support for a burlesque encounter with a wide array of literary and cultural representations of Argentina. At one point, the famous *Espíritu de la Tierra* makes its appearance in the form of an enormous glyptodon, a prehistoric indigenous dinosaur. The entity demands to speak with his "Gran Sacerdote" ["High Priest"], Bernini and, to the latter's dismay, refutes his theory that the pampa had once been an ocean floor. The content of this exchange is in itself trite; its rhetorical politics are not. That Bernini is cast in jest as a "priest" is an obvious distortion of Scalabrini's rhetorical stance as author of *El hombre que está solo y espera*. It is more likely that the true target of the satire is not Scalabrini, but rather the telluric topos itself, especially as used in the discourse of Ricardo Rojas, who in fact is mocked more than once in the novel (Marechal 1948, 56, 188). Indeed, that Bernini is humorously and hyperbolically portrayed as "High Priest" of the telluric commonplace can be understood as an indirect homage to its demystification in Scalabrini's essay.[21]

Remarkably, the *Hombre de Corrientes y Esmeralda* is not once mentioned in *Adán Buenosayres*, much less satirized, not even in the animated debate, at the Amundsen tertulia, on the burning topic of *criollismo* and Argentine identity (Marechal 1948, 162–68). At one point, Adán Buenosayres (caricature of Marechal himself) and Bernini (caricature of the creator of the Hombre C&E) come into direct confrontation. A third character (Arturo del Solar) has just alleged the following thesis: "Es verdad que la ola extranjera nos metió en la línea del progreso. En cambio, nos ha destruído la forma tradicional del país: y nos ha tentado y corrompido!" (164) ["It's true that the wave of foreign immigration put us on the path to progress. On the other hand, it has destroyed the traditional form of our country. It has tempted and corrupted us!"]. Adán Buenosayres turns the proposition around: "Yo diría que sucedió al contrario.... Que nuestro país es el tentador y el corruptor, que el extranjero es el tentado y el corrompido" (164) ["I'd say it happened the other way around.... That our country is the tempter that corrupts, and the foreigners are the tempted and corrupted"]. An irate Bernini considers that Adán has uttered a *boutade* (164).

Adán's reversal is possible because the term "foreigner" is a heterogeneous quantity. There is an abysmal difference between English capitalists, on the one hand, and poor Italian and Spanish immigrants on the other; the first are the movers and beneficiaries, the second are the pawns and victims of neocolonial trans-Atlantic capitalism. Adán in effect lays bare the contradiction of the liberal establishment's attitude to immigration, dating back to Sarmiento: they wanted foreign capital and labour, but deplored the "hordes of intruders" mentioned by Scalabrini. Ricardo Rojas, for example, attempted to manage this contradiction with the typically ideological gesture of "spiritualizing" national identity, recasting Sarmiento's dichotomy civilization/barbarism as exoticism/*indianismo* and ostensibly inverting it: whereas (European) civilization was positive, exoticism is now negative, and the negative term barbarism has given way to the positive term *indianismo*. Yet this inversion of valences is only apparent. Rojas maintains that the railways and utilities financed by foreign capital were not an "exotic" influence, but "a work of international solidarity," arguing that "European investments ... would not have come without our guarantee of order and our support of progress" (qtd. in Miller 1999, 169). This is the same disingenuous argument that Marechal's fictional del Solar rehearses in the passage quoted above, and which exposes the ideological contradiction in the discourses of both *indianismo* and *criollismo*. Scalabrini himself (1931, 19) begins by uncritically accepting the category of European foreigner, envisioning English and French, as well as Italians and Spaniards, as undifferentiated fodder for his rhetorical construct of Argentine identity.

Adán's contestatory inversion, however, comes out of a traditionalist discourse rather than a progressive one. Asked about his "posición de argentino" ["position as an Argentine"], he responds that it is: "[m]uy confusa.... No pudiendo solidarizarme con la realidad que hoy vive el país, *estoy solo e inmóvil: soy un argentino en esperanza*" (Marechal 1948, 166; emphasis added) ["Very confused.... Unable to feel solidarity with the reality currently experienced by the country, *I am alone and immobile: I am an Argentine in hopeful expectancy*"]. Here, the argument is no longer between the fictional characters Adán and Bernini; it is rather a direct textual confrontation between the novel *Adán Buenosayres* and Scalabrini's essay: the latter's definition of the Hombre C&E is clearly paraphrased in the former, but from a contrasting point of view. Adán elaborates:

En cuanto a mí mismo, la cosa varía: si al llegar a esta tierra mis abuelos cortaron el hilo de su tradición y destruyeron su tabla de valores, a mí me toca reanudar ese hilo y reconstruirme según los valores de mi raza. En eso ando. Y me parece que cuando todos hagan lo mismo el país tendrá una forma espiritual. (166)

[As for me, the situation is different: if upon arriving in this land my grandparents cut the thread of their tradition and destroyed their table of values, it's up to me to re-tie that thread and reconstruct myself according to the values of my race. That's what I'm trying to do. And

it seems to me that when everybody does the same, the country will
have a spiritual form.]

Again, Scalabrini's language and ideas are redeployed, but from an opposing point of view. What Scalabrini celebrates, Adán laments. Whereas
the Hombre C&E "desciende de cuatro razas distintas que se anulan
mutuamente y sedimentan en él sin prevalecimientos," (Scalabrini 1931,
37) leaving only "individuos yuxtapuestos, aglutinados por una sola vener-
ación: la raza que están formando" (38) ["descends from four different races
that mutually cancel each other out and settle within him, with not one
of them prevailing [leaving only] juxtaposed individuals, cohering in a
single veneration: the race that they are forming"], Adán speaks of "*my*
race." The Hombre C&E must "construct everything" (23) and elaborate
"una nueva tabla de valores" (94) ["a new table of values"]; Adán wishes to
"*re*-construct" himself according to his Galician Spanish grandparents'
traditional table of values. In short, the Hombre C&E, "the mystic without
God," puts his hope in his invented future; Adán's hope, tethered to an
authoritarian God, is a confused nostalgia for a traditionalist golden age
that may somehow be resurrected in the future.

  Clearly, Adán's values resonate with those of fundamentalist· or right-
wing Catholicism, as opposed to the democratic progressivism of Bernini/
Scalabrini. And yet they are both on the same side of the liberal/revisionist
divide. The discussion on *argentinidad* ends with all participants, including
Adán, rallying together in their common opposition to *míster* Chisholm,
who defends "la misión civilizadora de Inglaterra" Marechal 1948, 168)
["the civilizing mission of England"], so welcomed by Sarmiento, Mitre,
and other nineteenth-century liberals for their program to modernize
Argentina.

  Adán Buenosayres and Bernini, then, are at loggerheads on many issues,
but in solidarity on the big issue of Argentina's place within the trans-
Altantic capitalist order of their time. This situation is reflected in Bernini's
paradoxical role in the novel. On the one hand, it is not surprising that the
novel's narrator – apparently reflecting Catholic prejudice – should be
at pains to specify that, among the seven mock heroes, the sex-obsessed
Bernini is the one with the dimmest lights (Marechal 1948, 190). And yet
a peculiar narratorial construction in the "Indispensable Prologue" of
Adán Buenosayres suggests a major role for the unenlightened *petizo*.[22]
This prologue is both fictional, entering into the diegesis of the novel's
plot, and an extra-diegetical presentation of the novel signed by "L.M.,"
apparently Leopoldo Marechal. The narrator speaks in the first person to
recount how "six of us" buried the deceased Adán Buenosayres in spring-
time. Logically, this narratorial "I" must be Bernini, the only one of the

seven heroes who is not mentioned by name in the opening paragraph. Which also means that it is Bernini who claims authorship of the first five books of *Adán Buenosayres*, which are to be followed by the transcription of two manuscripts attributed to Adán, the "Cuaderno de Tapas Azules" ["The Blue-Covered Notebook"] and the "Viaje a la oscura ciudad de Cacodelphia" ["Journey to the Dark City of Cacodelphia"] as the sixth and seventh books of the novel.

Who, then, narrates the main body of the novel, the intradiegetic Bernini or the extradiegetic Marechal? Is this merely a literary practical joke? The culturally traditionalist Adán Buenosayres, younger version of Marechal, dies and becomes a symbolic "vacancy," as Marechal himself has interpreted him (Marechal 1966, 13). Bernini is left to tell his tale. Surely we are entitled to infer something about the implied chiasmic relationship between the writer Scalabrini Ortiz and the fictitious Adán Buenosayres. If Bernini becomes the amanuensis of Adán Buenosayres, and narrator of his novel, then perhaps Scalabrini is being tacitly acknowledged as the apostle of Adam Buenos Aires, of *homo bonaerense*. The traditionalist Marechal, figured in the moribund protagonist of his novel, appears to be abdicating in favour of the prophet of the *Hombre de Corrientes y Esmeralda*, to whom he has elsewhere paid homage.[23]

At the very least, we can read this paradoxical scriptural gesture, made by Marechal towards Raúl Scalabrini Ortiz, as figuring a dialectical cross between traditionalist Catholicism and democratic progressivism, both of them contesting authoritarian liberalism. Both challenge the ideology serving capitalist modernization, which in the late twentieth century entered a new globalizing phase and now seems, as in Beatriz Sarlo's reading of the present, to have disastrously triumphed. Nevertheless, the texts of *El hombre que está solo y espera* and *Adán Buenosayres* are deeply embedded in Argentine culture and will continue to serve as supports of cultural resistance and identity formation.

Works Cited

Altamirano, Carlos. 2001. Cristianos en el siglo. In *La batalla de las ideas: 1943–1973*, ed. Beatriz Sarlo, 43–62. Buenos Aires: Ariel.

Andrés, Alfredo. 1969. Introd. to *Antología poética*, by Leopoldo Marechal, 7–10. Buenos Aires: de la Flor.

Barcia, Pedro Luis. 1994. Introd. to *Adán Buenosayres*, by Leopoldo Marechal, 9–138. Madrid: Castalia.

Bianchi, Susana. 2001. *Catolicismo y peronismo. Religión y política en la Argentina 1943–1955*. Tandil, Argentina: Instituto de Estudios Histórico-Sociales "Prof. Juan Carlos Gross."

Cheadle, Norman. 2000. *The Ironic Apocalypse in the Novels of Leopoldo Marechal*. London: Támesis.

Cortázar, Julio. 1966. Leopoldo Marechal: *Adán Buenosayres*. In *Las claves de Adán Buenosayres*, Leopoldo Marechal et al, 23–32. Mendoza, Argentina: Azor.

Foster, David William. 1986. Defining Strategies in Raúl Scalabrini Ortiz's *El hombre que está solo y espera*. In *Social Realism in the Argentine Narrative*, 50–59. Chapel Hill: Univ. of North Carolina Press.

Galasso, Norberto. 1998. *La búsqueda de la identidad nacional en Jorge Luis Borges y Raúl Scalabrini Ortiz*. Rosario, Argentina: Homo Sapiens.

———. 1970. *Vida de Scalabrini Ortiz*. Buenos Aires: Mar Dulce.

Hutcheon, Linda. 1985. *A Theory of Parody: The Teachings of Twentieth-Century Art Forms*. New York: Methuen.

Mallea, Eduardo. 1961–1965. *Obras completas*. 2 vols. Buenos Aires: Emecé.

Marechal, Leopoldo. 1937. *Historia de la calle Corrientes*. Buenos Aires: Paidós, 1967.

———. 1948. *Adán Buenosayres*. 14th ed. Buenos Aires: Sudamericana, 1992.

———. 1966. Las claves de *Adán Buenosayres*. In *Las claves de Adán Buenosayres*, Marechal et al, 7–22. Mendoza, Argentina: Azor.

———. 1998. Carta al Dr. Atilio Dell'Oro Maini. In *Obras completas: Los cuentos y otros escritos*, vol. 5, 322–23. Buenos Aires: Perfil.

———. 2000. *Largo día de cólera*. Buenos Aires: Colihue.

Martínez Estrada, Ezequiel. 1976. *Radiografía de la pampa*. 8th ed. Buenos Aires: Losada.

Mignolo, Walter D. 1995. Occidentalización, imperialismo, globalización: Herencias coloniales y teorías postcoloniales. *Revista Iberoamericana* 60 (170–71): 27–40.

Miller, Nicola. 1999. *In the Shadow of the State: Intellectuals and the Quest for National Identity in Twentieth-Century Spanish America*. London: Verso.

Moraña, Mabel. 1997. Ideología de la transculturación. In *Angel Rama y los estudios latinoamericanos*, ed. Mabel Moraña, 137–45. Pittsburgh, PA: Instituto Internacional de Literatura Iberoamericana.

Prieto, Adolfo. 1969. El hombre que está solo y espera. In *Estudios de literatura argentina*, 57–81. Buenos Aires: Galerna.

Rama, Ángel. 1983. Rodolfo Walsh: La narrativa en el conflicto de las culturas. In *Literatura y clase social*, 195–230. México: Folio.

Rojas, Ricardo. 1924. *Eurindia: Ensayo de estética fundado en la experiencia histórica de las culturas americanas*. Buenos Aires: Librería "La Facultad."

Rosa, José María. 1971. Prólogo to *El hombre que está solo y espera*, by Raúl Scalabrini Ortiz, 9–15. 11th ed. Buenos Aires: Plus Ultra.

Sarlo, Beatriz. 1988. *Una modernidad periférica: Buenos Aires 1920 y 1930*. Buenos Aires: Nueva Visión.

———. 2001a. Fantastic Invention and Cultural Nationality: The case of Xul Solar. *Borges Studies on Line* April. http://www.hum.au.dk/romansk/borges/bsol/bsfi.htm.

———. 2001b. Ya nada será igual. *Punto de Vista* (Buenos Aires) 70 (agosto): 2–11.

Scalabrini Ortiz, Raúl. 1931. *El hombre que está solo y espera*. 11th ed. Buenos Aires: Plus Ultra.

Senkman, Leonardo. 1992. Discurso histórico y ficción en *Adán Buenosayres*. *Hispamérica* 61 (April): 3–21.

Viñas, David. 1971. Cotidianeidad, clasicismo y tercera posición: Marechal. In *Literatura argentina y realidad política*, 103–9. Buenos Aires: Siglo XX.

Zubieta, Ana María. 1994. *Humor, nación y diferencias: Arturo Cancela y Leopoldo Marechal*. Rosario, Argentina: Beatriz Viterbo.

Notes

1 All quotations from *Adán Buenosayres* refer to the fourteenth Sudamericana edition (1992). Plus Ultra published its seventeenth edition of *El hombre que está solo y espera* in 1991, but I cite from their eleventh edition of 1971.

2 Sarlo does mention Marechal's novel in "Fantastic Invention."

3 Mabel Moraña (1997, 144n) attributes the comment to Patricia D'Allemand.

4 "Me miró a los ojos y con rabia y amargura, me dijo sólo estas palabras: – Hay que empezar a hacer todo de nuevo. Todo otra vez...." According to Norberto Galasso (1998, 153), Marechal told him this in conversation.

5 "El Hombre [con mayúscula] de Corrientes y Esmeralda es un ente ubicuo: es el hombre de las muchedumbres.... Es, además, el protagonista de una novela planeada por mí, que ojalá alguna vez alcance el mérito de no haber sido publicada" (Scalabrini 1931, 34) ["The Man [with a capital M] at the Corner of Corrientes and Esmeralda is a ubiquitous entity: he is the man of the multitudes.... He is, moreover, the protagonist of a novel I've planned, which hopefully at some time will achieve the merit of not having been published."] The enigmatic comment, with its grammatical aporia, is typical of Macedonio Fernández's utterances. Marechal introduced Scalabrini to Macedonio in 1923 (Galasso 1970, 57). Scalabrini never did write his novel; it is as though Marechal wrote it instead.

6 The term was popularized with the publication of *La argentinidad* (1916) by Ricardo Rojas.

7 Ezequiel Martínez Estrada's powerful essay *Radiografía de la pampa* (1933) [*X-Ray of the Pampa*] is an interesting exception to the general tendency. His thesis that the Argentine nation is built on illusions is clearly at odds with the prevailing message of hope and optimism. However, he is neither populist nor anti-populist; his ambivalent and paradoxical position on Sarmiento is that the great man was too noble and idealistic to see that, in Argentina, "civilización y barbarie eran una misma cosa" (341) ["civilization and barbarism were the same thing"]. Though he admits that from the nineteenth-century types identified by Sarmiento –the *caudillo* [strongman], the *payador* [gaucho minstrel], and the *baquiano* [guide in the pampa]) – there has emerged a new man or "improvisor," this new/old type is condemned to failure (336).

8 He characterizes this movement with the metaphor of a beating heart, a rhetorical choice indicating both his sympathy with its cause and his expectation that it will prevail:

> En el medio siglo transcurrido [de los 1920 a los 1970] se asiste, como en un sístole y un diástole, a la emergencia y a la represión de las subculturas: 1928, arrasadora elección de Yrigoyen, que convoca una aglutinación nacionalista y populista con demandas sociales claras; 1930, golpe militar de Uriburu en que se refrena el avance popular apelando al ejército, al servicio de los intereses oligárquicos; 1946, elección de Juan Domingo Perón que apunta a una fragmentación del ejército, a la aparición de un proletariado reciente ajeno al enmarcamiento de la izquierda; 1955, revolución libertadora en que el ejército juega otra vez la carta conservadora contando con el apoyo de la clase media urbana y un vasto sector intelectual; 1973, reelección por insólito margen de Perón. (204)

> > [In the half-century [between the 1920s and the 1970s], we have seen, as in a systole and a diastole, the emergence and repression of the subcultures: 1928, Yrigoyen's sweeping second election as president, in which nationalist and populist concerns coalesce and put forward clear social demands; 1930, Uriburu's military coup, stopping the advancement of the people by calling on the army, in the service of the oligarchy's interests; 1946, Juan Domingo

Perón's election, initiating the army's fragmentation and the appearance of a new proletariat not oriented toward the left; 1955, *revolución libertadora* in which the army again plays the conservative card, counting on the support of the urban middle class and a vast number of intellectuals; 1973, Perón's overwhelming re-election.]

9   Rama uses eight pages (211–19) to discuss Marechal, a page-and-a-half for Cortázar, and only five pages for Rodolfo Walsh. He contends that *Adán Buenosayres* is "un texto fundacional de la narrativa nueva hispanoamericana" (212) ["a foundational text of the Spanish American new narrative"] of the 1960s, comparable only to José Lezama Lima's *Paradiso* of 1966. This literary appreciation aside, Rama's assessment of Marechal's novel remains one of the most insightful that has been offered to date in the field of Argentine cultural studies.

10   Rama cites Marechal's account of his experience of 17 October 1945, when he joined the mass demonstration in support of Perón: "Me vestí apresuradamente, bajé a la calle y me uní a la multitud que avanzaba rumbo a la Plaza de Mayo. Vi, reconocí y amé los miles de rostros que la integraban" (213) ["I dressed quickly, went down to the street, and joined the multitude that was advancing toward the Plaza de Mayo. I saw, I recognized, and I loved the thousands of faces making up the multitude"].

11   "[S]i la novela resultaba paradigmática es porque se trataba de una reconversión: él [Marechal] encontró a Adán Buenosayres en su camino a Damasco" (Rama 1983, 212) ["If the novel turned out to be paradigmatic it is because it involved a restructuring/re-conversion: he [Marechal] found Adán Buenosayres on his road to Damascus"].

12   The quote is from his 1936 poem/book *Laberinto de amor*, anthologized in *Largo día de cólera* (75). In the 1960s, Marechal would declare to Alfredo Andrés: "Yo no soy de estos pagos, yo soy de Arriba" (Andrés 1969, 7) ["I don't come from around here, I'm from Above"].

13   This paragraph resumes Bianchi's sub-chapter "Entre el totalitarismo y la democracia" (39–51).

14   "Aristóteles y Santo Tomás son tan míos como Jacques Maritain. Somos legítimos herederos, profesores y continuadores de la civilización occidental" (Marechal 1998, 322) ["Aristotle and St. Thomas are as much mine as Jacques Maritain. We are the legitimate inheritors, professors, and continuers of Western civilization"].

15   "Obviamente, no es nuestro propósito incluir a Marechal dentro de esta fanática y militante fracción del campo intelectual de la época que se ensañaba tanto contra el capitalismo-del-oro-judío como contra su inversión mítica: el judío-bolchevique" (Senkman 1992, 10) ["Obviously, it is not our intention to include Marechal within this fanatical and militant fraction of the intellectual field of the time, which raged both against the capitalism-of-Jewish-gold and its mythical inversion: the Jewish Bolshevik"].

16   This use of the term "ethos" follows Linda Hutcheon (1985, 6ff.).

17   In fact, Scalabrini had sketched out, in *Síntesis*, the *Hombre de Corrientes y Esmeralda* in 1928 (Prieto 1969, 60).

18   For example, the *Hombre de Corrientes y Esmeralda* is at once a product of the city and of the spirit of the land, two antagonistic geographical and cultural spaces. This contradiction is bridged with the simple assertion that "Buenos Aires es nuevamente la capital del campo" (Scalabrini 1931, 51) ["Buenos Aires is once again the capital of the countryside"].

19   Contrast Scalabrini's rhetorical pact with the reader with Eduardo Mallea's superficially similar gambit in *Historia de una pasión argentina* (1937), wherein he addresses, in confessional intimacy, a "lector que me has de juzgar, querer, abominar o padecer"

(1961–1965, vol 1, 313) [you, reader, who must judge, love, abominate o suffer me]. But his reader is certainly not the man-on-the-street, "el argentino que se levanta, calcula el alba según términos de comercio, vegeta, especula y procrea" (1, 308) [the Argentine who gets up, calculates the dawning day in commercial terms, vegetates, speculates, and procreates]. Scorning this "irrational animal," he seeks his ideal reader in a mysterious spiritual elite that has been living, hidden beneath the vulgar hurly-burly of everyday life, in a "submerged Argentina" (1, 308). Few are the Argentine readers who ever recognized themselves in this elitist, phantasmatic entelechy, and Mallea's work has not suprisingly fallen into oblivion.

20   Besides Bernini/Scalabrini, the most transparent caricatures are of Borges (Luis Pereda), Xul Solar (Schultze), Jacobo Fijman (Samuel Tesler), Oliverio Girondo (Franky Amundsen), as well as Marechal himself (Adán).

21   As I have tried to show in *The Ironic Apocalypse in the Novels of Leopoldo Marechal*, Marechal deploys parody and humour in complicated rhetorical strategies that are not necessarily directly satirical. For Marechal's use of humour in *Adán Buenosayres*, see Zubieta's *Humor, nación y diferencias: Arturo Cancela y Leopoldo Marechal*.

22   For a close reading of the "Prólogo indispensable," see Cheadle (23–31).

23   In his essay *Historia de la calle Corrientes* (1937): "Pero algo le faltaba a la calle: una metafísica; y Raúl Scalabrini Ortiz se la dio, en la figura casi mítica de aquel hombre de Esmeralda y Corrientes que parado en la esquina famosa era símbolo del ser 'que está solo y espera'" (93) ["But the street was missing something; and Raúl Scalabrini Ortiz supplied it, in the almost mythical figure of that man of Esmeralda and Corrientes who, standing at the famous corner, was the symbol of the being 'who is alone and hopes'"]. In the 1967 re-edition, Marechal again recalls him: "¡Esmeralda y Corrientes! En esa esquina ... Raúl Scalabrini Ortiz (que aún no pensaba en los ferrocarriles argentinos) concebía su drama filosófico de un Hombre en soledad y en esperanza" (8–9) ["Esmeralda and Corrientes! On that corner ... Raúl Scalabrini Ortiz [who was not yet thinking about Argentine railways] conceived his philosophical drama of a Man in solitude and in hope"].

Urban Identity: Buenos Aires and the French Connection

Richard Young, University of Alberta

The novel *Mireya* (1998) by the Argentinean writer Alicia Dujovne Ortiz is the story of a woman named Mireille, who began her adult life as a prostitute in a brothel in Paris during the *Belle Époque* before immigrating to Argentina. In Paris she was the redhead Mireille, the lover of Henri de Toulouse-Lautrec, and one of the models for his celebrated painting *Au salon de la rue des Moulins*. In Buenos Aires, when the sex trade and tango gave the city international notoriety, she became Mireya. She was the lover of the young Carlos Gardel and was immortalised as "la rubia Mireya" in the song "Tiempos viejos." In the period of time covered by the novel, from the late 1800s to the 1940s, the cultures of France and Argentina and their capital cities intersected. However, the intersection of the two spaces in the novel is not solely a function of Mireille/Mireya's movement between them and her passage through the lives of two important icons of the age. The age is embodied in her, not just through her life, but also in the traces of her body that remain in the cultural artefacts of the time, in painting and tango in particular. She is the figure that mediates an exchange of images, from one locale to another and from one form of cultural expression to another, in a process that engages everyday life, painting, architecture and interior décor, costume, dance, music, and gendered identities. In light of these attributes, this essay will consider how the novel represents the formation of Mireille's identity in the context of the process of the formation of identities attached to the cities of Buenos Aires and Paris.

The identity of a city is far more than the name of a place on a map. "Sites are not simply locations," Rob Shields (1991, 6) has remarked. The personality of a city is often evoked through reference to attributes derived from the character and lifestyle of its inhabitants, the images of its architecture and landscape, or the sounds of its streets, language, and music. In some cases such attributes – London Cockneys, the Viennese waltz, the Eiffel Tower, or the River Seine, for example – acquire iconic status as essentialized images, widely circulated and repeated, of a particular urban reality. Above all, as with any social phenomenon, the identity of a city is also embedded in narratives associated with it, in the stories of individual inhabitants, as well as in the human history of the societies that have made the city into the place it has become, inscribing and have inscribed their past on its spaces, its streets, buildings, and monuments. These narratives have important historical significance as repositories of the past, although the meaning and the identity they give to a city are highly symbolic. Founded on a mix of historical documentation, memories, popular myth, tradition, a sense of nostalgia, and received images, they are themselves often derived from other narratives. As such, they too are therefore based on a pre-conceived identity, which they perpetuate at the same time as they embroider it by incorporating additional perspectives and references to the events and conditions of the more recent past. To an appreciable degree, then, both the content and form of city identities are constructed from what is already known.

Although it may often be thought that literary narratives tell new stories, they are also inclined to tell old stories anew. The novelty in this case frequently consists of new textualizations of the human experience, or re-contextualizations of experience in light of the changing circumstances of human life and its social condition. Historical fiction, notwithstanding its status as a re-telling of the past, is far from immune from this kind of novelty. Since history and how it is seen and understood have as much to do with the present as with the past, history in the historical novel is affected by perspectives that derive from the present; it is not simply a re-telling of what is already known. Symbolic meanings inherited from the past are re-examined, re-constituted, and presented again in a new light. Thus, fictional narratives focused on the history of cities, even as they contend with urban identities that have taken shape over time and are already invested with considerable cultural capital, endeavour nonetheless to re-interpret them.

Bearing in mind the general context elaborated by the preceding remarks, the objective of this essay is to consider how a contemporary work of fiction draws on the history of a city in a way that lays out aspects of its identity at the same time as it reveals some of the process by which identity is formed. The text that will serve this purpose is Alicia Dujovne Ortiz's novel, *Mireya*, first published in 1998.[1] The heroine of her novel, the fictional Mireya of the title, is a French prostitute, born in Albi in the late 1870s, whose youthful "indiscretion" and subsequent social shame appear to leave her with no alternative but to enter one of her home town's brothels. She moves from there to another brothel in the French capital of the 1890s before immigrating to Argentina. In Paris of the *Belle Époque* she was the redhead Mireille, the lover of Henri de Toulouse-Lautrec (1864–1901), and his model, as the novel proposes, for one of the women painted by the artist in *Au salon de la rue des Moulins* (1894), a work to which I shall return in more detail momentarily. In Buenos Aires she went from redhead to blonde and her name was changed from Mireille to Mireya.[2] She became the lover of the young Carlos Gardel (1890–1936), the great Argentinean singer of tangos, who also hailed from France, ironically enough from Toulouse, the same region as the painter and the prostitute. She was immortalised in song as the fair-haired Mireya (*la rubia Mireya*) in the lyrics of the 1926 tango "Tiempos viejos," to which I shall return shortly. In the period of time covered by the novel, from the late 1800s to the 1940s, Buenos Aires became known for the tango and, especially during the earlier part of that period, acquired considerable notoriety as the site of a flourishing sex trade trafficking of women. During the same period, the cultures of Argentina and France and their capital cities intersected in various ways. After Buenos Aires grew out of its nineteenth-century identity as a big little town (*la gran aldea*), with a population of not much more than a quarter of a million, to become, before the mid-twentieth century, a metropolis of close to three million inhabitants,[3] it endeavoured to do so in the style of Haussmann and the Second Empire. Francophiles vied with anglophiles for cultural supremacy, but it was to Paris, not London, that most sons of the elite and the well-to-do migrated to complete their education, or just become men of the world, before returning to their family enterprises in South America. In Paris Argentineans engendered a myth for wealth and profligacy, and sparked a tango mania that would eventually enthrall Argentina itself and profoundly affect the cultural spaces of Buenos Aires.

In Dujovne Ortiz's novel, the intersection of these elements is not solely a function of Mireille's transformation into Mireya, her movement from one place to another, and her passage through the lives of two of the cultural icons of the age, Toulouse-Lautrec in Paris and Gardel in Buenos Aires. The age is, so to speak, embodied in her, not just through how she makes her living, but in the traces of her body that remain in the cultural artefacts and practices of the time, in painting and tango in particular, which are themselves also markers of certain historical spaces. Mireille, as we shall see, is a figure who mediates an exchange between locales and from one form of cultural expression to another, in a process that results in the construction of spaces through an engagement with practices from everyday life, painting, architecture and interior décor, costume, dance, music, sexual behaviours and gendered identities. By the same process, she is also a figure through which past spaces and times are reconstructed and iconicized.[4]

As an historical novel written in the 1990s, *Mireya* tells a story about the past, but does so with a consciousness of the role of memory, how the past is perceived from the present, and how the past is also transformed through a process of textualization. The novel begins with Mireille's encounter with Toulouse-Lautrec in the salon of a brothel on the Rue d'Amboise in Paris.

Its final episodes include Mireille's return to her hometown of Albi almost forty years later. There she visits the Toulouse-Lautrec museum and sees again the artist's painting of the salon in which she is portrayed seated in almost exactly the same pose as when he first saw her. However, in addition to other changes he introduced to the scene, the picture is called *Au salon de la rue des Moulins*, identifying it with a place that it does not seem to represent. The significance of those changes and their implications for an understanding of the novel will be taken up in due course. For the moment, suffice it to notice that the narrative completes a circle. It returns Mireille to Albi where she began and where other re-encounters take place – with Berthe Gardes, mother of the late Carlos Gardel, and with the accomplice of her disgrace so long ago, which had led to her life of prostitution.

The joining of the end of the novel to its beginning completes a circular movement between past and present that is repeated in several ways in the course of the text. Although Mireille's life is narrated according to a linear chronology, the novel begins with her first encounter with Toulouse-Lautrec when she is already installed in the brothel on the Rue d'Amboise. Her earlier life, a loop back to the past, is therefore told retrospectively. Moreover, as her life moves forward, there are constant reminders of what had preceded. In Paris she remembers Albi: her mother's house, the River Tarn and places in the town, the cassoulets typical of the region, and the people she knew. In Buenos Aires she not only remembers Albi, but also her life in Paris in the house on the Rue d'Amboise and her liaison with Toulouse-Lautrec, both of which are frequently recalled. Above all, each novelty in her life appears to be a repetition or reconstruction of something she has already experienced. Raúl, her first Argentinean pimp, is repeated in El Loco Cepeda, and both are murdered at a milonga over jealous rivalry for her. Her sexual initiation of the young Gardel, given his stature and his age (thirteen!), reminds her of the dwarfish Toulouse-Lautrec. The madame and the three other women in the house on the Rue d'Amboise (Rolande, Marcelle, and Lucie) reappear in Le Régine on Sarmiento and Libertad in the persons of Madame Rose and her three charges (Yvonne, Yvette, and Margot), with the similarities among the two groups of three drawn to our attention by their differences in hair colour and repeated collective references to each group rather than separate references to each individual.[5] The salon in the house in Paris is compared with the one in Le Régine in Buenos Aires, and when Mireille is set up in her own house she models its salon on the one she had known in Paris as painted by Toulouse-Lautrec in *Au salon de la rue des Moulins*. Lastly, when Mireille buys Le Régine herself, she restores it to its former "dignity," as if attempting to bring back the past. There she installs four Uruguayan women, in imitation of the groups that she and her three companions had earlier formed, of similarly different complexions as custom dictated: "la rosa, la violeta, la pelirroja y la negra" (Dujovne Ortiz 1998, 191) ["pink, purple, redhead and black"].[6] They too are referred to collectively, even if they are not named (205, 216), and they will later be replaced by another equally anonymous group of four women: "cuatro esqueléticas desenterradas, todas rubias iguales porque los hombres de hoy en día ni lo diverso valoraban" (213) ["four disinterred skeletons, all blondes alike, since men today don't even value variety"].

The idea that the present is constituted by an identity that originates in the past from the constant repetition of the same images, as suggested by the preceding commentary, has its corollary in the idea that the present therefore must anticipate the future. For in returning to the past as it constitutes its own identity, the future will, in due course, also look to the here-and now-once it has become the past. In Dujovne Ortiz's *Mireya* there are many occasions when an earlier part of the story is retrieved, but there are also times when a later moment is anticipated. There is, of course, nothing unusual about this. A narrator hypothetically in possession of the full story told in the novel is able to refer to its past or future at will.[7] Rather than reviewing the structural implications of these moments of anticipation or determining their general characteristics, however, I will focus on two of them in particular, both related to a textualization through tango of social conditions or personal experience.

The first refers to Mireille's isolation during the crossing from France to Argentina. Shut up in a cabin all day, she is taken by Raúl for a stroll around the deck at night, but can only peer into the dining room as they pass it by, unable to enter: "ella se acercó a los ventanales del salón comedor, huerfanita, deseosa, boquiabierta, la ñata contra el vidrio antes de que el tango lo dijera" (Dujovne Ortiz 1998, 87) ["she approached the dining room windows, a little orphan, full of wishes, gaping in wonder, her nose pressed against the glass long before the tango would use the phrase"]. The reference is to Discépolo's 1948 lyrics for "Cafetín de Buenos Aires" ["Café in Buenos Aires"], although, in contrast to the lyric subject of the tango, Mireille will never belong to the world on the other side of the glass.[8] The second reference is to Gaston Viala, also an émigré from France, who frequents Le Régine with a view to making one of the French women his wife. He eventually takes Mireille to his ranch on the pampas: "De haber sabido que algún día el tango las llamaría flor de cerco, quizá no habría ido, pero fue" (171) ["Had he known that one day the tango would describe them as common weeds, perhaps he wouldn't have gone, but he went"]. The phrase would indeed become commonplace,[9] although I am less interested in tracing its history than in considering the implications of its presence, as well as the presence of the allusion to "Cafetín de Buenos Aires" in *Mireya*. In both cases they draw attention to the prototypical character of Mireille's story. If the tango lyrics of the 1920s through to the 1940s are textualizations of aspects of life in Buenos Aires that symbolically represent an earlier period in the history of the city, then Mireille's story may be thought of as the source from which those textualizations are in part derived.

Mireille arrived in Argentina in late 1896 (Dujovne Ortiz 1998, 74), and lived there for almost forty years before returning to France in 1935 after the death of Gardel and the closure of the brothels in Buenos Aires (218). During that time she lived through the early history of tango as a popular dance in Buenos Aires, and its later triumph as a popular song. As the novel relates, she was not just a witness to these processes, but a participant, often on the margins, but occasionally as a leading protagonist. She learns to tango in Le Régine, where she soon surpasses Margot her teacher and is taken by Raúl to cafés where her partners will pay to dance with her. The cafés are historical: Lo de Laura at Paraguay 2512 (117), María la Vasca's establishment, where Raúl is killed by El Loco Cepeda (126), and Lo de Hansen, later known as Café Jarana, in Palermo, where Mireille danced the night that the first performance of Villoldo's "El esquinazo" ["The Street Corner Fight"] provoked such a disturbance (159–61) that the tango was subsequently banned from the café.[10] While still at Le Régine, Mireille also made the acquaintance of Berthe Gardes, whom she would re-encounter at intervals during her life. She had, as already noted, an intimate relationship with Gardel, and she organized a concert for the Gardel-Razzano duo on one of their tours through rural Argentina while she was living with Gaston Viala at Pigüé. In 1917, as Gardel was about to make a greater vocal commitment to tango, he sang to her "Mi noche triste" ["My Sad Night"], the first of his successful tango recordings. By then she had already been following his career assiduously and continued to do so until his death in Medellín in 1935.

The preceding comments by no means identify all the moments and conditions in which the fictional life of Mireille intersects with history. Nevertheless, they are sufficient to illustrate the scope of the relationship between the two, and they indicate how the story of her life in Buenos Aires also serves to convey a sense of the cultural ethos of a particular historical period. The ethos of this period, however, is not to be felt necessarily in the literal meaning of the events and circumstances that constitute it, but in the meaning it acquires through the symbolic narratives that represent it. The events in Mireille's life are significant above all because they are typical of the kind of person she is, the age in which she lived, and the places she frequented. In this respect, her story conforms to a version of history already configured through previous textualizations, one of which, as has been mentioned, is the body of tango lyrics that have become part of the city's traditions. Remarkably, a version of the process by which this textualization occurs is imbedded in the novel.

Almost thirty years after she had made a name for herself in the tango cafés of Buenos Aires, Mireille discovers that she has become the subject of a tango titled "Tiempos viejos" ["Old Times"]. The song is a lament for past times, the last stanza of which runs as follows:

¿Te acordás, hermano, la rubia Mireya
que quité en lo de Hansen al guapo Rivera?
Casi me suicido una noche por ella
y hoy es una pobre mendiga harapienta.
¿Te acordás, hermano, lo linda que era?
Se formaba rueda pa'verla bailar.
Cuando por la calle la veo tan vieja
doy vuelta la cara y me pongo a llorar. (Romano 1991, 103)

> [Do you remember, my friend, the blonde Mireya
> whom I took from the tough guy Rivera in Hansen's café?
> I almost killed myself for her one night
> and today she is a poor beggar in rags.
> Do you remember, my friend, how beautiful she was?
> They formed a circle around her to see her dance.
> When I see her on the street how old she has become
> I turn my head away and weep]

These lines are reproduced in the novel (Dujovne Ortiz 1998, 205–6) and are indeed from an historically authentic text. They are in fact taken from a tango titled "Tiempos viejos," with lyrics by Manuel Romero and music by Francisco Canaro, first recorded by Carlos Gardel in 1926. Through the narrator's discourse, however, Mireille protests against their veracity. It is "un tango plagado de mentiras" (205) ["a tango full of lies]: "Pavadas. Nadie se la había quitado nunca en lo de Hansen al Guapo Rivera … Y ella ni andaba en harapos ni estaba muy descangallada. Era una Madama muy chic, un poco gorda, como siempre, pero tan bien conservada y aún pelirroja" (206) ["What nonsense. Nobody had ever taken her from Rivera in Hansen's café … And she was not in rags nor was she very skinny. She was a very chic Madame, a little plump, as always, but well-preserved and still a redhead"]. The reader of the novel, who knows Mireille's past, is also led to believe that the story told by the tango is false. Besides, the reader knows that texts such as tango lyrics do not embody a literal or historical truth, but rather a cultural truth that captures more of the spirit than the reality of the time they represent, its sense of pathos, and the melancholy attributed to urban life during the period to which it refers.[11] Mireille's protestations aside, it is a lyric or melodramatic version of her life that the lyricist of "Tiempos viejos" has sought, and Mireille ironically seems to confirm the point through the choice of words intended to dismiss his representation of her. Her affirmation that she was not "muy descangallada" ["very skinny"] brings to mind, almost inescapably, an equally well-known tango of the same vintage as "Tiempos viejos," in which the lyric subject also laments the physical decline of a former lover. This is Discépolo's 1928 "Esta noche me emborracho" ["Tonight I'll get drunk"], which begins with the lines: "Sola, fané, descangayada, / la vi esta madrugada / salir de un cabaret" (Romano 1991, 147) ["Alone, well past her prime, just skin and bone / I saw her early this morning / come out of a bar"]. The similarity of the two tangos and Mireille's apparent familiarity with Discépolo's verses, affirmed by her use of the word "descangallada," suggests that their content had already become a cliché. Regardless of Mireille's history, as represented in the novel, or the history of "la rubia Mireya" as narrated in Romero's lyrics, it is the narrative of the moral and physical decline of a former lover that has prospered in tango lore and has become the more recognized form of textualization of the sentimental life of Buenos Aires in the early part of the twentieth century. The tango "Tiempos viejos" in fact has a long history and a rich discography, and has left its mark on cultural memory. First recorded by Gardel in 1926, as noted above, it was also recorded by a number of other celebrated singers such as Mercedes Simone, Julio Sosa, and Hugo del Carril. Its first performance, however, was in a stage revue and its narrative content later provided the basis for two films, both directed by the lyricist Manuel Romero. The first of these, taking a line from the tango as its title, was *Los muchachos de antes no usaban gomina*, made in 1937. The second was *La rubia Mireya*, shot in 1948. Neither film is mentioned in the novel, perhaps because the text places Mireille's death in 1945, ten years after her return to France, and she would not have had the opportunity to know of them.

"Tiempos viejos," then, is a real text, an authentic tango, but to judge from Mireille's comments about it in the novel, it does not tell her story accurately. Whether or not Manuel Romero, the lyricist, in reality transformed the life of an historical person, and whether he invented the story or conveyed it accurately, are matters of little concern for the moment. In any case, it is not necessarily the original version of a narrative that has the most impact; rather, it is the version of it that obtains currency and freely circulates in a cultural community that matters most here. Narrative truth is a relative concept. The truth of a matter is often not a question of the historical veracity of any given event or individual's life experience, but of what has come to be believed about it. It is cultural and not historical truth that is at stake. In this respect, the process described in *Mireya* that sees the transformation of her life into text in the composition of "Tiempos viejos" is not an isolated phenomenon. Indeed, it is just one example of several that occur in the novel and that make of the book a work founded on the notion of the creation and transformation of texts as an essential ingredient in the formation of identity.

The source of Mireille's Argentinean identity is undoubtedly "la rubia Mireya" of Romero's lyrics, but it is not presented as the immediate source of the novel. This is provided by another text that Dujovne Ortiz reproduces at the beginning of her book under the following heading: "Mireya está inspirada en los siguientes párrafos de un texto de Julio Cortázar, 'Monsieur Lautrec'" (13) ["Mireya was inspired by the following paragraphs of a text by Julio Cortázar, 'Monsieur Lautrec'"].[12] There follows a description of Mireille as she was painted in 1894 by Toulouse-Lautrec in *Au salon de la rue des Moulins*, an account of Mireille's friendship with the artist, the jealousy that this likely provoked among the other women in the brothel, and her decision, taken against the advice of the painter, to accompany a cattle baron to Argentina. The existence of Cortázar's text is real enough and was published in 1980, but there is nothing to indicate whether or not his anecdote has any historical foundation, and he does not refer to the tango "Tiempos viejos," or to the transformation of Mireille into "la rubia Mireya" in Buenos Aires. His story has the character of a literary *trompe-l'oeil* by Borges, but is nevertheless quite plausible. Toulouse-Lautrec produced a number of paintings of the Paris brothels and his friendships with prostitutes amounted to more than professional interest. Moreover, the story of a French woman bought in Paris and pimped in Buenos Aires by an Argentinean cattle baron is a commonplace of the history of the city in the late nineteenth century that has been consolidated by a number of tango texts.

Mireille, once she has become Mireya, is not the only character in the novel whose name and fortunes are associated with well-known texts. The four other women at Le Régine are also connected to tangos through their names. The names of Madame Rose and Margot both figure in the 1932 "Melodía de arrabal" ["Suburban Melody"],[13] while the names of Yvonne, Yvette, and Margot all figure as the titles of tango (see Romano 1991, 34–35, 40–42, and 244–45). The lyrics of two of the songs, "Madame Ivonne" (1933) and "Margot" (1919), are stories that focus either on moral or physical decline and therefore have elements in common with "Tiempos viejos." "Madame Ivonne," in particular, traces a story not unlike that of Mireille in the novel. The trajectory followed by the protagonist of the tango, from "Mamuasel" to "Madam," is comparable to that of Mireille and to that followed by the character Yvonne in the novel. In the case of the latter the wording in the novel used to describe this transformation ("Yvonne había puesto casa propia. Ahora la llamaban Madame Yvonne" [195] ["Yvonne had set up her own house. Now she was called Madame Yvonne"]) clearly echoes that of the tango ("Mamuasel Ivonne hoy sólo es Madame" [Romano 1991, 245] ["Mademoiselle Ivonne now is just Madame"]), while in the last lines of the tango there is a summary of the experience that both women have undergone:

Ya no es la papusa del Barrio Latino,
ya no es la mistonga florcita de lis ...
ya nada le queda ... ni aquel argentino
que entre tango y mate la alzó de París. (Romano 1991, 245)

> [No longer is she the belle of the Barrio Latino
> no longer is she the humble little *fleur de lis* ...
> now she has nothing left ... not even the Argentinean
> who between tango and maté carried her off from Paris.]

As may be gathered from the preceding paragraphs, *Mireya* presents a conventional narrative, one that re-textualizes a familiar tale, already shaped by tradition, of transformation through transplantation from one side of the world to the other. By displaying its relationship to an assortment of tango lyrics and Cortázar's anecdote of Mireille and her association with Toulouse-Lautrec, the novel reveals the process of its own construction and shows how the identity and meaning of a place is tied to the narratives that have accrued around it, and through which it is represented. Important as this relationship is, however, there is one other developed in the novel that takes us yet further in illuminating that process, namely the relationship that the novel establishes with the painting by Toulouse-Lautrec, *Au salon de la rue des moulins*.[14]

In all its variety – posters, paintings, drawings – the artistry of Henri de Toulouse-Lautrec has left us a visual record of an era, or at least of that particular facet of the cultural life of Paris with which he is customarily associated, not unlike how the world of the tango in Buenos Aires during the first half of the twentieth century has left us a record of particular facets of that time. Toulouse-Lautrec has given us not just a gallery of portraits of the personalities of his age, but has represented the costumes, the conduct, and moods of his subjects, as well as the interiors in which they are placed. In this way his work has become an icon of the era and its spirit. So close is the identification now established between the historical reality and the images that represent it that it is difficult to visualize that the world could have been other than how he has depicted it. Yet, for all that, although Toulouse-Lautrec's images have come to represent reality in such a definitive way, they are nonetheless constructions.

Au salon de la rue des Moulins was painted in 1894 and is one of a series of canvasses Toulouse-Lautrec completed of the occupants and interiors of the "maisons closes."[15] These were the legalised brothels of the late nineteenth and early twentieth centuries where the prostitutes lived an enclosed, convent-like existence under the watchful eye of a "madame" rather than a mother superior, and dedicated to the pleasures of the flesh rather than the discipline of the spirit. Here, contrary to what the law allowed, Toulouse-Lautrec occasionally lived and set up his easel to paint, and among the images he produced were not just the scenes of public life in the houses, but of its inhabitants in seclusion, in moments of reflection and, occasionally, in moments of shared intimacy. *Au salon de la rue des Moulins* has this general character as a collective portrait of the women of such a house, but I wish to draw attention to its character as a studied composition and an artefact. Toulouse-Lautrec made a number of preliminary sketches, both of the salon and its furnishings and the positioning of the figures that would eventually be portrayed in the painting. Moreover, although the work is titled *Au salon de la rue des Moulins*, thereby identifying it with the interior of one of the most celebrated establishments of Montmartre, at number 6 on the rue des Moulins, it lacks, as art critics and historians have suggested, the extravagantly exotic décor of that place, and shows the plush but simpler decoration of the so-called "maisons de quartier," such as the one on the Rue d'Amboise represented in Dujovne Ortiz's novel. All of this is to say that the picture is a contrived reality, a condition that Toulouse-Lautrec may well have recognized when he had himself, one of his models, and his painting photographed. Here the painter and his model stand on either side of the picture, and others from his "maisons closes" series are also included. As a portrait of the artist with the images he has created, the photograph is as posed as the pictures it portrays, a condition that highlights how perceptions of the real are often derived indirectly from the texts that represent them as much as from the real itself. In his self-portrait with model and paintings, Toulouse-Lautrec presents himself as the creator of such perceptions.

Toulouse-Lautrec's work serves a number of purposes in Alicia Dujovne Ortiz's novel. Several paintings from the "maisons closes" series are alluded to in *Mireya*, and there are references to the artist's style and his subjects, but I will only consider *Au salon de la rue des Moulins*. As a reflection of the reality of a Paris brothel and as a real artefact created by Toulouse-Lautrec, the painting serves to connect characters and events of the novel to nineteenth-century history. As a configuration of the real world, it also reinforces the notion of the constructedness of images of reality, and is therefore both part of and a model for the process at work in the novel. As an image of the past, it is also the projection of a memory that serves both to remind us of what is gone and to represent it, providing at the same time a source from which to imitate and recreate it. As such, it is a key element in a process exemplified by the novel, namely the production of social spaces in Buenos Aires and the investiture of that space with meaning. These purposes are all, in their way, evoked or anticipated in the first paragraph of the novel, in which the first encounter between Toulouse-Lautrec and Mireille is described in terms of how she will eventually be posed in the painting:

Era la única que esperaba a los hombres sin ponerse corset. Un poco para levantar lo derrumbado y otro por guardar las apariencias, las demás, entre cada cliente, se fajaban con saña. El pintor apreció la franqueza de esta rubia rojiza, apenas cubierta por un camisolín transparente que le llovía suelto sobre las carnes, desparramadas a lo ancho sobre el diván. Las piernas, enfundadas en medias de un verde oscuro, casi negro, yacían extendida la una y replegada la otra (aunque necesitaba de un mano para quedar doblada). Tenía los ojos semicerrados. Todo en ella era ausencia de sostenes y esqueleto. (Dujovne Ortiz 1998, 17)

> [She was the only one waiting for the men without wearing a corset. Partly to lift what had sagged, partly to keep up appearances, the others rigorously corseted themselves between each customer. The painter appreciated the openness of this reddish blond woman barely covered by a transparent shift that flowed loosely over her body spread across the width of the divan. Her legs were sheathed in dark green, almost black, stockings, one of them stretched out, the other folded, although she had to hold it to keep it doubled. Her eyes were half closed. Everything about her conveyed an absence of corsets and bones.]

This description acquires for a reader a distinct aura of reality because it is possible to relate it to a painting that is known to exist and known to represent a particular time and persons in history. But it also sets off a play of images, a confrontation between two artefacts. The description in the text is an imitation of the painting at the same time as it subordinates the painting to itself by pretending to be the moment or source from which the work of art is derived. In effect, the first three chapters of the novel also include an account of how the painting came to be produced and the impact it had on the subjects portrayed in it when it was first presented to them. Standing out above all, however, is how reality has been transformed, not just the particular ways in which the physical idiosyncrasies of individuals are represented, but how the entire scene has been endowed with its own character. The changes are especially visible to Mireille, who had seen the painting while it was being completed:

Mireille contemplaba fascinada la transformación del cuadro. En el primer boceto, el que ella conocía, aparecía con un camisón verde agua, alegre pero opaco. Y a Madame se la veía de blanco. También las otras llevaban ropas de tonos diferentes. En cambio ahora sólo quedaban dos colores. Aunque transparentaba el rosa de la carne, el camisón de Mireille seguía verdoso. El batón de Madame se había vuelto lila, los de Marcelle y Lucie se habían oscurecido hasta perder su identidad (la figura de espaldas, con media nalga a la vista, carecía de ello por completo) y los nobles ropajes de Rolande, muy erguida y solemne (majestad desmentida por la extraña nariz), se confundían con el granate de los vastos divanes. (Dujovne Ortiz 1998, 75)

> [Mireille stared in fascination at the transformation of the picture. In the first sketch, which she had seen, she appeared in a watery green shift, bright but opaque. Madame was in white. Also the others wore clothes of different tones. Now it had changed, only two colours remained. Although the pink of her flesh showed through, Mireille's shift was still greenish. Madame's gown had become lilac, those of Marcelle and Lucie had been darkened so much they lost their identity (the figure seen from the back with half her buttocks in view lacked identity entirely) and the noble clothing of Rolande, sitting stiff and solemn (a majesty belied by her strange nose), blended into the crimson red of the wide divans.]

The novel also includes an account of the photographic session that resulted in the picture of Toulouse-Lautrec and his model alongside his work, and it refers to the title of his painting, explaining that he had changed the name of the house where Mireille worked from the Rue d'Amboise to the Rue des Moulins as an act of revenge for her imminent departure for Buenos Aires.

By doing so, he has also completed the transformation of the real into the image of it he has created, an image that will endure, to use the liturgical formula cited in the text, "por los siglos de los siglos" (76) ["throughout the centuries"].

Thus, at the same time as it offers an accurate description of the painting, the novel *Mireya* also undermines its accuracy as a representation fully faithful to the subject it depicts, drawing, of course, on the doubts I have already mentioned that art critics and historians also have about the identity of the scene depicted in the painting. Yet, in the end, whatever discrepancy there is between the painting and its subject may be of little consequence since it is not the historical reality, but Toulouse-Lautrec's representation of it, that has remained lodged in the universal imagination. Meaning replaces matter, for want of another expression. When Mireille goes to Buenos Aires, purchased from the madame of the house on the Rue d'Amboise by an Argentinean beef baron who will profit from her earnings in her new location, she is transformed through a change in colour not unlike that she noted in Toulouse-Lautrec's painting: once the redhead Mireille, she becomes the blonde Mireya (*la rubia Mireya*), a transformation that fixes her identity in Buenos Aires in the terms of her exchange value as a French woman and a prostitute in her new environment.[16] Like any immigrant, however, she also carries with her the images of the spaces she has left behind. Of these there are many, including the memories of her mother and childhood in Albi and the first house of prostitution she knew in her hometown, but the image of the house on the Rue d'Amboise in Paris and the way that Toulouse-Lautrec had represented it in *Au salon de la rue des Moulins* is a constant, at times present through the evocation of its absence in the new environment, at times made real through imitation. Whatever the case, however, the evocation of the painting serves to illustrate a process whereby the new social spaces of Buenos Aires were modelled on constructions brought from Paris.

When Mireille goes to Buenos Aires, her situation does not really change. She goes from one house in Paris to another in the Argentine capital. She is pimped by a series of three men, lives with another on a ranch on the pampas, and eventually sets up as a "madame" in her own house. Her story is representative of one of the narratives that constitute the identity of Buenos Aires, the same story of Madama Yvonne told in the tango of that name. Throughout this experience she is accompanied by the image of her origins in Paris, as configured by Toulouse-Lautrec. Her first impressions of Le Régine are framed in terms of the presence and absence of images of familiar spaces remembered from the house on the Rue d'Amboise in Paris:

Casi no había sillones pero sí muchas sillas, mucho espacio en el centro de la sala y un piso de madera, sin alfombra, pulcramente encerado. Cierto es que las paredes estaban tapizadas con una tela verde y malva a rayas, una brillante y la otra no, como en la rue d'Amboise, como en el cuadro, pero ni un diván ni una almohadón de terciopelo granate surgían ante la vista. Por lo visto, en la Régine algo se hacía, algo seguramente mejor que estarse apoltronadas. (Dujovne Ortiz 1998, 92)

> [There were almost no armchairs, but many chairs, a lot of space in the centre of the room and a wooden floor, with no carpet, scrupulously waxed. Certainly the walls were covered in green and mauve cloth, striped, one shiny and the other not, like in the Rue d'Amboise, like in the picture, but neither a divan nor a crimson velvet cushion came into view. It seemed that in the Régine you did something, certainly something better than sitting idly about.]

The "something" that Mireille will shortly discover, of course, is tango, a cultural practice associated in particular with the River Plate cities of Montevideo and Buenos Aires, especially the latter. Although it is a distinctively South America phenomenon, the image that the growing city of Buenos Aires projects, as the novel suggests, both in elements of its culture and its appearance, is dependent on Paris. When Mireille takes to tango like a duck to water, it all becomes for her what the music hall and the cabaret are to Paris: "… la idea de ser bailarina le hizo latir las sienes. ¡Cuánto había envidiado a la Goulue, a Jane Avril, a Nini-pattes-en-l'air! Ahora, gracias al tango, ya no era la cataplasma de aquel tiempo. ¡Si la viera Monsieur Henri!" (112) ["… the idea of being a dancer caused her temples to throb. How much she had envied La Goulue, Jane Avril, Nini-pattes-en-l'air! Now, thanks to tango, she was no longer the boring person she was before. If Monsieur Henri could see her!"]. As Mireille's engagement with tango unfolds, the story of her life is woven into the history of the dance. The dance steps she devises and the venues where she performs, mainly cafés notorious for their association with prostitution and the dance, are part of tango lore. Her association with the young Carlos Gardel and the friendship she maintains with him, even during the height of his international career, draws her into the artistic milieu of Buenos Aires, similar to her association with Toulouse-Lautrec and the artistic milieu of Paris, as if her life in one location were a continuation of the one in the other.

When Mireille leaves Le Régine, the house where her first Argentinean pimp had placed her, she is set up in another house by other men. Her private room is decorated in white, in imitation of the private room of a madame she had seen in another house in Buenos Aires, but the salon is a different matter: "de común acuerdo, resolvieron decorarlo como se debe, con paredes a rayas verde y malva, molduras doradas y terciopelo granate" (Dujovne Ortiz 1998, 148) ["by common agreement, they decided to decorate it as it ought to be, with green and mauve stripes, gilded mouldings and crimson velvet"]. It is, in effect, a reproduction of Toulouse-Lautrec's *Au salon de la rue des Moulins*. And in this setting, Mireille also plays her part:

… quizás sin darse cuenta, o quizá guiñándole el ojo a sus recuerdos, Mireille esperó a su primer cliente someramente vestida con un camisoncito transparente y unas medias de un verde oscuro, casi negro.

Su primer cliente, un hombre fino … entró al salón y exclamó tapándose la boca:

—¡Pero esto es un cuadro de Toulouse-Lautrec!

…

… el pelo rojo, el vestidito de gasa, las medias verdes…

Claro que usted no se parece para nada a la matrona del cuadro: es más finita de cintura. Pero el resto, tal cual. Hasta ese pedacito de piel entre el vestido y la media que provocó el escándalo. (149)

> [… perhaps without realizing it, or perhaps with a wink to her memories, Mireille waited for her first customer scantily clad in a transparent shift and dark green, almost black stockings.

> Her first customer, a cultivated man, … entered the salon and with his hand to his mouth exclaimed: "But this is a painting by Toulouse-Lautrec!"

> …

> "… the red hair, the chiffon dress, the green stockings…. Of course, you don't look anything like the woman in the painting: you're thinner about the waist. But the rest is just the same. Even that patch of skin between the dress and the stocking that provoked such a scandal."]

The real life and surroundings of Mireille are the image of herself as represented by Toulouse-Lautrec. This is not entirely inconsistent with how her daily life has come to be, given that she habitually dresses up for her clients and acts out the roles they request. However, reflection on the representation of her in the painting and especially that small triangle of flesh visible between her dress and her stockings, "situado estratégicamente a cierta distancia del triángulo central" (151) ["strategically situated at a certain distance from the central triangle"], causes her to realize that she is really nothing more than the embodiment of an image which has created an expectation about how reality should be: "Una francesa, para un argentino –le decían– es una rubia culta, refinada y viciosa" (153) ["'For an Argentinean man,' they told her, 'a French woman is cultivated, refined, blond, and given to vice'"]. She understands all these characteristics save the first and asks herself why she should be cultivated, to which she promptly replies: "Porque Francia es el país de la cultura, idiota. ¿O vos qué te pensás, que vienen acá a patinarse una fortuna por tu linda cara? No, m'hijita: vienen porque hacen de cuenta que se acuestan con Madame Pompadour" (153) ["Because France is the country of culture, you idiot. Or what do you think, that they come here to hand over a fortune for your pretty face? No, my girl: they come because they kid themselves they're going to bed with Madame Pompadour"]. Mireille herself is an icon, a mere image of what other configurations of reality have made of her.

This conclusion and the capacity of the image to provide a basis for both the creation and perception of real spaces are emphasized once more at the end of the novel. After her return to France following the death of Gardel in 1935, and the earlier de-legalizing of brothels in Argentina in 1934, Mireille visits the Toulouse-Lautrec Museum in Albi where the painting *Au salon de la rue des Moulins* is held, hanging in a place of honour. She wonders as she enters the building if the English tourists will recognize her as one of the artist's models. Certainly they look at her, but more because of her dress and her carriage, and because of what she has come to represent: "aunque no la identificaran concretamente con *Au salon de la rue des Moulins*, igual parecía escapada de todo cuadro con burdeles pintado por Monsieur Henri. Un cuadro vivo" (Dujovne Ortiz 1998, 234) ["even if they didn't identify her precisely with *Salon de la rue des Moulins*, she seemed nonetheless to have escaped from every brothel painting ever painted by Monsieur Henri. A living image"]. As she looks at the painting of herself hanging on the wall, with the earlier sketch that she had also known on the wall opposite the finished work, she reflects on the transformation that the painting entailed, and on the falsehood of its title and what it claims to represent. She also reflects on how she had changed in Buenos Aires in comparison with how she appears in the painting: "Aún hoy, a sus años, tenía más cintura que entonces. Los ochos del tango la habían vuelto a ella como un ocho" (235) ["Even today, at her age, she had more of a waist than then. The tango figures-of-eight had made her figure like an eight"]. This was the reason why the first customer to come to her house years before recognized the setting, but failed to identify her. Her confrontation with the image of herself thus brings together the elements that have been in play throughout the novel: the process of transformation engaged in through representations of the real; the degree to which the constructed image establishes perceptions of the real and replaces it, but is subject to further transformation each time it is deployed and confronted with other realities; the effects of time; the growing ambiguities that arise each time an original or its representation is faced. By the same token, this multiple interplay is cause for reflection concerning the kind of history of Buenos Aires that is told in the novel. By the time Mireille appears in the city, she is already a construction and it is as such that part of the history of the city is told through her association with it. Her life story is thus a reminder of how the history of the city and of urban spaces is also a history of constructions, of ways of viewing the place and its story that have as much to do with perceptions and representations of spaces and events that took place there, or of people who passed through, as with any narration based on an objective catalogue of events and their protagonists, or with the streets, buildings, monuments, or geography of the city itself.

Works Cited

Bossio, Jorge A. 1995. *Los cafés de Buenos Aires: reportaje a la nostalgia*. Buenos Aires: Plus Ultra.

Genette, Gérard. 1980. *Narrative Discourse: An Essay in Method.* Ithaca: Cornell Univ. Press.

Dujovne Ortiz, Alicia. 1993. *Maradona soy yo*. Buenos Aires: Emecé.

———. 1995. *Eva Perón: la biografía*. Buenos Aires: Aguilar.

———. 1998. *Mireya*. Buenos Aires: Alfaguara.

Keeling, David J. 1996. *Buenos Aires: Global Dreams, Local Crises*. Chichester, UK: Wiley.

Romano, Eduardo, ed. 1991. *Las letras del tango: antología cronológica 1900–1980*. Rosario, Argentina: Fundación Ross.

Sabat, Hermenegildo, and Julio Cortázar. 1980. *Monsieur Lautrec*. Madrid: Ameris.

Shields, Rob. 1991. *Spaces on the Margin*. New York: Routledge.

Thomson, Richard. 1991. Images of the *maisons closes*. In *Toulouse-Lautrec*, 405–61. New Haven: Yale Univ. Press.

Notes

1   Quotations are taken from this edition and are identified by the page references added in parentheses at the end of each one.

2   For the sake of consistency, however, I shall refer to the character throughout as Mireille, except in quotations from the novel where Mireya is used.

3   Greater Buenos Aires now has a population approaching 13 million (see Keeling 1996, 6).

4   Alicia Dujovne Ortiz has also written biographies of Eva Perón (*Eva Perón: La biografía*) and Diego Maradona (*Maradona soy yo*), individuals whose lives might also be perceived as iconic representations of their times.

5   For Rolande, Marcelle, and Lucie, see pages 19, 21, 23, 26, 27, 35, 57, 64, 70, and 75 of the novel. For Yvonne, Yvette, and Margot, see 91, 93, 94, 95, 99, 112, 118, 127, 135, 144, 157, and 195.

6   All translations are mine.

7   See Gérard Genette's study of temporal shifts in narrative in relation to Proust's *Remembrance of Things Past* in *Narrative Discourse: An Essay in Method* (1980, 33–85).

8   "Cafetín de Buenos Aires" begins: "De chiquilín te miraba de afuera / como a esas cosas que nunca se alcanzan; / la ñata contra el vidrio" (Romano 1991, 376) ["As a little boy I looked in at you from the outside / like one of those things that are never obtained; / my nose pressed against the glass"]. There are two further echoes of the same tango later in the novel: "Defino [el apoderado de Gardel] era su vidrio. El vidrio de la ventana en que apoyar su ñata de huerfanita deseosa para espiar a una estrella refulgente que se llamaba Carlos Gardel" (Dujovne Ortiz 1998, 209) ["I define [Gardel's representative] was his glass. The glass of the window on which to press her little orphan's nose, desiring to spy on a shining star who was called Carlos Gardel"] and "Cuando contemplamos una ventana iluminada, la ñata contra el vidrio desde las sombras de afuera ..." (224) ["When we look through a lighted window, our nosed pressed against the glass in the shadows outside ..."].

9   See, for example, Luis Castineira's 1938 lyrics to "Desaliento" ["Despair"], which tell the conventional story of a man whose moral decline results from his having pursued a prostitute: "iba tan ciego y orgulloso como terco / que por una flor de cerco / por el mundo me arrastré" (lyrics found online at www.todotango.com) ["I was as blind and proud as I was stubborn / that for a common flower / I crawled through life"]. In the hands of a lyricist such as Homero Manzi, the image of the humble flower acquires a more poetic turn. In "Malena" (1942) he writes of the effects of the singer's voice: "A yuyo del suburbio su voz perfuma" (Romano 1991, 309) ["Her voice gives off the scent of a common flower of the suburb"].

10   The history and culture of the cafés of Buenos Aires are documented by Jorge A. Bossio (1995) in *Los cafés de Buenos Aires: reportaje a la nostalgia*. The incident at the Café Jarana is narrated on page 272.

11   Moreover, although many tango lyrics have a point of departure in the real world, they generally include more fiction than history. See, for example, the explanatory notes in Romano's *Las letras del tango* indicating the origin of some of the lyrics in his anthology.

12   Since the word "Mireya" is written without any typographical convention to suggest that Dujovne Ortiz is referring to the novel, she is presumably alluding to the source of its main character.

13   "Rosa la milonguita / era rubia Margot" (Romano 1991, 241) ["Rosa the prostitute / Margot was blond"].

14 This is not the only painting and Toulouse-Lautrec is not the only artist alluded to in the novel. There is an oblique reference to Manet's *Déjeuner sur l'herbe*: "Por ahora sólo podía sonreír con timidez, buscando sus ropas, como si a ella también le divirtiese verse desnuda y gorda entre esa gente vestida" (Dujovne Ortiz 1998, 36) ["For now she could only smile, looking for her clothes, as if she too were amused at seeing herself fat and naked among those fully clothed people"]. There is also a running reference to the slippers in the same painter's *Olympia* (see, for example, page 149).

15 This appreciation of Toulouse-Lautrec and information about his life and work are drawn principally from Richard Thomson's essay "Images of the maisons closes," *Toulouse-Lautrec* (New Haven: Yale University Press, 1991), 405–61.

16 I am grateful to Elizabeth Montes for reminding me of this reading.

3 EXILE AND IDENTITY

Exile and Community

Luis Torres, University of Calgary

Despite the present-day claims made by the proponents[1] of globalization concerning the supposed disappearance of the borders that separate nations (just as similar claims were made in the past[2]) the experience of forced displacement, life in refugee camps, migration, and exile still haunts the social imaginary. No claims in favour of the contraction of distance and the compression of time into the fleeting present of technologies and consumption can erase the yearning for attachment and belonging; in spite of the aesthetics of fragmentation and loss of identity, the struggle for identity and community still continues.

Exile is perhaps one experience that can show what is hidden from the view of many by the so-called global community: life in camps at the border of nations, the marginality of many in the metropolis, the pathos implicit in the loss of community, and in the break of the ties to the land. Without giving exile and literature an undue privilege, it is in the artistic representations of this experience that we find an important source for thinking about territorial displacement, attachment to a locality, and the struggle for community.

We understand exile as the forced uprooting of the person from a community and of inhabiting a place while wishing for another. The etymology of the word exile indicates this separation from the place: "saltar afuera" (["jump outside"]; my translation) is the primary sense of *exsilire*, according to Joan Corominas (1954, 129). Another connotation of the word, found in the *Oxford English Dictionary* (1989), points both to the crisis of

55

the community and the negativity of the space: "*essil*, state of banishment, also ... devastation, destruction" (540). This sense of crisis and loss is even more movingly articulated in another meaning of the word: "to have been 'disemboweled'" (541), which refers to the existential crisis of the banished and to how that condition is imagined in the materiality of the body.[3]

Out of these definitions, I would also like to articulate a distinction between the exile in the world of experience or in the reality of everyday life, and the exile represented in artistic expression, those exiles who inhabit imaginary worlds. We should keep in mind, though, that the need for this methodological separation between the two does not inhibit the difficulties of such a division. As can be seen in the definitions above, for example, in the last one we speak of the exile's experience in a poetic or fictional mode, although we are speaking of a real-life experience. Ovid, however, provides a paradigmatic example of a poetic subject who wants to be seen as the real, based only on the wish of the poet who gives life to his poetic persona. In Ovid's *Tristia* (1975), the author sends his book back home to Rome as a substitute for himself. Exiled in Tomis and clothed, as he says, "in disheveled dress as is proper for exiles" (1), he commands: "But go you, however, in place of me to see Rome (it's permitted). / Gods above bring it about! I wish I could now be my book" (3). Perhaps the book and the imaginary character that returns in its pages are nothing but a sad proxy for the exiled author, but who can deny the blurring of the separation and the desire that the representation be the real? We will speak, thus, of poetic subjects or of poetic experience to distinguish the world of fiction from the world of everyday life.

From the previous definitions one can also conclude that the experience of exile can be related to a traumatic event: in some cases, a violent action directed at the person and, in others, an indirect violence originated in the sudden and radical transformation of the surrounding world and the expectations of ordinary life. There is a traumatic dimension attached to the break with the known localities of the subject and in the experience of displacement to the land of asylum. Under these circumstances, the world of the present is transformed into something foreign and menacing, while the world of the past, the one before the upheaval, becomes an object of the imagination or an otherness the exile cannot recover. These aspects underlining the separation from the home determine the character of the experience of exile as one of personal devastation and loss of community.

Despite the traumas and personal instability, in the exile's condition one can also identify an attitude or an ethics that question the identity of the exile as victim and, consequently, the culture of suffering and false compassion. As discussed by Liisa H. Malkki (1997, 64), there has been an inclination to see refugees as anomalous or as victims of a pathological condition: "our sedentarist assumptions about attachment to place lead us to define displacement not as a fact about sociopolitical context but as an inner, pathological condition of the displaced." At the same time, however, it is necessary to distinguish the imposition of this identity of victim from the fact that the exile is in many ways the injured party in the social process that lead to the expulsion. In that sense, he or she really is a victim. Consequently, on the one hand, there is a suffering subject (because of the trauma of displacement) and, on the other hand, there might be an identity imposed from outside by the victimizers or by society.[4]

The victim is also the one who stays in the suffering and whose injury is the mark of his or her identity; this is a subject subordinated to a one-dimensional discourse that always circles back to the trauma.[5] In everyday life the trauma has many dimensions that has been represented in literary works not only as the product of a violence directed at the person, but also as a psychological inability to integrate into the new society, an effect of what one might call the trauma of displacement. This is the condition of the main characters in novels such as *Collect Call* by Leandro Urbina, *De chácharas y largavistas* by Jorge Etcheverry, and *Exile* by Ann Ireland. The questioning of the integration of Ireland's protagonist, Carlos Romero Estévez, is also the product of the heavy burden of expectations from the host society: the desire that he acts as a victim and that he complies with the image imposed on him by the group in Vancouver. The undue expectations forced on Carlos and his lack of adjustment are shown in his confusion, his doubts about himself, and in the many small accidents he suffers: "Again my knees banged against the table and again the peanuts spun off, this time safely to the ground. My head was throbbing: they all had stories constructed for me, much better tales than mine. How would I avoid disappointing them?" (Ireland 2002, 43). Ironically, the exile is expected to retell his traumatic experiences, but he is also required to project himself as a hero who was able to overcome and triumph over adversity. In *Exile*, Carlos refuses to play this identity because it seems he has never been a direct victim of violence and because he rejects the formalities and constant moralistic evaluation of his actions.

As I have mentioned before, in contrast with the identity of the exile as a victim, always returning to the pain or accepting the identity expected by society, one cannot ignore an attitude that is also found in everyday life and in the artistic representations of forced migration and exile: that the same individual, the victim, has the potential to overcome the suffering of trauma and the pain of separation and displacement. This is the attitude towards life that I call the ethics of struggle. Following this ethics, perhaps it is possible to say that in exile one might be witnessing the experience of the one who perseveres in spite of the trauma. Alain Badiou, in *Ethics: An Essay on the Understanding of Evil*, writes about the victim and the immortal in the conditions of concentration camps, where some, against the dehumanization, "remain human beings" (Badiou 2002, 11). This, according to Badiou, "is always achieved precisely through enormous effort, an effort acknowledged by witnesses ... as an almost incomprehensible resistance on the part of that which, in them, *does not coincide with the identity of victim*" (original emphasis; 11). For Badiou that resistance transforms the person into "something other than a mortal being" (12): an immortal.[6] Keeping in mind the circumstances of which Badiou is writing about – the Holocaust – and the condition of exile, one can argue that this resistance is not uncommon. In many cases it is the basis of survival in refugee camps or in the struggle for a new life in exile.

The ethics of struggle radicalizes the notion of perseverance and brings forth the idea that perseverance is an effort and not a given. The effort, following Badiou, is to be "other than a victim, other than a being-for-death" (2002, 12).[7] The fact of perseverance and its radicalization in the struggle is seen in a number of works dealing with the topic of exile and forced migration. Touching on both the trauma of torture in prison and life in exile, Nela Rio's *Túnel de proa verde / Tunnel of the Green Prow* (1998) is exemplary in the way it develops the struggle for life when life itself has become unbearable because of pain and uncertainty. The female character in the poems finds strength in the life of the imagination and in the recognition of silence as a form of resistance to the torturers and of solidarity with the persecuted. This perseverance and the struggle for life is seen in many poems of the collection, but is especially poignant in poem "XVII," which deals with the experience of torture:

Ellos obstinadamente inquisidores
yo obstinadamente silenciosa
en esta noche en que han venido a buscarme.
Ahora sé que volveré
definitivamente victoriosa
aferrando con mi carne dolorida
una palabra escrita que ellos jamás podrán violar. (58)

> They are stubborn inquisitors
> I am stubbornly silent
> in this night when they have come for me.
> Now I know I shall return

finally victorious
grasping with my painful flesh
a written word they shall never violate. (59)

She thus rejects the identity of victim that the torturers try to impose on her, but not as a heroic act of resistance; rather, she does this simply as an act of dignity available to everyone, even in the worst of conditions.

As I have noted so far, exile seems to entail the possibility of an ethics that contradicts the identity of the exile as victim. This ethics is found in the struggle and perseverance that help sustain the individual in the face of despair and loss of community. In what follows, I will maintain these ideas as the ethical framework for the study of the relationship between the loss of community and the effort to imagine and build new ones in exile. I will develop my argument in three stages: first, I will identify some of the images of space in exile; in particular, I am interested in the sense of locality found in the relation of the person to space and community. Second, I will briefly discuss the contradictory meaning of the knowledge implied in those images and in the diaspora. Third, in the conclusion, I will focus on the creation of a new sense of community and belonging in the context of forced displacement.

The many representations of space in relation to exile seem to coalesce in at least two major extremes: on the one hand, there are those of a world in ruins in which space is seen as chaotic, foreign, and menacing; while on the other, the images of space appear to have a positive meaning for the subject, who sees the possibility of an encounter and reconciliation with the world. The image of the storm while crossing the sea towards exile in the case of Ovid's *Tristia* is the paradigmatic example of the chaos that affects the world and the spirit of the exile. This is how the crisis of the poetic subject is described in the poem:

> We are lost! There's no doubt of disaster, our hope of salvation has
> vanished,
> And while I am talking the waters are splashing all over my face.
> The billows are crushing my spirit, in vain all my prayers to protect
> me,
> My mouth will receive the wild breakers, they'll overwhelm me at
> last.
> But my loyal wife is weeping for nothing except that I'm exiled:
> Only this evil of mine is she conscious of, this she deplores.
> She knows not I'm tossed on an ocean immense, where my body is
> floating,

She knows not that the winds are driving nor that my end is at hand.
(1975, 7)

The poetry of the Latin-Canadian writers, such as in *Tequila Sunrise* (1985) by the Chilean poet Erik Martínez, is also haunted by the images of a menacing world that seems to overflow the consciousness of the poetic voice. The poem "Tequila Sunrise," for example, develops the topic of creation as an experience in which the poetic subject tries to affirm himself in the face of his own vision of a transforming world:

De repente hubo una gran explosión.
Un relámpago incandescente iluminó el cielo.
Las estrellas comenzaron a girar y fulguraron
más brillantes que el cielo ardiendo.
La tierra se abrió y yo pude ver sus dimensiones interiores.
¡Había llamas por todas partes!
Agitadas y turbulentas como un océano atormentado.
El espacio entero parecía girar.
Creo que yo era lo único que permanecía estático. (57)

   Suddenly there was a great explosion.
   An incandescent lightning-bolt lit up the sky
   The stars began to whirl and flared
   more brightly than the burning sky
   the earth opened and I could see the depths within
   There were flames on all sides!
   Agitated, turbulent, like a stormy sea.
   Space itself seemed to revolve,
   I believe I was the only static thing (56)

As I have mentioned, parallel to this alienating view, in exiles' writings the world has also been represented in a more positive light. In Luciano A. Díaz's poem, "The Streets," from his book, *The Thin Man and Me* (1994), the streets of the city, though "angular and orderly," become open and inviting:

   The streets, somewhat timidly,
   invited us to burst through the winter.
   The main streets invited us,
   with their sweet and cold indifference,
   to fill spaces,

the emptiness left in moments of boredom and lifelessness.
The streets led us to cafés, bookstores and meetings:
train stops in this labyrinth,
in the search to
reach life.
The streets carried us far. (21)

For Julio Torres-Recinos, in "He bajado a los infiernos," from *Crisol de tiempo* (2000), there is also a possibility for an embrace between the exile, the peripatetic Ulysses in this case, and the world of the diaspora and its inhabitants:

He bajado a los infiernos, a los fijos,
a los reales como una piedra en el rostro,
los que se nombran países, naciones,
territorios que en mi cara tornan

sus nombres en exilio, en tránsito, en ajeno.
He conocido buenas gentes, a qué negarlo,
que me han ayudado, que se han acercado
a la tripulación con un vaso de vino,
....
Por esas gentes soy hombre en reino extraño ...(3)

> [I have walked down to hell, to the never-changing ones,
> to those as real as a stone hitting the face,
> those named countries, nations,
> territories that in my face change
> their names into exile, into transitoriness, into foreignness
> I have meet good people, why deny it,
> who have helped me, who have come near
> the crew with a glass of wine
>
> Because of those people I am person in a foreign land ...]
> (My translation)

The Spaniard Jesús López Pacheco is another poet who is able to find a connection with the land of exile in his poem "Poetic Asylum":

> Canada, page of snow. I am beginning
> to write slowly in you the steps

of the second part of my life.
I almost fear to stain your whiteness
with prints of the pain I have brought.
To write new verses in the snow,
I would want to be white. But I have
the colour of the life I've lived. (1991, 19)

Here, in spite of the desire to be part of and embrace the Canadian space, there is a distance between the subject's life, the "prints of pain," and the purity of the world represented in the snow. That distance, as I have mentioned concerning the image of the victim, can also turn into an artistic representation of the inability or indifference towards integration, as it happens to the "Sociólogo" in *Collect Call* (Urbina 1999), or to Carlos, the exile character in Ireland's novel. Sex, drinking, and a propensity to accidents appear to symbolize their lack of social acumen and, consequently, indicate their marginality. These and other characters, such as the man with the binoculars in *De chácharas y largavistas* (Etcheverry 1995), come to a point where the process of integration is subverted by the realization of the artificiality of the encounter. What was considered an embrace soon becomes an empty gesture and the space of unity turns into a site of social and existential marginality.[8]

Among some postmodern thinkers, such as Julia Kristeva in her essay "A New Type of Intellectual: The Dissident," and Thomas Docherty in *Alterities: Criticism, History, Representation*, exile has also been regarded as a desired space of creativity or a territory that would allow the person to escape from the restrictions imposed on life and imagination in the modern world.[9] Exile is not a place from which one should flee but a locality one should embrace. Another significant image is the one based on the Scriptures, wherein exile is seen as a universal condition: we are all exiles because we have been expelled from paradise to a world of suffering. The world, then, is the space of exile. These two dimensions of space vis-à-vis exile, the space one desires and the space of the universal, either flatten the pathos of the experience or erase its subversive force in non-differentiating universality. In contrast, it is important for us to consider what is implicit in the sense of space and in the particularities of the subject's relation with the world in exile, and not to transform the experience into an all-encompassing image.

Based on these generalities, it might be relevant to stress that the notion of space has a geometrical connotation that is not completely appropriate for the description of place in the context of the human habitat in general, and in the exile's experience in particular. In contrast, the idea of locality, as noted by Arjun Appadurai, "is an aspect of social life" (1995, 204)[10] and represents a broad system of relationships with emphasis in the context of the experience. Locality, as seen in both the world of experience and in the fictional world of texts, is a social dimension codified by a complex system of production and reproduction of a sense of place and belonging. While it is in the sense of locality that we understand the references to space in the context of exile, we do not ignore the tension present in the images of the territories, or the materiality of the place and the feelings implicated in that vision. Such is the case, for instance, in the representations we noticed before: the world in ruins, the site of a possible reconciliation, the desired space, and the universal space of the same.

It is clear then that the images of locality in the context of exile are strongly associated with the territory or the materiality of space, but they also are concerned with the relationships between the subject and the surrounding world. Now, if exile implies a break with locality and displacement from the known territories to the unknown, then one wonders about what is broken in that relationship in the context of real-life experience, and also in its representation in artistic form. In my opinion, this is not only a break with a naturalized system of relations, but mainly the crisis of a structure that is more difficult to erase and that persists in the feelings of belonging and fidelity to the place that are not controlled by the official ideology of the state. This implies that, in addition to the general crisis of belonging, a belonging formalized and co-opted by the structures of the nation, what seems to be more important is the loss of that which constitutes the *particularity of the situation* of the person or the group regarding the place and the community.[11]

Let us note, briefly again, that belonging is in many ways constructed as a fiction of the state's ideology and that the loss of the particularity of the situation could also be described and communicated to others by artistic means. Moreover, as can be seen from the definitions of exile, the limit between life and fiction is sometimes erased by the ways in which we imagine and speak that borderline condition. In the next examples, I will be touching on several expressions that can be called poetic, but which are found not only in the realm of poetry, but also in the ways cultural theorists and ethnologists speak of exile. In poetry, for instance, the social break of the subject with the surrounding world, as locality and community, is imagined in the metaphor of the uprooted tree. The Spaniard poet Rafael Alberti, exiled in Argentina after the Spanish Civil War, used this metaphor in "Canción" from his *Baladas y canciones del Paraná (1953–1954)* to convey the trauma of separation:

... mi canto
puede ser de cualquier parte.
Pero estas rotas raíces,
ay, estas rotas raíces! ...
....
... Amigos,
aunque mi canto quisiera
ser del mundo,
tiene al aire sus raíces,
y le falta el alimento
de la tierra conocida.
Y es como el árbol que sube
sin ser de ninguna parte ... (1976, 58")[12]

> [... my song
> could be of any place.
> But these broken roots,
> alas, these broken roots
> ....
> ... My friends,
> even though my song would like
> to belong to the world,
> it has its roots in the air,
> and it lacks the nourishment
> of the motherland.
> And it is like a tree that grows
> And does not belong ...] (My translation)

Notably, as in Ovid's poem, in these verses there is also the claim of a transposed identity between the writer, the poetic persona, and his poetry ("mi canto"): to describe his condition Alberti writes of the uprootedness of his poetry. The separation of the poetic subject and of Alberti himself from the nurturing environment of home displayed in the image of the uprooted tree is also taken up by critical anthropology, such as in the case of Liisa H. Malkki in her investigations of the modern condition of resettlement and diaspora. For example, Malkki studies the root metaphor or what she calls "botanical metaphors" (1997, 56) and their functions "in the natural-izing of the links between people and place" because, she adds, "[P]eople are often thought of, and think of themselves, as being rooted in place and as deriving their identity from that rootedness" (56). To be rooted, then, both in the world of poetry and in the world of experience, implies that one belongs and is tied to a territory in which the self can be projected in unity with others. To be uprooted, on the other hand, questions the relation with the place and the community and, as a result, the subject's identity. Poetic discourse, in Alberti, deals with the objectivities of the condition as well as with the emotive side of the experience, without separating the two. Critical discourses in the social sciences and literature, I may add, are at pains when confronted with the question of emotions, and want to separate the factual from the metaphysical. Even Malkki's essay, which seems to arrive at the questions of emotions implicated in the root metaphor, leaves them aside to emphasize the more objective aspects of the "naturalizing" process of settlement and belonging.

As we have seen, uprooting questions the exile's identity and brings forth the notion that the image of oneself in the world is constructed in contact with the surrounding environment and the community and, as the exile's artistic representations appear to dramatize, especially with the particularity of the situation of the person in the locality. In view of the lack of the specificity of the situation, the space is transformed into a site with parameters that must be constantly rearticulated, while the subject who creates those relations is herself/himself involved in a process to reconstruct her/his own integrity in the middle of the ruins. Space becomes a frontier and the person a liminal being, situated between the familiar world and a world that is foreign and, sometimes, threatening.

Robert Edwards, in his literary study of exile, describes this liminal space as one of transition "from organized space invested with meaning to a boundary where the conditions of experience are problematic" (1988, 16–17). Exile, then, is a frontier torn by different drives that have an unsettling effect on the subject's experiences and expectations. Two forces seem to be at work at the border locality: on one side, the structures of the known and significant, those familiar signs that can be read in the surrounding world and, on the other, the frontier space itself, a site of unexpected and sudden openness and transformations.

That frontier is the location where the exile struggles to find a basis on which to organize his or her experiences and to make sense of the new signs. But if exile is a frontier, and if on this side the space responds to some categories of order and knowledge, then it is appropriate to ask about the nature of the space away from the limit: Is that space always a frontier or is it the site of a possible new order? In my own poetic work, in *El exilio y las ruinas* (2002), I have written of that border in the image of the ruins: a known locality but also an open site for the imagination. In the ruins, as life is seen from exile, there seems to emerge the presence of those who have returned only to find the destruction of themselves and the world. In my poem "Los descarnados," the border and liminal space of transition of which the critic speaks is that of an encounter and of a sending off back to the north towards life again:

Ellos me empujaban a las fronteras,
        la asesinada,
        el poeta,
        el pintor,
        los colgados
que murieron por nosotros,
        los descarnados
que salían llamando,
        sus presencias que tocaba.
Allí estaban con sus rostros que borraron
        porque eran los únicos
                que me quedaban
                    en esa
                        despedida. (2002, 75–76)

        [They pushed me towards the frontiers,
            the murdered one,
            the poet,
            the painter,
            the ones who hanged themselves
        and died for us,
            the ones without flesh
        who were coming out calling me,
                their presence I could touch.

        There they were with their fleshless faces
            because they were the only ones
                left for me
                    when
                        I departed.] (My translation)

James Clifford (1997, 254) defines *diaspora* as a condition of "dwelling-in-displacement." This is an "in-between" locality where one lives in constant ambivalence and in the tension between the order one had before and the new state of unexpected openness. Similar to exile, diaspora is a space of experience that cannot be fixed or defined by stable borders.[13] The alliance between the subject and the world is dislocated by this instability and by the ambiguity affecting the relationship with the new space. The desire for what was left behind, the old space that occupies the imagination, does not allow the projection of a non-mediated relation with the localities of asylum. As it happens to some exiles represented in novels and poetry, they appear to be always returning (in their imagination) to the old spaces of home while traversing the cities of asylum. Alberti in Argentina imagines Spain and his beloved Cádiz, and Chile is on the minds of many characters in the stories of *De cuerpo entero* (1997) by Carmen Rodríguez as well as that of Jorquera, the main character in the *De chácharas y largavistas*.

Clifford's notion of diaspora, in the sense of residing or the being in place while in movement, is also close to the ethics of struggle we have mentioned before. Perseverance, in this case, is that of the need for home or for settlement in the open space of displacement. Dwelling is also a form of lingering, an insisting, which, for us, concerns the person's persevering for being in residence and in community. It can be argued that writing is in itself a form of dwelling and a way of attempting the permanence of the representation of certain experiences. It is also a perseverance to sustain a language and its cultures, and a struggle to affirm the self and the possible community in the face of the uncertainties of exile.

Edward Said in "The Mind of Winter" (1984) also studies the condition of space in exile. Said writes that exile is "the unhealable rift forced between a human being and a native place, between the self and its true home" (49). Here, exile becomes a tearing or a wound that separates the subject from one's familiar world. At the same time, exile as rift seems to plunge the self into the very wound that is one's own image. In front of the rift that cannot be healed, one is the witness and the victim. There is neither remedy to cure the break in the relationship between the person and the space in this border life nor a reprieve in the landscape on the other side of that frontier. Hence, it appears that this condition, in its radicality, points to the nature of the knowledge found in exile and begins to answer the question about what is there on the other side of the border: the unhealable (49). Perhaps the marginality of "el sociólogo" in Urbina's *Collect Call*, the sadness of Alberti, or the crisis of identity of the subject in my own work in *El exilio y las ruinas* are a testimony of this condition without remedy.

We should keep in mind, though, that the unhealability of the situation does not exclude the struggle and the hope for a better condition. From this point of view, and considering that the image does not refer necessarily to a pathology of the individual (which is also possible), the evil of the situation is its lack of resolution. Strictly speaking, this evil, the unhealable, is the same presence that inhabits the images of the uprooting, the border, and the displacement. It is also the presence that undermines the community, because the unhealable is what corrodes the sense of being near others and transforms the locality into a site not of communion, but of separation. In a more general and less literary sense, "the unhealable rift" allows us to see more clearly the shortcomings of the community when it becomes an artificial imposition, reified in the myths of the nation or in the idea of a cohesive whole situated inside fixed boundaries. On the other hand, what is left of community in exile is precisely its character as project; not what is given by the system, but the effort to build it. This idea brings us closer to the imperatives of perseverance in the localities and the experiences of that which, according to Said, cannot be cured. This is a perseverance that appears in the struggle to construct a sense of community from the specificity of the subject's circumstances. The roots of this poesis of community, as we will see in its literary representations, rest in the interpellation of shared memories.

The instability of the place in exile can also be imagined in the presence of an otherness that haunts the space of the familiar. This idea is an extrapolation of what Homi Bhabha (1994a, 9) calls the "unhomely" or "the condition of extra-territorial and cross-cultural initiations." This condition, explains Bhabha, does not imply a negation of home, but it refers to a moment when something that was hidden appears on the surface of experience. Life in exile, in many instances, is similar to this "unhomely moment" when the displaced images, such as those of the home, come to the surface to break the order one is seeking. The individual who walks the streets of the city of asylum perceives in them another familiarity, one that has persisted in her/his memory and comes to break the logic of the new locality. Estela de Ramírez, the main character in the story "Agujero negro" by Carmen Rodríguez, suffers a similar experience when in her confusion a street in Santiago, Monjitas, appears superimposed on a street in Vancouver:

De día, mientras jugaba con los niños en la guardería o manejaba por el tráfico de Vancouver, se esforzaba por recordar lugares, caras, olores, colores, acentos. Pero nunca lograba la claridad que buscaba. Todo se le aparecía borroneado, pálido, distorsionado. Cuando pensaba que sí, que así era la calle Monjitas, se daba cuenta de que no estaba segura si ese café estaba en verdad ahí, o en la calle Main. (1994, 65)

> [During the day, while playing with the children in the day-care or while driving in the Vancouver traffic, she tried to remember places, faces, smells, colours, accents. But was never able to find the clarity she was seeking. Everything appeared to her as if diffused, paled, distorted. When she though she was sure that Monjitas looked the same, she

realized that she was not sure if that café was truly there or in Main Street.] (My translation)

In its social connotation, as well, exile seems to formulate an "unhomely moment" of the order of the nations. This is because exile, in its ambiguity, subverts the basis of the reification of community, such as the myths of nationhood and the naturalized and unproblematic ties to the territory. In addition, since exile implies the sudden and traumatic break of the bonds of the person and the world, it tends to cast doubt on the generalities surrounding the "jouissance" of displacement. The festive promotion of travel across borders, fragmentation, liminality, and globality has its opposite image in the life in refugee camps at the borders of nations, in the marginality of the "aliens" in the metropolis, in the nostalgia for home, and in the struggle for identity. Exile, that unhomely moment that haunts the global, remind us of the specificity of the subject's situation – the being-there and the yearning attached to one's places of origin after the forced separation.

Since it is possible to think of the unhomely as a symbolic and momentary relocation of home (the familiar), this moment entails the break of the borders that separates the public and the private. As we have seen, the private comes to the surface in the reappearance of suppressed images, and those images fracture the order of the world or the public space of the land of asylum. This instance of the fracture of the two realities contains an ethical dimension since, according to Bhabha (1994a, 15), following Levinas, "it effects an 'externality of the inward' ..." that we understand as the expression of the dimension of the suppressed in the experience of exile. The instant in which the unhomely breaks the surface is the moment in which exile announces its truths to the world.

The metaphors and images we have mentioned, the uprooted tree, the frontier, the dwelling in displacement, the unhealable rift and the unhomely, not only portray a sense of space and locality in the everyday-life experience of the exile, but they are also a picture of the poetic subject in crisis. The image as such, however, does not totalize and cannot integrate the representations of exile into a new and stable state of coherence. The unhealable rift, for example, is also incurable in that the image continues producing different meanings. The rift is just one instance among many of the struggle to imagine exile and, whatever we capture of its meaning, it cannot be made a totality or a single truth. Despite these uncertainties, the instances of this imaginary of exile can be thought of as a kind of symbolic map that allows us to get near its dilemmas and ambiguities.

This indirect or metaphorical approach to the exile's locality, according to Michael Seidel, is similar to the cognitive act in Søren Kierkegaard's story about the imagination in *Either/Or*, where "the line marking the end of the familiar is the same as that marking the beginning of the unknown. The line that limits is also the line that dares" (Seidel 1986, 3). According to Seidel, following Kierkegaard, it is possible to imagine the other side by the shape of the boundaries of the known country. The imagined space is not completely foreign since it is structured by what Robert Edwards (1988, 16) calls the "eidetic structure" of the familiar territories: the space left behind because of exile or the place of asylum, which in time might become a known territory. In metaphors there is a familiarity at the literal level or on the side of the known, and this familiarity is in tension with the unfamiliarity of poetic signification or the side of the unknown. As we have seen, the new projections from the images and metaphors referring to space, together with the challenging sense of locality in the exile's representations, are the means to explore that border and the other side. In this sense, the metaphor, such as the uprooted tree, is the "line that dares" (Seidel 1986, 3) to imagine the inside of that liminal experience. As a result, the other side is neither muted nor unknowable; it speaks to us in the direct testimony of the exile and in the languages of art.

The tension implicit in the instability and contradictory nature of space in exile, and the effort to make sense of it in language, suggests a question about the possibility of achieving some knowledge out of those localities and experiences. Without doubt, there is already knowledge implicit in the images and metaphors we have seen. The creative exploration of the border externalizes the contents of the pathos of exile and, in that sense, produces knowledge and an awareness of the possible truths of the situation and of what exceeds the specificity of the condition. The knowledge of what exceeds the specificity of exile is what the metaphor is there to enunciate: the wound without remedy, the uprooted tree; in other words, the dimension that cannot be articulated in literal terms.[14] Knowledge, therefore, situated in the condition of the one who suffers the experience but also knowledge in the openness of what exceeds the event of suffering. Let us keep in mind, though, that in literary representation these two instances of knowledge are not separated from one another; instead, they are present, as we have seen, in the tensional structure of the metaphors.

However, while taking into account the particularity of the situation, we cannot leave aside the truths of exile in their general significations: their value in light of concepts such as community and belonging. Knowledge, in this case, is what the situation tells us of the meanings of the contact of the individual or the group with the community and the localities; it is also the lessons one can learn when faced with the traumatic loss of the ties to the land and the struggle to renew or establish new relations in the space of displacement. In any event, we should note that these lessons are framed by the particular experiences of those confronted with the task to imagine the home and belonging in the space of the absence of home or, as Liisa Malkki (1997, 52) points out, of places that cannot be inhabited any longer.

My intention is not to make of exile a privileged experience based on the supposed value of its contents; what is important is what the illumination the study of exile can bring to the ethical dilemmas that confront us as critics. We also have the possibility of exploring the other side of the politics of displacement and of the "unhomely moment" that haunts the order of the global world and the pleasures of non-belonging. Thinking of localities and belonging, imagining the land and exploring the basis of old and new ties, giving shape to a new sense of community: all of these can have an important critical value that could help challenge the traditional ideas of the nation-state and the intention of our elites to create a global community dominated by capital and technologies.

I recognize that this interpretation of the situation of exile as a critique of the modern world and the supposed inevitability of progress towards the global at the cost of displacement, marginality, and the evil of military and cultural conquest, does present some problems when one considers the pathos of exile: the possible critical force of exile that I propose is based on a condition that can offer knowledge but also hopelessness. Here, the ethical dilemma is implicit in the fact of extracting knowledge from an experience impregnated by subjectivities, conflicting desires, and emotions; that is, of forcing the supposed objectivity of exegesis over the subjectivity of speaking from inside the experience or of reifying the moment when the private comes to the surface and is made public. However, for critical work, one possible way to interpret the exile's condition without transforming it into another instrument of knowledge may be the ethical recognition of its contradictory condition and the possibility of learning that come from it. This is what Homi Bhabha (1994b, 172) argues in one of his essays when he writes: "a range of contemporary critical theories suggest that it is from those who have suffered the sentence of history – subjugation, domination, diaspora, displacement – that we learn our most enduring lessons for living and thinking." The recognition of the condition of exile, its otherness, localities, feelings and ethics of struggle, and the ethical problem traced on the terrain of criticism gives an open character to those "enduring lessons." It does not empty its pathos or transform it into a totalizing revelation that would allow the exile to escape from contradiction.

On the other hand, to seek a lesson from the experience of exile, to consider, for example, the meaning of the structures of feelings in that experience and the struggle to give form to the self and to community in the space of loss, is in itself to seek for knowledge. For us this knowledge or lesson "for living and thinking" is found in the liberating possibilities of the ethics of struggle in exile. We see this ethics in the perseverance of the person, who persists despite the negativity of the condition. This is the individual who resists the identity of victim and becomes another, not a being previous to the trauma or superior to it, simply another that affirms his or her existence over the contingencies of life. This effort does not erase the trauma, but imagining the ethics of struggle in exile is a recognition of the perseverance that sustains the truths of the one who resists the injustice.

On the basis of that perseverance and under the conditions of what Homi Bhabha (1994b, 172) calls "cultures of survival," in what follows I would like to explore the ways in which the exile thinks about or imagines the community represented in the artistic work. In general, community can be understood as a structured whole organized around a communality of interests that unites the social nucleus and , because of its claims, excludes others from its association. It could also originate out of a strong sense of belonging to a place and to the social world achieved through personal experiences, and not as something given by the state's ideology. These forms of community are not exempt from criticism when, for example, the community of the nation becomes a reified entity whose institutions are there to serve not the members of society, but its own bureaucratic reproduction. Even the idea of community based on the specificity of an individual's feelings of belonging to a locality, for instance, can develop into images of transcendence that negate the possibilities of developing a creative relationship with new experiences and localities.

Against the supposed transparency of belonging, of a belonging framed in the legalities of citizenship and on the idea of a naturalized relationship between a culture or group to a territory, and also against the temptation of transforming the home into an idealized entity, exile sharpens the ways of thinking and of giving form to community and to the idea of belonging. As we have seen in the cases discussed before, in the context of loss the force of perseverance and the affirmation of the individual are both examples and celebrations of the struggles to imagine new forms of community. Such communities are not tied to a locality or to reified notions of the *sensus communis* but can still sustain a sense of belonging that has some value to assert the continuity of the individual. The emotions implicated in the loss, the passing of time and the distance from the places of origin, as we saw in López Pacheco and others, have already undermined the possible reification of the community of home in the imaginings of these writers. What was the totality of home has become fragmented and immersed with feelings that cannot be reduced to a single truth. Exile, then, entails the forced displacement of people from home and the breaking of bonds between community and territory; this trauma of displacement and deracination has a critical force that points to the shortcomings of the community of the nation and the idea of a global community. As we will see next, it also highlights the "imagined" character of community in the space of transition.

Akhil Gupta and James Ferguson (1997, 39) write that it is under conditions of personal and collective displacement that

> it becomes most visible how imagined communities (Anderson 1983) come to be attached to imagined places, as displaced peoples cluster around remembered or imagined homelands, places, or communities in a world that seems increasingly to deny such firm territorialized anchors in their actuality.

Before concentrating on the particularities of the imagined character of the diasporic communities and of their textual representations, I should clarify Anderson's ideas concerning the "imagined community" alluded to by Gupta and Ferguson. According to Anderson (1983, 15), the community of the nation "is *imagined* because the members of even the smallest nation will never know most of their fellow-members, meet them, or even hear of them, yet in the minds of each lives the image of their communion." In addition, the community of the nation is situated inside frontiers that are more or less defined and which, as a national community, excludes those who are outside the borders. It is worth noting, then, that at the roots of the community there is this violence of exclusion, and also the fact that the "image of the communion" of the members of the group is generally based on a mythology of the nation imposed and promoted by the state's institutions. Such imaginary of nationhood is, of course, never monolithic. According to Bhabha (1994c, 231) the myths and images of the project that unites the anonymous inhabitants are subverted by what he calls "group identifications," and by the emergence of "minority discourses" that do not coincide with the national project and the nation's identity. Exile is another possible discourse that comes to question the notion of the national community. It is a minority discourse that is better excluded from the national referents since it is seen as dangerous to the state's unity.

Judging by the ideas proposed by Gupta and Ferguson, Anderson's "imagined community" can be applied to the condition of territorial displacement in the modern world and, by extension, to the problem of how community is imagined and represented in exile. In exile, this question comes to the surface at the time when the order of collective images is broken and the person comes to think of communalities as the shared feelings and memories of separation and traumatic loss of the links to the place. This is the case, for example, in the poetry of *El exilio y las ruinas*, in which the community is founded and projected out of the rubble of the ruins, and in the communion with the disappeared and the ones who have returned but have never found the other's embrace. To think about the community in this context is to think about the loss of the immediate relation with the place (now the ruins), and of the break affecting the proximity with others, which leads to what may be called a community of loss and desire. When considering the traumas implicit in exile, such as seen in those who have suffered torture, life in concentration camps, and marginality in cities of transition, those shared experiences take the shape of a new communality: that of the memory of those events.

Liisa Malkki (1997b, 92) calls the communities imagined out of experiences such as wars, revolutions, and life in concentration camps or refugee camps "accidental communities of memory." She explains in the following manner the communality in these communities of memory:

People who have experienced such things together carry something in common – something that deposits in them *traces* that can have a peculiar resistance to appropriation by others who were not there. These momentary, out-of-the-ordinary periods of shared history can produce (more or less silent) communities of memory that neither correspond to any ethnologically recognizable community, nor form with any inevitability (original emphasis).

Because they are based on accidental encounters, these communities are thought of as being formed around memories of events and circumstances that have shattered the order of daily life. Further, as stated by Malkki, they have left traces that are difficult to share with those who have not experienced them. Without pretending to explore those memories, it should be stressed that it is not only a communality based on trauma or suffering; for many there is also the memory of struggle and the perseverance for life that overcomes the identity of the victim in those circumstances.

Many communities of memory inhabit the imaginary of exile. The poets Rafael Alberti and Jesús López Pacheco, for example, create a sense of community in their remembrance of the uprooting and out of the yearning for the Spanish landscape and its people. Nela Rio, in *Túnel de proa verde / Tunnel of the Green Prow*, writes about life in prison and of torture of the woman prisoner and thus gives form to a communality of memory that is also a recovery of the presence of the forgotten other. Carmen Rodríguez's stories, as well as the poems of *Guerra prolongada – Protracted War*, not only create community out of traumatic memories, but also in solidarity with the persecuted and in the acknowledgment of being part of a chain of memories and presences, as exemplified in "Su memoria":

> and those
> still to come
> who will they be
> great-great-grandchildren
> of miner and washerwoman
> great-grandchildren
> of teacher and housewife
> children of the three
> children of
> daughter
> granddaughter
> mother
> woman
>
> working towards definition
> at the tip of
> two tongues (Rodríguez 1992, 31)

In "Exiliados," *Vitral con pájaros*, Jorge Etcheverry (2002, 20) imagines the other side of the moment of separation, of those who stayed behind and are thinking of those who are leaving and will put down new roots in another land:

Nos dijeron que se iban
Que muy pronto volverían

Pero nosotros sabíamos en nuestro corazón
que no veríamos de nuevo esas caras ansiosas
de pupilas dilatadas por el miedo
por sueños imposibles
Ellos habrán de echar sus raíces lejos
fuera de nosotros

> [They told us they were leaving
> That soon they would come back.

But we knew in our hearts
That we were not going to see those anxious faces again
With their pupils dilated by fear
By impossible dreams
They would put down their roots far
away from us] (My translation)

Here, Etcheverry brings us closer to the break of community as well as to its future reconstruction. The same writer has dealt with the question of community and solidarity in that future, his now of asylum. In *A vuelo de pájaro: Miniantología personal*, the possibility of community seems to imply the recovery of the marginalized (the rebel, the prophet, the vagabonds that inhabit the margins of the city, and the immigrants):

Los inmigrantes con que nos topamos por ejemplo en el bus
de repente
....
La mujer, el marido, los niños chicos
en el último asiento
hablando en español de sus cosas
y uno como un ladrón furtivo
escuchándolos
....
Y quizás ha valido la pena
venir a dar aquí ... (1998, 42)

> [The immigrants that we bump into for example on the bus
> suddenly
> ....
> The wife, the husband, the children
> in the last seat
> speaking in Spanish of their things
> and I like a furtive thief
> listening to them
> And perhaps it was worthwhile
> to have come to this land ...] (My translation)

On the one hand, the forms of community in these texts, based on memories and desires for belonging, are saved from reification by the contradictory feelings implicit in them: the remembrance and the need to overcome the separation. Novels such as *Collect Call*, *De chácharas y largavistas* and *Exile*, on the other hand, present the reader with the difficulties of establishing a sense of belonging and of giving a positive direction to the struggle for community. The ethics of struggle and perseverance is marred in these novels by the inability to overcome the marginality or simply by being indifferent to the process of integration, especially when that process is being determined by their hosts, as it happens in Ann Ireland's novel.

As can be seen in these cases, the accidental communities of memory subvert the rigidity of the community of the nation because they are open, personal, and charged with feelings and emotions. Its subjective nature also unsettles the idea of the global community when it shows us the other side of displacement: suffering, nostalgia for home or for a sense of belonging, and the ethic of struggle that leads to the imagining of new communities in the context of loss. We should not ignore, though, the possible negative impulses of communities in exile, of the desire to impose a single truth when this is what sustains its memories and identity. However, this danger does not erase the subversive force of the exile's experience and of the communities of memory. Exile helps bring to light the false naturality of the community of the nation and of its fictions, and it reveals the failings of the enjoyment of displacement. Without insisting on the negative, exile shows the loss of the specificity of the subject's situation in the community, of one's familiar surroundings, and of the ties with the immediate group. Considering this loss, one can hopefully see the contradictory nature of the sense of community represented in exile itself: on the one hand, the loss and the effort to create it, and on the other, its instability and the struggle against it when the community becomes an alienating imposition.

In "Community after Devastation: Culture, Politics, and the 'Public Space'" (1993), David Carroll writes about the possibility of thinking about the community after its destruction. His essay focuses on the study of the sense of community in Hannah Arendt, Jean-François Lyotard, and Jean-Luc Nancy, authors who have as their referent Kant's ideas about critical judgement. The main point developed by Carroll, seen in his reading of Nancy, is to come to an understanding of an open sense of community. Similar to the questions opened up by exile, the problem, according to Carroll is "how to think community, how to act in the name of community, in the absence of any reliable foundation for community and without recourse to an ideal or myth of community" (180).

To think about the community of memory after devastation does not presume a desire to recover a lost community, nor the privileging of a foundational moment situated at the origin of trauma, nor the structuring of the future community around an idealized notion. It is to think the community as a way of being, of acting with others and of imagining it in a process that has in itself the seeds of its own critique. This is a critique of community that, at the same time that it resists its call, does not forget the need to be with others. That is what Carroll brings forth in his reading of Nancy in *La Communauté Désoeuvrée*:

Nancy implies ... that the resistance that constitutes a response to the demands of community must be double: first, a resistance to community as work or to the working (fashioning) of a people, an identity or a social space ... and, at the same time, second, a resistance to the obliteration of community, which is already in itself the extreme form of devastation. (1993, 186–87)

Together with the exigencies of the struggle for community, it is important to note here a relationship between community and the idea of evil. In this context, evil is the act of announcing the community, with its impositions and its possible exclusionary nature. According to Alain Badiou (2002, 86), "the community and the collective are the unnameables of political truth: every attempt 'politically' to name a community induces a disastrous evil." The communities of memory are not exempted from this danger; rather, this danger is underscored by what the very enunciation of community allows us to see: that its devastation is a form of evil and that from its ruins the individual and the group resist, as Carroll states, their destruction. As we have seen, each act of the artistic imagination, the writing of a poem, a story, or a film, is an example of this drive to build a community, but at the same time it is the testimony of the consequences of its devastation.

In summary, we have seen that the geography of exile could be explored through the mediation of images and metaphors that seek to capture the foreignness of its spaces, the traumas that inhabit and the catastrophe that marks the separation, the wound, between the "I" and locality.[15] In this manner, we come close to a sense of place and of its lost materiality in expressions such as the border, the dwelling in displacement, the unhealable rift, and the moment of the negation of the familiar. This way of referring to the experience of exile and of thinking about its localities presents a dilemma concerning the knowledge of those places and its voices; this is the ethical conflict implicit in the search for knowledge and for a social critique based on borderline experiences that have a high emotional value. This dilemma, it seems to us, is in danger of being resolved by the imposition of an exclusionary criterion and, thus, by the formulation of a single and all-encompassing truth. Perhaps it is the recognition of the exemplary character of those liminal experiences, as proposed by Bhabha, which can help overcome the ethical problem implicit in the knowledge of that condition. From this point of view, the knowledge or the lessons of exile are contained in the ethics of struggle and in the perseverance of the individual in the face of evil.

Concerning the community, as we have seen, exile dramatizes the break in the relationship between community and territory, between the subject and the locality. But, let us insist, not only the contact with the material space and the others is lost but also, and perhaps more importantly, the network of relationships that creates the locality and the belonging to the community. I am referring to the emotional investment one makes in the ways we build a sense of being part of the community, of giving it materiality, of imagining it, and of projecting oneself as an active being in the world. That which is lost in exile, then, is a sense of the world that combines the image of space with the personal and collective threads by which one is tied to a place.

Not all is devastation regarding the community and the exile. The ethics of struggle and the perseverance evident in the negation of the condition of the subject as victim entail the projection of new sense of community: that of a process which, while calling for community, does not hide from the critique of the forces that could transform it into an oppressive entity. Finally, as we have seen, to imagine the community in the liminal space of exile might take the form of the accidental communities of memory, a dwelling that is also a remembrance. The presence of those memories is a strong influence on the modes of thinking about a new sense of belonging and the task of building communities in the localities of asylum.

Works Cited

Alberti, Rafael. 1976. *Baladas y canciones del Paraná (1953–1954): Poemas del Destierro y de la espera*. Madrid: Espasa-Calpe.

Appadurai, Arjun. The Production of Locality. In *Counterworks: Managing the Diversity of Knowledge*, ed. Richard Fardon, 204–25. London: Routledge.

Anderson, Benedict. 1983. *Imagined Communities: Reflections on the Origin and Spread of Nationalism*. London: Verso.

Badiou, Alain. 2002. *Ethics: An Essay on the Understanding of Evil*. Trans. Peter Hallward. London: Verso.

Bhabha, Homi. 1994a. Introd. to *The Location of Culture*, 1–18. London: Routledge.

———. 1994b. The Postcolonial and the Postmodern: The Question of Agency. In *The Location of Culture*, 171–97. London: Routledge.

———. 1994c. How Newness Enters the World: Postmodern Space, Postcolonial Times and the Trials of Cultural Translation. In *The Location of Culture*, 212–35. London: Routledge.

Carroll, David. 1993. Community after Devastation: Culture, Politics, and the 'Public Space.' In *Politics, Theory, and Contemporary Culture*, ed. Mark Poster, 159–96. New York: Columbia Univ. Press.

Clifford, James. 1997. Diasporas. In *Routes: Travel and Translation in the Late Twentieth Century*, 244–77. Cambridge, MA: Harvard Univ. Press.

Corominas, Joan. 1954. *Diccionario crítico etimológico de la lengua castellana*, vol. 4. Bern: Francke.

Díaz, Luciano A. 1994. *The Thin Man and Me*. Ottawa: Split Quotation.

Edwards, Robert. 1988. Exile, Self, and Society. In *Exile in Literature*, ed. María-Inés Lagos-Pope, 15–31. Cranbury, NJ: Associated Univ. Press.

Etcheverry, Jorge. 1993. *De chácharas y largavistas*. Ottawa: Split Quotation.

———. 1998. *A vuelo de pájaro: Miniantología personal*. Ottawa: Verbum Veritas.

———. 2002. *Vitral con pájaros*. Ottawa: Poetas Antiimperialistas de América.

Griffin, Keith. 2004. Globalization and Culture. In *Globalization, Culture, and the Limits of the Market: Essays in Economics and Philosophy*, ed. Stephen Cullenberg and Prasanta K. Pattanaik, 241–64. Oxford: Oxford Univ. Press.

Gupta, Akhil, and James Ferguson. 1997. Beyond 'Culture': Space, Identity, and the Politics of Difference. In *Culture, Power, Place: Explorations in Critical Anthropology*, ed. Akhil Gupta and James Ferguson, 33–51. Durham, NC: Duke Univ. Press.

Ireland, Ann. 2002. *Exile*. Toronto: Dundurn.

López Pacheco, Jesús. 1991. *Poetic Asylum: Poems Written in Canada (1968–1990)*. Trans. Fabio López Lázaro. London, ON: Brick Books.

Malkki, Liisa H. 1997a. National Geographic: The Rooting of Peoples and the Territorialization of National Identity among Scholars and Refugees. In *Culture, Power, Place: Explorations in Critical Anthropology*, ed. Akhil Gupta and James Ferguson, 52–74. Durham, NC: Duke Univ. Press.

———. 1997b. News and Culture: Transitory Phenomena and the Fieldwork Tradition. In *Anthropological Locations. Boundaries and Grounds of a Field Science*, ed. Akhil Gupta and James Ferguson, 86–101. Berkeley: Univ. of California Press.

Martínez, Erik. 1985. *Tequila Sunrise*. Ottawa: Cordillera.

Ovid. 1975. *Tristia*. Trans. L.R. Lind. Athens, GA: Univ. of Georgia Press.

Oxford University Press. 1989. *Oxford English Dictionary*, vol 5. 2nd ed. New York: Oxford Univ. Press. 1989.

Rio, Nela. 1998. *Túnel de proa verde / Tunnel of the Green Prow*. Trans. Hugh Hazelton. Fredericton, NB: Broken Jaw.

Rodríguez, Carmen. 1997. Agujero negro. In *De cuerpo entero*, 48–67. Santiago, Chile: Los Andes.

———. 1992. *Guerra prolongada- Protracted War*. Trans. Heidi Neufeld Raine and Carmen Rodríguez. Toronto: Women's Press.

Said, Edward. 1984. The Mind of Winter. Reflections on Life in Exile. *Harper's* (September): 49–55.

Seidel, Michael. 1986. *Exile and the Narrative Imagination*. New Haven, CT: Yale Univ. Press.

Torres, Luis A. 2001–2. Writings of the Latin-Canadian Exile. *Revista Canadiense de Estudios Hispánicos* 26 (1–2): 179–98.

———. 2002. *El exilio y las ruinas*. Santiago, Chile: RIL.

Torres-Recinos, Julio. 2000. *Crisol de tiempo*. Saskatoon: Amaranta.

Urbina, José Leandro. 1999. *Collect Call*. Trans. Beverly J. DeLong-Tonelli. Ottawa: Split Quotation.

Notes

1   I am referring mainly to the supporters of economic liberalization: the World Trade Organization, the International Monetary Fund, and the World Bank, among others.

2   Globalization is not a recent phenomenon, though it has increased in speed due to the dominance of the capitalist system in the last decades. Keith Griffin, in his 2004 article "Globalization and Culture," points out that human societies have always been in some kind of contact with each other: "The movement of people has been a constant force in shaping the global economy and bringing about cultural change" (243). This view of globalization as a normal process of economic and cultural exchange has a negative side, which is also recognized by Griffin: that it is unequal. According to Griffin, "[c]ultural contact has not historically been equalizing, and often not liberating. On the contrary, it has been accompanied by conquest and enslavement, by uneven development and inequalities of income, wealth, opportunities, and freedoms" (256). Thus, the break of international barriers to free trade and cultural flow accompanied by a lack of globalization of justice and wealth and the continuous political and military interventions across the planet have the unpleasant consequences of creating thousands of refugees and exiles, forced to migrate in search of security and better opportunities.

3   I have discussed some of these issues in my 2001–2 article "Writings of the Latin-Canadian Exile."

4   Programs of psychological recovery promoted by governments, for example, would deal with the trauma but are unable to lead to solutions at the social level. In Canada, the politics of multiculturalism that create a space for expression of national identities is also a form of a collective therapeutics oriented to localize the yearning for home and to play and replay its images (in music, dance, clothes and foods, and other manifestations of the countries of origin), as occurs in the festival of nations in many cities across the country. In these celebrations the immigrant can display his or her allegiances but the activity does not have consequences in terms of a better understanding of the individual. The festivity, in many ways, erases the particularity of the immigrant in the stereotyping of culture and difference.

5   The notion of the exile as victim originates in my study of the representations of violence in the arts. The literature of the Holocaust, for example, is a telling example of the evil of violence and of the purpose of the torturers to make the prisoner into a victim incapable of overcoming the dehumanization of the camps. At a different scale this is the same objective of the torturers in the Latin American countries during the period of the dictatorships. Exile is also a form of punishment and dehumanization by forcing the person to leave her or his community. Even when the pain of exile is transformed into opportunities for personal and collective growth, there is a sense of the cost and the losses, and of the "what could have been" back at home if it were not for the forced separation. The victimization, then, is always there, but so is the possibility of moving on.

6   Later on Badiou explains this immortality: "The fact that in the end we all die, that only dust remains, in no way alters Man's identity as immortal at the instant in which he affirms himself as someone who runs counter to the temptation of wanting-to-be-an-animal to which circumstances may expose him" (2002, 12).

7   Concerning the concept of perseverance and the overcoming of the identity of victim, my referent is Alain Badiou. This philosopher explains that in the process of constituting ourselves as subjects, the "somebody" we are remains faithful to a truth and to the situation surrounding that truth. He also adds that fidelity is a form of perseverance that allows us to move away from our singularity (2002, 44–45). As a result, for Badiou the ethics of a truth implies the following imperative: "Do all that you can to persevere in

that which exceeds your perseverance. Persevere in the interruption. Seize in your being that which has seized and broken you" (47).

8   Pedro/Pablo Jorquera or "PJ" in *De cháchaças y largavistas* (1993) symbolizes the radical marginality of the exile after the situation in Chile is no longer important. The following lines represent some of his thinking about his present marginality:

> Pero ninguna noticia del país de origen, cuyos avatares históricos parecen haberse disuelto en los últimos años, que con su avalancha de guerras, masacres y desastres ecológicos, y ahora el derrumbe del Este, han ido reduciendo la dimensión de los sucesos que lo convirtieron en exilado al rango módico de una escaramuza, de una pelea de barrio, de perros chicos, de sencillo en las cajas del Banco de la Historia. (43–44)

>> [But no news of his country of origin, whose historical avatars seem to have dissolved in the last years, with its many wars, massacres and ecological disasters, and now the end of the East block, have been reducing the dimension of the events that made him into an exile to the cheap price of a skirmish, of a fight among neighbours, among small dogs, of pennies in the Banks of History.] (My translation.)

9   I have discussed Kristeva, Docherty, and other writers' ideas about exile in "Writings of the Latin-Canadian Exile" (2001–2).

10 Appadurai writes: "I view locality as primarily relational and contextual rather than as scalar or spatial. I see it as a complex phenomenological quality, constituted by a series of links between the sense of social immediacy, the technologies on interactivity and the relativity of context" (1995, 10).

11 In the novel *Exile* this particularity is what Carlos remembers and misses in the novel *Exile*: "Yet I felt a stab of longing as I listen to the poet's words. He had been there, in my town, in my café, just a week ago. And why haven't I once ventured into Colonia Milagro, out of simple curiosity if nothing else?" (Ireland 2002, 74–75). He also regrets the lost chances of not having visited places back home and of not having their familiarity at the moment of remembering.

12 In Alberti's poetry there are many examples of the image of the uprooted tree. Jesús López Pacheco has also used the image of the tree to portray the experience of exile and the struggle to overcome the separation:

> No one ever dies from being cold,
> or from being distant.
> Like the trees, let yourself
> freeze solid, that life may be hard protected
> while life around you is hard and cold.
> See the tips of the trees' fingers –
> they have not lost the colour of hope.
> (1991, 21)

I would like to thank Tamara Schurch for her insights into the tree metaphor in Alberti and Rio in her study "El árbol y el exilio en la poesía de Nela Rio y Rafael Alberti" (master's thesis, University of Calgary, 2004).

13 Clifford quotes Khachig Tololian to support the idea that the concept of diaspora shares a number of meanings "with a larger semantic domain that includes words like immigrant, expatriate, refugee, guest-worker, [and] exile community ..." (1997, 245).

14 To ascertain the possibility of this knowledge, I use Badiou's vocabulary when he speaks of an ethic founded on the situation: "The concept of situation is especially important, since I maintain that there can be no ethics in general, but only an ethic of singular

truths, and thus an ethic relative to a particular situation" (2001, ivi). In the situation, the person that is faithful to the conditions of the event carries the truth of that event to its final consequences. For us, this implies a break with normative language and with canonical knowledge. According to Badiou, "a truth-process is heterogeneous to the instituted knowledges of the situation. Or – to use an expression of Lacan's – it punches a 'hole' [*trouée*] in these knowledges" (43).

15 It should be said, though, that the representation and study of the experience of exile is not the exclusive territory of literature or the arts. Psychology, sociology, anthropology and other disciplines are also implicated in its study. Each one can give us certain insights that may not be available to another because of differing methodologies. The openness of literature makes it a limitless space for the exploration and representation of this liminal condition.

Exile and the Search for Identity

Mercedes Rowinsky-Guerts, Wilfrid Laurier University

According to Andrew Brennan, identity is regularly associated with other things that matter. Those things, in the case of humans, could be our language, our surroundings, the space in which we live, and the objects that offer us a sense of familiarity: everything that provides us with a sense of "continuity." When this state is interrupted unexpectedly and a sudden change occurs, the imbalance produced by the abruptness of such a change could create a situation where survival takes precedence over identity. The individual, in such a case, can find himself/herself trying to balance the "self." If we believe that the self predominates over the social (Cohen 1994, 33), then it is possible to accept the premise that the self could survive, even when the underlined support of his/her identity is destabilized. The surviving self is different from the previous one and contains characteristics that pertain to both the old and the new.

In this paper I will examine the need that the exile (writer Cristina Peri Rossi, who abandoned Uruguay and has lived in Spain since 1972) has to create a sense of balance between the "self" and the new environment. As a consequence of this process, the identity of the individual has to be readjusted and reconsidered. In the case of a writer, the problem is even more profound. Hana Píchová (2002, 7) explains: "... the challenges of exile are especially acute for those who make their living by writing, who must confront, in addition to physical uprootedness, problems of linguistic and cultural differentiation."

When exile occurs, the individual is removed from everything that is familiar. Amy Kaminsky (1999, 11) states that: "This process of uprooting is a literal *desarticulación*,[1] a term that evokes the physical processes of both speech and touch." In exile, the experience of displacement is accentuated by the abruptness that the action entails. Before leaving, the individual doesn't have time to gaze on the most loved objects and is not able to gather precious mementos that form part of the familiar, of that which we call "ours." Leaving, in most cases empty-handed, implies that a part of who the individual is stays behind. The person feels abandoned, as though drifting in a space that is not his/hers anymore. In its place, the exile tries to compensate for the discontinuity with the replacement of new objects that are part of the new environment, such as places, tastes, colours and, in some cases, even language. Frequently, the exile finds that the process of assimilation becomes easier when connections are made with the new environment at various levels. This helps to ease the fears that come with the abrupt extrication and placement of the being into a completely different setting.

In the case of Peri Rossi, the fear of not being able to write in exile was one that was very present as she left. She states (2003, 8):

When I left Montevideo on an Italian ship (the Giulio Cesare from the Trans Mediterranean Company), I had, fundamentally, one fear: not being able to write. Fear that my identity as a writer would suffer such an abysmal fracture that would induce me to silence. In other words: exile as castration.

The worry of not being able to write is common among writers.[2] Eduardo Galeano, for example, thought that he could never write again when he left Uruguay; similarly, "Julio Cortázar's sense of exile sprang from being unread by his 'natural' audience" (Kaminsky 1999, 67). In the case of Peri Rossi, the fact that the Uruguayan government banned her work upon her departure was an added disconnection. She not only had to try to establish herself in Spain, but she had also lost her reading public in Uruguay. The dislocation, in the case of writers, is even more complex than other professions. Píchová (2002, 8) explains:

For a once-active writer, to respond with a blank page is to confirm and participate in personal and public forgetting. Silence erases the person from the collective memory of those left behind on the native shore and prevents him or her from ever being recognized by the inhabitants of the new shore. Silence, moreover, diminishes personal memory, inasmuch as writing provides for a recovery of past mementos via an imaginary journey back home, when physically such return is impossible.

We all know by now that this was not the case for Peri Rossi: exile, she explains, "questions identity" (2003, 7). This questioning emerges from the disarticulation or scission of the self, which creates countless searches for who the self is in exile. In this unexpected state where everything is different, strange, and foreign, the essence of who the self is stays the same. However, the referentiality and the commonality of the familiar is absent, and that absence becomes more of a presence because it creates the need to have, to see, to smell, to taste, to feel, to do, and to say all the components of what constituted one's life prior to exile.

Consciously or unconsciously, the self in exile tries to reach out for memories, those faulty recollections that in time escape and betray the self, playing tricks on those who try intensely to keep them in order and to protect everything as it was, at least in one's mind.[3] This is a constant battle in exile. A memory can appear when least expected and, in a fraction of a second, it can take the self far away, splitting one's existence and fractioning the experience of the present.

The uncontrollable emergence of memories could be the result of the sudden smell of humid soil after rain, the taste of familiar foods cooked in a small hidden restaurant that the exile never thought could exist so far away from home, or the sound of foreign waves breaking on new shores: any of these elements could elicit a memory. Unexpectedly, the self feels the disarticulation, accentuating the already physically and emotionally unbalanced situation. This disarticulation, at the same time, reinforces the turmoil already in existence.

The continuity of the scission of the self persists in exile; what varies with time in many cases is the frequency of the events in which, even for a short period of time, memories of the past take over. In a way, the fact that memory is not reliable, and that the self is not able to remember everything (as one produces, at best, a vague recollection), could be a blessing. It allows the self to create and store new memories. In the event of a possible return, it also helps the exile to accept the fact that things, places and people have changed or do not appear as they were remembered. We tend to forgive memory. Time and distance make the exile more kind and grateful towards memory.

The absence or faultiness of memory also allows the self to accept the need to create new memories. In the process of making these new memories, the self creates connections with others, allowing, at the same time, the opportunity to know oneself within the contours of the strangeness of the new environment. Following Martin Heidegger's (1962, 161) premise that "knowing oneself [Sichkennen] is grounded in Being-with, which understands primordially ... [and that it] operates proximally in accordance with the kind of Being which is closest to us – Being-in-the-world as Being-with," we can surmise that allowing the creation of new memories offers the exile the opportunity to establish relationships with others and with new surroundings. Exiles respond to this challenge in many ways: by learning the new language, by accommodating to new norms and customs while trying to maintain the ones they brought with them, and by searching for new ways of "Being-in-the world as Being-with," among others.

Peri Rossi (2003, 8) has responded to exile with her love for words; she says that "Exile asked me for words, asked me to write, asked me to fix my emotions." These quotes are from her latest book of poems *Estado de exilio* [*State of Exile*], winner of the XVIII International Prize for Poetry Unicaja Rafael Alberti. This collection, written soon after her arrival in Spain, was left in a drawer because she didn't want "to contribute to the collective pain" (2003, 8). She doesn't call this collection autobiographical; as a matter of fact, she explains that "only a few are written in first person" (9). As Carol Muske (1997, 18–19) explains, "A poem is different from autobiography and the negotiation between these differing 'truths' of the self *is* dialectical, exhilarating, and essential. It is a profound act of subversion." In this case, we are referring to Peri Rossi as a poetic subject represented through her poetry.

Peri Rossi's love for words, commitment to justice, wisdom, and acute alertness about the social and political events occurring in Uruguay had put her in jeopardy. She says (2003, 9) in the prologue to this edition that her actions and words had placed her in a foreign country: "Because I was ahead of my time, I found myself alone, sick, exiled, far away from my birthplace, from my family, from my books, from my friends and from all that that was my world for the first thirty years of my life." To publish this book when it was written in 1973 would have been too painful due to the personal and intimate content of her experience. It took another thirty years for Peri Rossi to find the balance, to find her/"self" and feel free to let these verses be read by others. During these thirty years, we have seen innumerable occasions where glimpses of *State of Exile* have appeared in Peri Rossi's other writings, and exile and its consequences have been a leitmotif in most of her literary work.[4]

The peculiarity of this edition comes not only from the richness of the verses and the profound emotional charge they carry, but also from the fact that the fifty-one poems come together with a brief but intense collection of Peri Rossi's poems for the Catalan writer and friend Ana María Moix under the title *Correspondence with Ana María Moix*. Peri Rossi found in Moix the "otherness" needed in order to be able to establish the human connection essential to survive in exile. After a night of exchanging life stories, Peri Rossi wrote this collection of poems all at once; she confesses (2003, 12): "I had some kind of revelation: if she had been born in Montevideo, she would have been me; and if I had been born in Barcelona, possibly, I would have been her."

The first poem of the book only has the number one for a title and reads as follows: "I have a pain here, / on the side of my homeland."[5] Written in free verse, the poems in *State of Exile* show the disarticulation felt by the author, a sense of physical and emotional displacement that leads to not being here nor there; in some instances, this state never reaches a complete resolution. In this poem, we see the use of visual devices to draw the reader into the idea of dismemberment. If we look at the poem from behind the page, we will notice that the second verse: "on the side of the homeland" it is located where our heart is: to the left. The position of the poems on the page in representational designs is a device that Peri Rossi uses frequently. This recourse adds to the idea of tension and disarticulation (Brogan 1994, 117).

It is not surprising that the first poem makes an implied reference to the body. The imbalance produced by the journey that took the individual away from the mother/land and everything that was called the home is linked to the physical as well as to the mental and spiritual components of being. Kaminsky (1999, xi) explains: "Exile and all the processes related to it have a material component, and that component is felt, experienced, and known through the body." What Kaminsky adds, and I completely disagree with, is that such is not the case for women exile writers. She explains (1999, 8) that: "Women exile writers themselves tend not to (con)fuse the maternal body with the lost homeland. References to the mother are rare."

In the case of *State of Exile*, this does not seem to be the case. Peri Rossi makes reference to her mother specifically in two poems, "Letter from Mom" and "Letter from Mom II." In both, Peri Rossi establishes the insurmountable distance that accentuates the sense of longing for what is secure: in her case, she expresses the need for both mother and motherland. The first poem reads (Peri Rossi 2003, 19): "Letter from Mom: / and if everyone leaves, my daughter, / what are those of us who are left behind going to do?" The poet plays with imagery related to both loved ones and loved objects. Reference to the sea and ships is always present in Peri Rossi's writings. For those who are familiar with her "loves" it is well known how much she loves anything related to the sea. Poem two reads:

I dreamt that I was leaving far away from here
the sea was rough
black and white waves
a dead seal on the beach
a piece of wood navigating
red lights in high seas
Did a city named Montevideo ever exist? (18)

In these verses, as well as in most of *State of Exile*, the reader senses the fluctuating experience that one feels while navigating by the iteration and reiteration of words and phrases of related imagery. This undulating experience is similar to the uncontrollable movements of the sea that make those on board a boat feel completely powerless. The constant drifting of objects in *State of Exile*, as well as the continuous nomadic sense of disconnection between what possessed and is now lost and what was left behind and is now longed for, create kinetic forces that swivel individuals who are search of stability and security while trying to rescue whatever is left of who they were/are as individuals. That is what exile is for Peri Rossi: a constant pulling and pushing of interior and exterior forces that provokes the turmoil of identity which is explained through the verses in a sophisticated linguistic play.

In some cases, the uncertainty remains unsolved forever, and the individual finds that belonging somewhere is almost impossible. For others, like Peri Rossi, the need to connect is a demand that comes from her need to express herself through words, and as Kaminsky (1999, 58) explains, it is also a way of gaining spaces: "language provides the means to establish as well as to recover a sense of place."[6] While searching, the individual tries to establish links with others. The failing and frustration that result from not achieving such communication is one that appears as a constant in this collection. This idea is what Peri Rossi presents in many of her poems where she defines exile. In "Telephone Booth 1975," for example, the poetic voice says (2003, 42):

Exile is to have a franc in the pocket
and the phone to swallow the coin
and not return it
– neither coin, nor call –
in the exact moment in which we realize
that the booth does not work.

As we can see, even when describing the loneliness and almost-desperation of this moment, Peri Rossi's poetic voice maintains one of her unique qualities: her distinctive sense of humour. In her poem "Exile II" she also represents this need to establish a link to those left behind and she writes:

We speak languages that don't belong to us
we don't carry passports
or identity cards
we write desperate letters
that we don't send
we are outsiders numerous unhappy
survivors
surviving
and sometimes that
makes us feel guilty. (2003, 36)

The impossibility of joining in and the desperate attempt to convey the pain without feeling guilty because others didn't have the chance to get away (and therefore paid with their lives) is a difficulty that many had to deal with constantly. Dragging their bodies through countries, attempting to create a new identity and at the same time trying not to change too much just in case they could come back, thousands of people lived their lives in a state of disassociation. Carrying very little with them, many felt what Milan Kundera (1984) called "the Unbearable Lightness of Being" as a blessing, because it allowed them to move with ease. However, it also symbolized the tremendous fracturing that had occurred.

In the poem "The Art of Loss," Peri Rossi (2003, 56) makes reference to the lightness of being and the consequences of such lightness. In this poem we find one of the most salient examples of allusions to other identifiable sources. The poem reads:

Exile and its countless losses
made me lighter with objects
less possessive
....
Exile and its countless losses
made me giving
I give away what I don't have – money, poems, orgasms –
I stayed floating – ship lost in high seas –
with roots in the air
like a carnation without a trunk to which to entwine

The allusions in her poem "Max Ernst" to Max Ernst's painting *Here Everything Is Still Floating* (2003, 70) and to the title of Milan Kundera's novel are obvious. The sense of dispossession and dislocation creates a void that lingers within the exiled while he or she tries to survive in alien surroundings.

In order to compensate for the loss, the poetic voice presents the subconscious with a way to recover from the disorientation created. Many of the poems make reference to dream experiences in which the poetic voice tries to reach a certain place; however, once the poetic subject reaches the place, she is rejected. Poem VI (Peri Rossi 2003, 22) says: "I dreamt that I came back / but once there / I was afraid / and I wanted to come back / anywhere." This idea of drifting is omnipresent in *State of Exile*. Peri Rossi, either by the syntactic units of the poems or by the imagery that she presents, always offers a vision of being immersed in the middle of a foggy night in some far away sea; a shipwreck. One of the best of numerous examples is the poem that shares its name with the book: "State of Exile." In the most representative example of free verse, Peri Rossi bombards the reader with a myriad of seemingly incongruent words that add to the tension and confusion that an exile experiences. The poem says:

very soon so far away pretty bad
                              always
difficulty words furious long
strange foreigner what more the tree
I only look different
everything
                    could be more human. (29)

Once more, the poetic voice uncovers the cruelty of the state of banishment. With a poetic speech that appears and feels discontinuous, Peri Rossi creates a sense of life that is interrupted and halted. The self appears confused and looks for words that sound strange even when they are their own. Places appear; new to some, and familiar to others. By breaking the lines and by the use of enjambment, the poet creates a sense of uncertainty that is very common among those who suffer exile. Peri Rossi exposes, in this poem, the state of fragmentation of being. She juxtaposes objects and experiences, almost in a Cubist style comparable to that of Apollinaire in his monumental poem "Zone" of 1912. The memory images in Apollinaire, as Suzanne Nalbantian (2003, 102) explains, "[create] in this poem a powerful impression of unleashing simultaneous memory images in the experience of the 'present' moment. It is what I have labeled 'zig-zag memory'."

We will understand better the notion of "zig-zag memory" if we follow Antonio R. Damasio's (1999, 17) precept that there is a difference between what he calls the "core self," which is "a transient entity, ceaselessly recreated for each and every object with which the brain interacts," and the "autobiographical self," the traditional notion of self which "is linked to the idea of identity and corresponds to a non-transient collection of unique facts and ways of being which characterize a person."

The individual in exile is composed of both the "core self" and the "autobiographical self." While in exile, he/she finds himself/herself fragmenting and linking memories. Memories of who he/she was before exile and who he/she is in exile become part of his/her existence, creating an uncontrollable "zig-zag" movement. What before was stable, secure, and familiar has become unstable, fragile, and foreign. In the process of adaptation, the self questions itself at every step. This creates a constant evaluation and re-evaluation of the concept of Being-in-the-world. The very feeling of "being" is questioned in exile, and the impossibility of the return makes this questioning more cumbersome as time goes by. Damasio (1999, 136) explains: "It is intriguing to think that the constancy of the internal milieu is essential to maintain life *and* that it might be a blueprint and anchor for what will eventually become a self in the mind." In exile, the external setting has been changed. This has a direct impact on the internal condition of being; it creates an unbalanced situation in which identity is constantly questioned. The constancy of the past has become the uncertainty of the present. The sense of "being" that was anchored and secure has become adrift and lost. Memories come and go, becoming confused, unreliable, and untrustworthy. Being tries to hold on to those memories that make him/her feel secure, while at the same time attempting to create a place of his/her own in the new setting. This "zig-zag" movement is constant, unrelenting, and exhausting. It provokes feelings of deep longing for what once was one's life.

The poet Rabindranath Tagore (1961, 93) expresses this feeling of longing for the unreachable and the impossibility of escaping the present when he says:

I am restless. I am athirst for far-away things.
My soul goes out in a longing to touch the skirt of the dim distance.
O Great Beyond. O the keen call of thy flute!
I forget, I ever forget, that I have no wings to fly, that I am bound in this spot evermore.
I am eager and wakeful, I am a stranger in a strange land.

....

Searching for an identity that was there not so long ago and now seems so unreachable, the being fights to maintain a certain inaccessible balance. The verse "I only look different" could apply to the fact the individual may look physically different from those around him/her, or that he/she sees things differently because everything appears foreign. In any case, the idea of being lost is one that stands out in these verses, as well as in the whole collection.

Peri Rossi makes the reader aware of the resources needed in order to survive exile. In exile the individual has saved the physical aspect of his/her existence but, in the process, identity has been altered. Identity is where the real adaptation of exile takes place, and the regaining of a new or revised identity may take years to find. Another of the resources to which Peri Rossi alludes as a way to try to regain identity is memory, which may recall things, places, or faces. However, even memories start to fade. Poem XXXV (Peri Rossi 2003, 52) says:

They dream to go back to a country that is no more
and they would not recognize it more than in the maps
of memory
maps that they built each night
in the fog of dreams
and that they travel in white ships
constantly moving.
....
If they would return
they would not recognize the place
the street, the house
they would doubt at each corner
they would think that they were somewhere else.

Memory can also be false. In an attempt to recover something that is intangible, anything of what made the self feel secure in the past, the individual constantly grasps for threads of the familiar. It is a way to escape the chaos created by the unknown. Petar Ramadonovic (2001, 72) expands on this issue:

[M]emory is a thoughtful, skillful, and artificial extension of order against the unknown. If this is so, the art of memory remembers only that part of the past which can be ordered; it sheds light on the things that can be ordered, and while it illuminates certain elements of the past, it – the luminosity itself, the shining itself – further obscures that which remains in the dark.

That is exactly what the poetic voice explains in poem XXXV. Even when the exile, tries to remember, some things are forgotten: What do the exiles miss the most? The poetic voice explains:

They miss
the rhythm of the cities
the dark sky full of smoke
the birds' singing
they miss the passage of time
the heat and the cold
sometimes they say one word instead of another
and they are afraid

when they discover that they have forgotten
a street's name.
.... (51)

The missed objects and people, slowly start being replaced by other objects
and different people. The new ones never occupy the same place as the ones
gone; they take refuge in other corners of the heart trying to find some kind
of resolution for the identity crisis that exile has provoked. This painfully
common human drama that has afflicted so many was, and still is, very real
for the poet. She found that her love for words and for the new country that
offered her asylum was the only way to rescue whatever was left of who she
was for thirty years of her life. She has built upon what she knew, but also
from what she learnt. Love was one of the ways to start anew. She explains:
"from all catastrophes, including exile, libido saves us" (9). Her last poem,
"Barnait," makes reference to love. It reads:

I believe that by loving you
I'm going to love your geography
 – "an ugly manufacturing city"
....
I believe that by loving you
I'm going to learn a new language
this archaic language
where fall is feminine
 – *la tardor* –
and the frozen wind
goes behind the mountain.
I believe that by loving you
I'm going to mumble the names
of your ancestors
and I will exchange an ocean nervous
and agitated – the Atlantic –
for a sea so serene
that it seems dead.
....
Cities are known by love
And all languages are loved. (76)

It is through language and in language that Peri Rossi has reconstructed her
sense of identity. It is through her extensive and internationally renowned
literary work that her sense of self became one with who she was and is as

a human being. Words were the reason for exile and they also became the source of reaffirmation and survival during this journey. The poet affirms: "there are forms of survival that are not worth it because they leave us without principles, without identity" (9). Peri Rossi has survived and has established herself as one of the most salient voices of Hispanic letters. Thirty years after her exile her identity as a woman, a writer and an exile, has empowered her to excel in what she does best: to express through words the unequivocal style connected with her commitment to who she is as a human being.

Works Cited

Brennan, Andrew. 1988. *Conditions of Identity: A Study in Identity and Survival.* Oxford: Clarendon.

Brogan, T.V.F., ed. 1994. *The New Princeton Handbook of Poetic Terms.* Princeton, NJ: Princeton Univ. Press.

Cohen, Anthony P. 1994. *Self Consciousness: An Alternative Anthropology of Identity.* London: Routledge.

Damasio, Antonio R. 1999. *The Feeling of What Happens: Body and Emotion in the Making of Consciousness.* New York: Harcourt.

Dejbord, Parizad Tamara. 1998. *Cristina Peri Rossi: Escritora del exilio.* Buenos Aires: Galerna.

Heidegger, Martin. 1962. *Being and Time.* Trans. John Macquarrie and Edward Robinson. San Francisco: Harper.

Kaminsky, Amy K. 1999. *After Exile: Wrting the Latin American Diaspora.* Minneapolis: Univ. of Minnesota Press.

Kundera, Milan. 1984. *The Unbearable Lightness of Being.* New York: Harper.

Muske, Carol. 1997. *Women and Poetry: Truth, Autobiography and the Shape of the Self.* Ann Arbor: Univ. of Michigan Press.

Nalbantian, Suzanne. 2003. *Memory in Literature: From Rousseau to Neuroscience.* Houndmills, England: Palgrave.

Peri Rossi, Cristina. 1975. *Descripción de un naufragio.* Barcelona: Lumen.

———. 1976. *Diáspora.* Barcelona: Lumen.

———. 1987. *Europa después de la lluvia.* Madrid: Fundación Banco Exterior.

———. 1997. *Inmovilidad de los barcos.* Vitoria, Spain: Bassarai.

———. 2003. *Estado de exilio.* Madrid: Visor.

Píchová, Hanna. 2002. *The Art of Memory in Exile: Vladimir Nabokov and Milan Kundera.* Carbondale: Southern Illinois Univ. Press.

Ramadanovic, Petar. 2001. *Forgetting Futures: On Memory, Trauma, and Identity.* Lanham, MD: Lexington.

Solomon R. Guggeheim Museum. 1975. *Max Ernst: A Retrospective.* New York: Solomon R. Guggeheim Museum.

Tagore, Rabindranath. 1961. *Collected Poems and Plays.* London: MacMillan.

Notes

1 Kaminsky deliberately uses the Spanish term *desarticulación* in her analysis of the multiple stages of the exiled while they try to adapt to a new environment.

2 Peri Rossi explains that writers like Galeano and Di Benedetto suffered the drama of feeling "that what they wrote was intrinsically connected to a geographical space, and without it, they doubted it if they could keep on writing" (Dejbord 1998, 229).

3 Peri Rossi refers to this faultiness as "a trick of unconsciousness" (2003, 35). Throughout the book, the poet presents the idea of memory as a tool to reconnect and to sustain the threads with what was left behind; at the same time, she refers to the impossibility of keeping all the memories alive.

4 Among some of her books of poetry in which the theme of exile appears we find *Descripción, Europa,* and *Inmovilidad.*

5 All the translations from *Estado de exilio* have been done by the author of this paper.

6 In an interview, Peri Rossi explains that writing in exile was a way of gaining spaces in Spain (Dejbord 1998, 225).

4 RE-READINGS OF GENDER REPRESENTATION

Retracing Genealogy: Mothers and Daughters
in *Las andariegas* by Albalucía Angel

Myriam Osorio, Memorial University of Newfoundland

Novelist, poet, playwright, and singer, Albalucía Angel is a Colombian writer whose literary career began in the 1970s when the Latin American literary "Boom" came to an end.[1] She published her first novel *Los girasoles en invierno* [*Sunflowers in Winter*] in 1970. In it she chronicles the voyages of a young woman in Europe. This initial interest in traveling, and in the permanent relocation of the self across time, space, and culture, would, in fact, become one of the most important threads that connect this novel to subsequent work. The other thread, women's personal history and its connection to national history, finds expression in a second novel, *Estaba la pájara pinta sentada en su verde limón* [*The Colored Bird Was Sitting on the Green Lemon Tree*] published in 1975.[2] Fourteen years later and after producing *Dos veces Alicia* [*Alice Twice Over*] in 1972, a detective novella, a collection of short stories entitled *Oh Gloria inmarcesible*,[3] and a third novel, *Misiá señora* [*Mrs. Madam*] in 1982, Angel published a synthesis of her interest both in traveling and in women's history: *Las andariegas* (1984). Inspired by *Les Guerrilleres* (1971) by the French writer Monique Wittig and written mostly in the third person plural, this volume goes beyond the voyages in Europe and the national history to develop a loose feminist cartography from which to examine, rewrite, and reconnect with ancient and colonial myths that have had an impact in the constitution of women's identities, women's roles, and in the mother and daughter relationship.[4]

The Trip

Travel writing has become an important subject of colonial and postcolonial studies. In the case of *Las andariegas*, travel writing "concerns the desire to speak to the Western paradigm of knowledge in the voice of otherness" (Goldberg and Quayson 2002, xii). The voice of otherness is, however, not one, but many: in *Las andariegas* Albalucía Angel presents a group of beautiful women, both young and old who, gripping each other's legs to form a symbolic umbilical chord, descend to the earth and in an operation similar to that of Genesis, begin their journey by naming the landscape and the colors they see. At the outset the travelers display a consciousness of the power of language and its ability to shape not only the world they come to inhabit, but also their constitution as subjects. Cynthia Tompkins (1997, 156) precisely remarks that in *Las andariegas* Angel deconstructs "the unified (humanist) subject" through the multiplicity of expressions used to designate the travelers: "peregrinas, buscadoras, náufragas" ("pilgrims, searchers, castaways").[5]

In *Las andariegas* the language of the narrative voices describe how, as searchers who move on foot, the women perform a trip of mythical proportions that includes, among others, a visit to three important places: ancient Greece, the Garden of Eden, and the Valley of Anáhuac. Along the way they find a number of important female figures like Electra and her mother Clytemnestra, Eve and Tecuichpo, or Copo de Algodón (Spanish name given in Angel's narrative), daughter of Moctezuma.[6] Since all of them have been conceived as by-products of men, and their stories told from the male perspective in the Greek plays, the Bible, and the chronicles of the conquest of America, *Las andariegas* provides them the opportunity to speak for themselves or be spoken about by the voices of other women. While undergoing their search for origins they display conflictive relationships, re-examine the fall of women, and essentially materialize a desire to go deep into their past to meet their female ancestors and witness their stories. Through the help and guidance of their ancestors they hope to ask questions, find some answers, and move forward in the process of locating and reconstituting identity.[7]

The readers, along with the travelers, enter an open-air theatre[8] where both witness important scenes that, however fragmentary, compel them to question how discourses on women's behaviour, feeling, and experience have been produced and interpreted. Beyond that, the accounts we are about to explore propose, in their move to relocate identity, that the widely accepted penis theories familiar to psychoanalytical thought, which explain women's development and separation from their mothers, are not completely acceptable: epistemologically, conceptually, and politically they promote binary oppositions intended to "subserve a project of power and hegemony" as "all binary oppositions are value-laden, with the first term often implicitly assumed to have an ethical or conceptual, normative or logical priority over the second" (Goldberg and Quayson 2002, xii).[9]

As an alternative, the vignettes suggest that a focus on the dynamics between the phallus and the breast would illuminate the shaded areas of women's relationships to their maternal ancestors. The relevance of the breast is clear as the three characters show their breasts, two of them at times of danger. The breast, moreover, is a reminder of that archaic (erotic) and seemingly lost connection to the mother. In the order of things, for a newborn, the first contact with the world is not through the phallus but through the breast. Therefore, by going back to the beginnings – the Greek tragedy, the Bible, and the chronicles of the early conquest of Mexico (whose audiences were predominantly male) – and re-enacting the conflict between Electra and her mother Clytemnestra, re-creating Eve, and unearthing Moctezuma's daughter, Angel attempts to establish relationships and connections among the past histories of the women noted, the group of women who travel and the readers. This operation, like genealogy, serves the purpose of reuniting families of women separated by centuries of oblivion, misunderstanding, and silence. These factors exacerbate the enormous difficulties women face in identifying with each other as mothers, wives, and daughters.

Genealogy

Where does genealogy begin?[10] With whom? Usually it begins with the father or with a conflation of mother and father, as most family systems are patrilinear. Thus, Luce Irigaray (1993) examines the cultural manifestations of women's genealogy and how it is constituted. Irigaray argues that Western history fuses female and male genealogies into one or two family triangles which are under male control. The origin of this model goes back to ancient Greece and constitutes the Oedipal pattern that has so strongly taken root in Western culture. According to Irigaray, in Greek tradition, it is necessary for God to blend two genealogical trees. By the same token, the Judeo-Christian tradition invokes God, a transcendental entity, to join two genealogical trees. This model, then, promotes man as the embodiment of holiness, identity, and genealogy. Angel (1984, 22) shares this perspective with Irigaray as the travelers recognize that "un hombre era el elegido. el heredero de la divinidad. el que regía los destinos, la construcción o destrucción. el hacedor del infortunio o la bonanza o decidía las vidas y las muertes con un movimiento de su cetro" ["a man was the chosen one. he inherited holiness. he controlled destiny, life and its destruction. he decided on matters of life and death just by a movement of his sceptre"].[11] Thus, the omnipotent father eclipses and controls the mother and seduces the daughter in her search for protection. This seduction is perhaps the core of the female inability to build a genuine self, which arises from the loss of relationship to the mother-world of early childhood and adolescence.

Contrary to this model, *Las andariegas* seeks to connect women with mythical origins, but not necessarily through the intervention of God, the institution of marriage, or restricted blood ties: the women travelers are not the wives of anybody and do not carry a family name. In this case they subvert the traditional definition of women by their relationship to men. They are outside concepts of property, as they do not belong to a male or, for that matter, to a country or nation-state. This lack of "respectable" origins presents them with the freedom to look for the mother, as she is not the representative of the nation or the giver of relevant surnames. Neither Electra nor Clytemnestra is connected by blood to Eve or Tecuichpo. Their connection lies more in the affinity of their stories and in what those can metaphorically tell their female descendants. The profiles, however, contain a drawing of Electra, Eve, and Tecuichpo[12] and, in addition, talk about privilege, honour, power, and their value in Western, patriarchal culture. Most importantly, instead of conflating the mother and the father in one single line, as most definitions of the genealogical practice do, Angel focuses on the mother's side. The author also draws attention to the fact that constituting a genealogy relies a great deal on memory, on remembering, and listening for crucial but unmentioned components in the definitions of genealogy. Thus, the travelers manage to make their way back to the lived recollections of Electra, particularly to the moments when she violently tears herself (and her brother) apart from Clytemnestra, their mother. The question asked here is: Why does Electra so passionately need to break such a fundamental bond?

Mother and Daughter

The group of women finds a young girl "cubierta con cenizas y el cabello rapado y un extravío de pesadumbre en el mirar" (Angel 1984, 42) ["covered with ashes and the hair shaved and her eyes revealing loss and sorrow"]. It is Electra who has just forced her brother Orestes to kill Clytemnestra.[13] Surprised by the travelers and perhaps tormented by feelings of remorse, Electra immediately starts to talk and confesses what, in her view, has happened. Freud would say that she is the hysterical daughter who suffers "not only from [her] reminiscences but from failure to have told her story" and therefore needs to express "a retrospective story about her father as beloved and lost or as seducer" (Froula 1989, 120). In fact, Electra tells of her intense love for her father and the great loss she has experienced. He is no longer alive because her mother Clytemnestra has assassinated him[14] and, therefore, Electra can no longer locate in him (again, according to Freud) her need for patriarchal protection. Not surprisingly, Freud is unable to imagine the primordial need for the safety mothers provide, "the need to be at one with her [and to] be made part of her power" (Chernin 1987, 91).[15] It is surprising, however, that Electra has forgotten that initial, powerful connection to the mother's breast in order to favour the view that Clytemnestra is a bad woman, a prostitute, an "escorpiona" (Angel 1984, 44) ["female scorpion"]. Her words are little different from the ones used by the character of Electra in *The Oresteia*. In it, the mother is a "monster, a mad woman, not a mother at all" (Sophocles 1957, 56). Therefore, Orestes in turn assassinates her in both the classical text and *Las andariegas*.

Even though the scene in which Clytemnestra is killed constitutes something close to a blank space in the classical texts as it is told indirectly, in *Las andariegas* that very scene takes center stage.[16] Besides, it is Electra who narrates the bloody killing because she was present and actively participated in it.[17] Electra determines the circumstances in which she would slay her mother: "llegó sin un presentimiento. las esclavas troyanas se retiraron a esperarla y comenzó la danza del terror" (Angel 1984, 44) ["she arrived without any suspicion. the Trojan slaves left to wait on her and then the dance of terror began"]. Realizing that her life is at stake, Clytemnestra appeals to several arguments directed not to the daughter, but to her son. First, she reminds him of the violent death perpetrated by Agamemnon on her daughter Iphigenia: As this fails, she cries and yells to Orestes: "no hieras, no asesines a tu madre" (44) ["do not harm, do not kill your mother"]; as a last resort, she shows him her breasts: "abrió la túnica mostrándole los pechos que él recordó tan blancos y amorosos" (44) ["she opened her tunic and showed him the breasts that he remembered so white and full of love"].[18] As when he was an infant, Clytemnestra's breasts awake in Orestes a desire to caress and to suck them (44). The verbs *to caress* and *to suck* contribute to the representation of the mother's breasts as a source of life, love, eroticism, protection, and power. There is, of course, a clear allusion to the Oedipus complex; however, that is not the course the events of this story take.

Seminude, Clytemnestra faces both her hesitant son (who is armed with a sword) and the daughter who witnesses the episode and observes her desperate attempts to survive. Despite her powerful last attempt to stay alive, Electra forcefully takes Orestes hand when he seems to doubt: "yo le aferré la mano que abandonaba ya la espada como si se pudiera burlar lo que el destino tiene escrito y le obligué a asestar dos golpes" (Angel 1984, 44) ["I grabbed his hand that was about to abandon the sword as if destiny could be played with and forced him to stab twice"]. As Hélène Cixous (1995) has commented regarding this case, Orestes' hesitation demonstrates his own dilemma in choosing between the mother's milk and the father's sperm. In contrast, the choice seems clear for Electra, whose commitment to the father compels her to impose a bloody patriarchal and indelible sign on her mother's body.

Needless to say, Electra regrets her actions but somehow justifies them because her mother is the agent of her tragedy. She killed Agamemnon, the incarnation of light and sunshine for Electra and, in his long absence, audaciously took a lover.[19] While the long-absent father represents light, warmth, sun, power, and force, the mother embodies the complete opposite: darkness, irrationality, passion, and desire. This dichotomy reinforces binary oppositions that promote a "ceaseless warfare between opposites" and "explain[s] why culture did not give a suitable place within itself to the Goddess and her daughters" (Chernin 1987, 76). The divide prevents Electra from finding out what her mothers' motivations, feelings, pains, and thoughts are. By so vehemently embracing the father, Electra is unable to question his long absence and his slaying of Iphigenia. There is no consequence for him. In fact, for Electra and the culture in which she has grown up, it was expected and valued that the father would be absent and detached, particularly when fighting a war in defence of state: women had little to do except instigate such business by their beauty.[20]

Without any apparent sense of communication between mother and daughter, Electra does not know the intimate motives or reasons for which her mother acts the way she does. Electra does not ask any questions (perhaps she is not allowed to); she repeats what the male imagination makes of Clytemnestra. Clytemnestra, in turn, never has a chance to explain or speak for herself. As a result tension, hostility and death ensue as Electra actively participates in the assassination of her mother.

By choosing this tragedy and re-enacting it, Angel allows us to remember that the murder of the father by Oedipus was preceded by the murder of the mother by Orestes and that despite long centuries of silence, Western history and culture are built on the basis of matricide and on the elimination of a crucial genealogical thread. At the same time, the author wants to explore and incorporate the darker, more destructive side of the complex and sometimes extremely turbulent relationship between mothers and daughters, each one working with totally different categories: Electra by means of the excessive identification with the father, and Clytemnestra through the equally excessive distancing from him.[21]

Julia Kristeva explains this rupture by asserting that "feminine disruption depends on a contradiction between the semiotic and the symbolic, so feminist disruption depends on a permanent contradiction between masculine/paternal and feminine/maternal identifications" (Leland 1992, 126). As presented by Kristeva, these options are bounded by two undesirable extremes, father-identification and mother-identification, which effectively create a double bind for women. Evidently, the father-identified woman is embodied by Electra, who takes the point of view of her father with respect to her mother: the mother's crime against the father has been to expose her jouissance to the world by taking a lover, an act forbidden by patriarchal law.[22] Electra's actions are expressions of her fear and hatred of the jouissance, not only of her mother's body, but potentially of her own as well. She must reject in herself what she abhors in her mother and, as a result, she perpetuates the patriarchal symbolic order.

If this picture of the woman identified with the father is unpleasant, Kristeva nonetheless accepts the view that the repression of both instinctual pleasure and continuous relation to the mother is the price to pay in order to enter history and social affairs. This is why the alternative of mother-identification is equally adverse: It condemns women to "forever remain in a sulk in the place of history, politics and social affairs" (Leland 1992, 127). Thus mother-identification results in a failure to enter the symbolic order, a path that ends in psychosis. On the other hand, father-identification entails taking over patriarchal conceptualizations and valuations. In the extreme case, this results in a rejection of attributes gendered as feminine and therefore incompatible with entry into the (masculine) realm of culture and history.

The choice, however, would be to refuse both extremes, something that unfortunately Electra is not capable of doing. However, after the matricide, she assumes the mother's role and sings and rocks Orestes as if he has become her child. One could say that underlining the re-elaboration of the myth there is a need for Electra to speak both of the crime and also of the need for reparation.[23] Electra demonstrates the formidable contradictions she encounters by identifying with the males (the father and the brother) of her family and by her total inability to reconcile such identification with the mother, a fact that leads to destruction and death. Death and destruction are, however, the very models Electra has observed at play both inside and outside her home, as Agamemnon had fought and killed in a war: Clytemnestra has, in turn, assassinated him. Nevertheless, the story also suggests that this kind of order is not sustainable as it ultimately brings only devastation and grief.

In an attempt to heal those wounds, Angel (1984, 18) suggests that it is important "to find, rediscover, invent the words, the sentences that speak of the most ancient and most current relationship to the mother's body." Those three active verbs, *find*, *rediscover*, and *invent*, are consistent with such a project and with the redefinition of Eve, the first mother, who apparently was not born of woman but of Adam's rib, according to the Bible story. Sharon Magnarelli in *The Lost Rib* (1985) mentions the reiteration of this story and its consequences for women as she notes that "[t]he rib story, by virtue of its endless repetition, has provided one of the principal sources for today's perception of women and one of the principal sources of concern for feminists, as evidenced by the frequent references to the question by feminist scholars and critics." (11) Angel is also concerned with the story itself, particularly with its linguistic mode of production. As Eve was not supposed to have had daughters, the travelers symbolically come to occupy that position and reconfigure her image. They challenge the established pattern by leading the reader to reconsider the story and go back to its source.

Eve, the Wicked Mother

Eve's daughters arrive at a sort of hell, "[un] albergue abarrotado de olores fetidos y llantos y cantos salmodiales" (Angel 1984, 74) ["[a] hostel full of fetid odours and cries and psalmodic songs"] where they find a statue of Eve carved in stone. Here, she shares the space with other evil figures punished by fire, such as "pigmeos con colas y con trinchos y otros pigmeos alados y otros metidos en el fuego y toda esa horridez como castigo" (74) ["pygmies with tails and with forks and other winged pygmies and others inside the fire and all that horridness as punishment"]. Punished and petrified, Eve's figure shows how persistent her image as evil, malicious, disobedient, and guilty has been. An older female voice, pointing a shaky finger towards the stone, accuses her of being a traitor, specifically a "fémina traidora" (74) ["female traitor"], a "criminal" trait she coincidentally shares with Clytemnestra. By presenting only a fragment of the story, Angel reminds us that the same process of production occurred to the story that the old woman repeats. Eve is accused of being a traitor, but there is no question about determining whether there was any treason or not: Whom did she betray? How? Why? There is no need to verify the claims, as the force of tradition has in some way rendered those questions unnecessary. As there is no possibility for a figure carved in stone to speak and answer any questions about what happened in paradise, neither she nor her story can change. Her silence, as Alicia Ostriker (1993, 31) explains, is pervasive "because the canonizing process throughout our history has rested, not accidentally, but essentially, on the silencing of women."

Angel therefore insists on the need to alter such practices even in a small way. To begin with, the choice of words to designate Eve is significant, as *fémina* is an unusual Latin term to name woman. Moreover, this word names an "animal of female sex," derives from *fecundus* and *fetus* and is, of course, associated with women's fertility. Angel avoids *mujer* (woman), the most common expression for *woman* in Spanish since, according to several dictionaries, the term represents the concept of *esposa* (wife). *Fémina* is also an alternative to the words Adam uses when God brings Eve to him: "Esta sí que es de mi propia carne y de mis propios huesos! Se va a llamar 'mujer,' porque Dios la sacó del hombre" (Genesis 2:23) ["This one is at last bone from my bones, flesh from my flesh! She shall be called 'woman,' for she was taken out of man"].[24] Due to the differences both in meaning and use, *fémina* is favoured because it generates life without being the "wife" of Adam, but a likely equal of God as Alicia Ostriker's investigations on Eve suggest. However, Eve's power over the process of childbirth "was appropriated by Yahweh" (Ostriker 1993, 37).

Despite that appropriation, in *Las andariegas*, Adam becomes the man next to Eve, although he is characterized ironically as "the first man" (Angel 1984, 74). In addition, there is no mention of any detail that describes her as his derivation or servant. This operation, of course, has an impact on the process of production. Seeing Eve first and Adam second alters the structure of the narrative and the way we think about it. Angel inscribes her revision of Eve along the lines of Phyllis Trible (1995) as the phrase "ese a su lado el primer hombre" is, in fact, a reinsertion of a similar sentence ("the man who was with her") that, Trible notes, has been elided in the majority of translations of the Bible. Such elision has, naturally, led to a number of mistaken interpretations.[25] As a corrective, Angel seems to suggest that

Eve does exist in her own right, undermining Adam's power and authority as well as his alleged dominance.

The order of appearance also suggests an acknowledged biological fact: man is born of woman and not vice versa, as the biblical rib story would like to imply. Nonetheless, the rib story talks of a wound on the body of Adam and perhaps of his unconscious desire to be a woman and give birth. One can read this wound as a sign of his powerlessness at creating life and nurturing it at the breast; his sleep can be interpreted as the casting out of the memory that could remind him of this primal power he would never possess. One can imagine how such inability brings God and man together to rule over the subdued, voiceless mother.[26]

Eve cannot talk but her daughters, the travelers, can. They describe Adam as silent, asleep, and unaware of the visitors. He is ignorant of what they do, see, or say, or of what Eve can be for them without his intervention. Moreover, Adam lacks some of the features attributed to Eve. The group of women travelers can see the stone-carved image and in it discover that she has an aesthetic dimension; she is a "figura en piedra con gesto acoquinado, menudita y desnuda" (Angel 1984, 74) ["figure in stone, with a shy gesture, slender and nude"]. This description brings us back to the mothers' breasts, to the fullness and abundance of the woman-body, to her beauty and power, features of Eve that the Bible never provides. Instead, it centers only on the dangerous acts she performs: talking with the serpent, desiring the forbidden fruit, eating it, and inciting Adam to eat it too. These actions, of course, have disastrous consequences for her. The first of these is shame as she discovers the naked body of Adam, and becomes similarly conscious of her own. Subsequently, she experiences the high cost of disobedience to God's orders: banishment from Eden. Finally, she is subjected to extraordinary pain as God warns her he will increase her pain when giving birth: "[A]umentaré tus dolores cuando tengas hijos, y con dolor los darás a luz. Pero tu deseo te llevará a tu marido, y él tendrá autoridad sobre ti" (Genesis 3:16) ["I shall give you great labour in childbearing; with labour you will bear children. You will desire your husband, but he will be your master"].

The punishment is certainly harsh and she has little opportunity to argue in her own defence. At that point the only one who has a right to speak is God. Apparently admitting her guilt, Eve becomes a silent embodiment of pain, the model of suffering and subjection. She will not have a choice when deciding on bearing children, as she, in the book of Genesis, gives birth to three males. By God's will she must transfer her desire from the tree of knowledge, equality, and understanding, to her husband's control. This further suggests the need to keep in check both her physical and intellectual desires.

In sum, the power both God and Adam have over her will ensure that she does not develop a sense of happiness. In Angel's version, however, the image that accompanies Eve's profile shows some signs that can be construed as the opposite: her face shows a sort of smile that reveals some degree of the happiness denied to her and, by extension, to the women who do not conform to the laws and prohibitions of a patriarchal culture. She is happy within her naked body, not showing the sense of shame she is supposed to have. This depiction of Eve also suggests that the women travelers, her daughters, can see her in a different light. For them she is not subject to Adam's or God's authority as she is no longer under the surveillance of God: he is absent from both the passage and the picture. He and his voice have disappeared, no longer making her a by-product of patriarchy.

For that reason, it is all the more important for Eve's daughters to revisit the story and make it talk to them. They rewrite a sacred book, paying attention even to a detail as unessential as the rib story. They attempt to create a new version or perception of Eve, to reshape an ideology by replacing old beliefs with new concepts created by language. They go against the grain to recreate a myth by women for women, in which Eve becomes a heroine of disobedience as she unstitches the authority of God. Eve is a rebel, the first woman to challenge the subjugation of woman in the patriarchal garden and suffer the consequences (Chernin 1987, xvi).

Connecting with female figures from different times and cultures, the travelers continue to the next crossroad to find another heroine in the Valley of Anáhuac.

Tecuichpo/Copo de algodón: "la chingada"

"¡Viva Mexico, hijos de la chingada!" ["Long live Mexico, sons of *la chingada!*"] is a key phrase that Octavio Paz uses to explain the identity of male Mexicans in *The Labyrinth of Solitude* (1950). For him, *la chingada* is the indigenous, passive mother raped by the European conquistador. Albalucía Angel, however, has a different vision of *la chingada*. In the fifth section of *Las andariegas* the author rewrites a segment of this particular myth that shaped the history of the new world: "El invasor había desembarcado con su angurria y sus barbas. sus cuadrúpedos. traían sed de oro y de la plata y de turquesas y esmeraldas y plumas de quetzal" (Angel 1984, 115) ["The invader had disembarked with his greed and his beard. his horses. they brought thirst for gold and silver and turquoise and emeralds and quetzal feathers"]. The travelers arrive at the Valley of Anáhuac to meet the protagonists of this centuries-old story: Tecuichpo, daughter of Moctezuma, the weak Aztec emperor who submitted to the Spaniards, Moctezuma himself, and Hernán Cortés, the Spanish conquistador. They observe one key scene in which the travelers, along with Tecuichpo, tell the story of her rape, a story contained neither in Paz's essay nor in Cortés's *Segunda carta de relación*.[27] Cortés, however, briefly makes mention of her as a present given to him by Moctezuma, "después de haberme él dado algunas joyas de oro y una hija suya" (1985, 59) ["after he had given me some gold jewellery and one of his daughters"]. Bernal Díaz del Castillo, a soldier who closely participated with Hernán Cortés in the conquest of Mexico and authored *The True History of the Conquest of Mexico*,[28] describes her as "bien hermosa mujer para ser india" (1984, 489) ["so beautiful a woman, for an Indian"]. More recent descriptions, like the one published by Maria Idalia in the *Exelsior* newspaper, erroneously qualify her as [una] *mujer española* ([a] Spanish woman) and also as another Malinche: "su papel no fue muy distinto del de la Malinche, ya que ayudó a los españoles a dominar a los indios, aunque lo hizo utilizando para ello la dulzura de su carácter"[29] ["her role was no different than the one of Malinche, since she helped the Spaniards dominate the Indians, although to accomplish that she used the sweetness of her character"]. She was a traitor, much like Clytemnestra and Eve.

By focusing her attention on the young indigenous woman, Angel redefines all four readings. First, in *Las andariegas*, Tecuichpo is character-ized as a virgin "[f]lor morena" (Angel 1984, 117) ["[b]rown flower"]. When confronted with the conquistador and his power, she speaks, audaciously challenges him, and performs a series of unexpected actions:

Tecuichpo se hincó como a besar la tierra y recogió un puñado de pantano. que el gañán invasor no tuvo tiempo a nada pues el asombro lo pasmó cuando ella tiró al suelo el casco de plumas, se embadurnó la cara y brazos con la greda, se desgarró la túnica de hilo, ¡aquí tienes a Copo de algodón ... verdugo de mi pueblo!, le anunció a voz en cuello y lo escupió. (119)

> [Tecuichpo kneeled down as if to kiss the ground and picked up a fistful of mud. the invader thief had no time for anything as astonishment paralyzed him when she threw her feathered crown to the ground, plastered her face and arms with the mud, opened up her cotton tunic, here, take *Copo de algodon* ... victimizer of my people! she yelled out and spat on him.]

The actions she performs constitute an appropriation of the movements reserved only for important men, particularly for Moctezuma and his lords. For example, the "Segunda carta de relación" mentions that kneeling down and kissing the soil is an activity only for Moctezuma: "yo me apeé y le fui a abrazar solo; e aquellos dos señores que con él iban me detuvieron con las manos para que no le tocase; ellos y él ficieron asimismo ceremonia de besar la tierra" (Cortés 1985, 57); "I dismounted and stepped forward to embrace him, but the two lords who were with him stopped me with their hands so that I should not touch him; and they likewise all performed the ceremony of kissing the earth" (Cortés 2001, 84). Spitting and yelling, on the other hand, are probably not proper behaviours for a young girl of noble standing either, but those very actions cause tremendous confusion and instability as *Copo de algodón* transforms the masculine gestures into feminine ones. Not satisfied with those transgressions, Tecuichpo performs an even more spectacular one than those. In what represents an uncanny similarity with Clytemnestra, she opens her tunic and apparently shows her breasts to Cortés. Such an act of defiance manifests, once again, the divide between the phallus and the breast and momentarily destabilizes the balance of power as the conquistador responds with complete astonishment: "El invasor no tuvo tiempo a nada pues el asombro lo pasmó" (Angel 1984, 119) ["The invader had no time for anything, as he was stupefied"]. He does not understand the meaning of Tecuichpo's gestures and predictably misreads them as a provocation.

Despite her resistance and challenge, the conquistador rapes her. Tecuichpo is nevertheless able to rearticulate the scene and show that her sacrifice is not for the emperor, but for her people. She subverts the image of the indigenous woman as no more than a *chingada*, a silent and passive victim. Instead, she becomes a heroine who speaks for all the other indigenous women who, as slaves, probably suffered the same fate. She offers her sacrifice to the people.[30] Beyond that, she is able to publicly expose the trap that the patriarchal system had reserved for her. She is caught between her father, who has given her to the foreigner with perhaps the expectation of something in return, the captain who rapes her, and the people who admire her but cannot and do not save her. Father and captain (the mother is conspicuously absent), therefore, share the responsibility for the rape of Tecuichpo. She, however, appears as a strong woman, a woman who raises her voice, a woman with dignity. Her voice and the silence of Moctezuma speak volumes about issues of courage, something Moctezuma seems to lack: "El cacique iba absorto" (Angel 1984, 117) ["The chief was absorbed in his thoughts"]. In sum, in *Las andariegas*, Tecuichpo allows the readers to configure a different, more positive and complex image of the indigenous woman, as she is able to expose the existing power structures that make her a pawn. In the end, Tecuichpo attempts a vindication of the indigenous woman, often represented as dispossessed and outcast.

While Tecuichpo is to be applauded for her actions and her resolution, the same cannot necessarily be said of Clytemnestra or, for that matter, Electra, both of whom engage in murder (matricide), an unthinkable crime. They seem to bring disgrace to women for generations to come. Angel, however, suggests that as a creation of myth and imagination those stories are fluid, and that women can reconcile themselves with our ancestors and rebuild torn connections with our foremothers. Clytemnestra represents a polarized extreme, the prostitute, while Electra portrays the opposite: the chaste young woman. Eve, petrified and silent, projects the image of punishment in hell. Tecuichpo emerges as an inversion of more traditional interpretations of history. Like all other human beings, she exemplifies a mixture of victory and defeat, not just one or the other.

In *Las andariegas* Angel writes of movement across time, space, and culture. Her writing configures a revision of master narratives without becoming another master narrative. She presents the reader with a validation of female genealogy, with a remaking of myths in an effort to recapture lost origins. Angel trains the readers to go beyond the deep divide between the breast and the phallus and read the signs of the experience of four women, not as markers of fixed identity, but as discourses that constantly change. As readers, we are shown the meaning of being both participants and privileged observers; we are being educated about the world and the multiplicity of ways to name the women who live in it. *Las andariegas* illustrates that Angel trusts the experience of women as imperfect (and perhaps indefinable) mothers, sisters, and daughters to bring us back to ourselves. As well, she expresses confidence in our desire to order the world according to figures of our own making. That is why the book concludes with a call for action by quoting from *Les guerrilleres*: "Ellas dicen que todas esas formas designan un lenguaje anticuado. dicen que hay que recomenzar todo. dicen que un gran viento barre la Tierra. ellas dicen que el sol va a salir" (Wittig 1971, 139) ["They say that all those forms designate an antiquated language, that every thing has to begin anew, that a great wind sweeps the Earth, they say that the sun is about to rise"].

Works Cited

Ángel, Albalucía. 1970. *Los girasoles en invierno*. Bogotá: Editorial Bolívar.
———. 1975. *Estaba la pájara pinta sentada en el verde limón*. Barcelona: Argos Vergara.

———. 1979. *Oh Gloria inmarcesible!* Bogotá: Instituto Colombiano de Cultura.

———. 1982. *Misiá señora.* Barcelona: Argos Vergara.

———. 1991. Siete lunas y un espejo. In *Voces en escena,* ed. Nora Eidelberg and María Mercedes Jaramillo, 18–102. Medellín, Colombia: Univ. de Antioquia.

———. 1984. *Las andariegas.* Barcelona: Argos Vergara.

Bal, Mieke. 1989. Introd. to *Anti-Covenant: Counter-reading women's lives in the Hebrew Bible,* 11–24. Decatur: Almond Press.

Blundell, Sue. 1995. *Women in Ancient Greece.* Cambridge: Harvard Univ. Press.

Chernin, Kim. 1987. *Reinventing Eve.* New York: Times Books.

Chodorow, Nancy. 1989. *Feminism and Psychoanalitic Theory.* New Haven: Yale Univ. Press.

Cixous, Helene. 1995. Salidas. In *La joven nacida,* 13–107. Trans. Ana Maria Moix. Barcelona: Anthropos.

Clendinnen, Inga. 1991. *Aztecs.* Cambridge Univ. Press.

Cortés, Hernán. 1985. Segunda carta de relación. In *Cartas de la conquista de México,* 39–95. Madrid: Sarpe.

———. 2001. The Second Letter. In *Letters from Mexico,* 47–159. Trans. Anthony Pagden. New Haven: Yale Univ. Press.

Díaz del Castillo, Bernal. 1984. *Historia verdadera de la conquista de la Nueva España.* Ed. Miguel León Portilla. Madrid: Historia 16.

Eliade, Mircea, ed. 1987. *The Encyclopedia of Religion,* vol. 5. New York: Macmillan.

Euripides. 1959. *Electra.* Ed. David Grene and Richmond Lattimore. New York: Random House.

Filer, Malva E. 1985. Autorescate e invención en *Las andariegas* de Albalucía Angel. *Revista Iberoamericana* 51 (132–33): 648–53.

Frasier, Nancy. 1992. Introduction: Revaluing French Feminism. In *Revaluing French Feminism: Critical Essays on Difference, Agency & Culture,* 1–24. Bloomington: Indiana Univ. Press.

Froula, Christine. 1989. The Daughter's Seduction: Sexual Violence and Literary History. In *Daughters and Fathers,* ed. Lynda E. Boose and Betty S. Flowers, 111–35. Baltimore: Johns Hopkins Univ. Press.

García Pinto, Magdalena. 1988. Entrevista con Albalucía Angel. In *Historias íntimas,* 27–66. Hanover, NH: Ediciones del norte.

Goldberg, David Theo, and Ato Quayson. 2002. Introduction: Scale and Sensibility. in *Relocating Postcolonialism,* xi–xxii. Oxford: Blackwell.

Graves, Robert. 1969. *Greek Myths.* London: Cassell.

Harris, Max. 1996. Moctezuma's Daughter. The Role of La Malinche in Mesoamerican Dance. *Journal of American Folklore* 109 (432): 149-77.

Irigaray, Luce. 1993a. Each Sex Must Have Its Own Rights. In *Sexes and Genealogies,* 1–5. Trans. Gillian C. Gill. New York: Columbia Univ. Press.

———. 1993b. Body Against Body: In Relation to the Mother. In *Sexes and Genealogies,* 9–21. Trans. Gillian C. Gill. New York: Columbia Univ. Press.

Jaramillo, María Mercedes. 1991. Albalucía Angel: El discurso de la insubordinación. In *¿Y las mujeres? Ensayos sobre literatura colombiana,* ed. María Mercedes Jaramillo, Angela Inés Robledo and Flor María Rodríguez-Arenas, 203–38. Medellín: Univ. de Antioquia Press.

Leland, Dorothy. 1992. Lacanian Psychoanalysis and French Feminism: Toward an Adequate Political Psychology. In *Revaluing French Feminism: Critical Essays on Difference, Agency & Culture,* 113–35. Bloomington: Indiana Univ. Press.

Magnarelli, Sharon. 1985. *The Lost Rib: Female Characters in the Spanish American Novel.* Lewisburg, PA: Bucknell Univ. Press.

Moi, Toril. 1985. Marginality and Subversion: Julia Kristeva. In *Sexual/Textual Politics,* 150–73. London: Routledge.

Ostriker, Alicia Suskin. 1993. Out of My Sight: The Buried Woman in Biblical Narrative. in *Feminist Revisions and the Bible*, 27–55. Cambridge: Blackwell.

Mueller, James R., Katharine Doob Sakenfeld, and M. Jack Sugs (eds). 1992. *Oxford Study Bible: Revised English Bible with the Apocrypha*. New York: Oxford Univ. Press.

Paz, Octavio. 1978. Los hijos de La Malinche. In *El laberinto de la soledad*, 59–80. México: Fondo de Cultura Económica.

Philip, Marlene Nourbese. 1997. A Genealogy of Resistance. In *A Genealogy of Resistance and Other Essays*, 9–30. Toronto: Mercury.

Sophocles. 1957. *Electra*. Ed. David Grene and Richmond Lattimore. Chicago: Univ. of Chicago Press.

Todorov, Tzvetan. 1985. *The Conquest of Mexico*. Trans. Richard Howard. New York: Harper.

Tompkins, Cynthia. 1997. Aporias resultantes de la deconstrucción del sujeto en *Como en la guerra* de Luisa Valenzuela, *Son vacas, somos puercos* de Carmen Boullosa y *Las andariegas* de Albalucía Angel. *Torre de papel* 7 (3): 148–65.

Trible, Phyllis. 1984. *Texts of Terror: Literary Feminist Readings of Biblical Narratives*. Philadelphia: Fortress.

———. 1995. Eve and Miriam: From the Margins to the Center. In *Feminist Approaches to the Bible*, ed. Hershel Shanks, 5–24. Washington: Biblical Archaeology Society.

Williams, Raymond L. 2004. Latin American Women Writers: An Interview with Women Writers in Colombia. Personal web page, http://faculty.ucr.edu/~williar1/womenwriter.htm.

Wittig, Monique. 1971. *Les Guerrilleres*. Trans. David Le Vay. Boston: Beacon Press.

Film

La otra conquista. 1998. Directed by Salvador Carrasco. Carrasco & Domingo Films Production, Twentieth Century Fox.

Notes

1   For a comprehensive discussion of the Latin American Boom see José Donoso, *Historia personal del Boom*.

2   This novel received the Vivencias Literary award in 1975. As a recipient, Angel found herself in the middle of a controversy covered in some of the national newspapers. Some readers hotly debated the merits of the novel because of its experimental nature.

3   The title comes from the Colombian national anthem, which is parodied in the book.

4   This topic is mentioned by Malva E. Filer in one of the few published discussions of *Las andariegas*. In her view, the conflictive aspects of the relationship between mothers and daughters require greater analysis and understanding (1985, 654).

5   All translations from the book are my own.

6   In his study of La Malinche in Mexican folkloric dance, Max Harris indicates Isabel was the Christian name given to her by the Spaniards.

7   *Las andariegas* seems to be, in a significant manner, ideologically shaped by the French feminist theories of the seventies and eighties. As Nancy Frasier remarks: "It was axiomatic that existing social relations and institutions were wholly repressive and that no mere reforms could put things right. On the contrary, the realization of the feminist vision would require the creation of an entirely new form of life-new social relations among new social subjects" (1992, 2).

8   Angel has also written a trilogy of plays, which include *La manzana de piedra* [*The Apple of Stone*], *Siete lunas y un espejo* [*Seven Moons and One Mirror*] and *Lilita mi amor* [*Lilita my Love*] (unpublished).

9   Referring to psychoanalysis, to Freud and the rereadings of him by critics like Nancy Chodorow and Kim Chernin has divided those theories in a number of categories: "[T]he penis as power; as nurturing symbol analogous to the breast; as a symbol of freedom from primal impotence; as a safe place to turn into from primal hostility to the mother; as token of the father's social power within the patriarchal world" (Chernin 1987).

10 A review of general definitions indicates that genealogy is the tracing of family pedigrees, the studying a family's descent from ancestors or a group of people related by blood or marriage. According to this model, members of families are joined together by a series of lines that contribute to ascertaining the relationship to each other, their location and their personal lives. Sometimes, pictures contribute to the wholeness and unity of a chart. Mircea Eliade, however, maintains that genealogy goes beyond the listings of pedigrees to establish itself as "an intellectual discipline" that allots "a share of human values that consist of privileges and honors, titles and powers. It draws implications for human conduct and for the structure of the social order. Most directly, genealogies connect human families with their mythical origins, joining them as kin" (1987, 502).

11 Lower-case letters are used in the original text. Angel also deliberately uses periods instead of commas throughout the text.

12 Lucy Tejada, a Colombian painter, is the artist who contributed them.

13 According to Robert Graves, Electra was totally neglected by Clytemnestra and lived in abject poverty. She was also under constant surveillance and forbidden to openly call her mother and Aegistus "murderous adulterers." If she did, she would go to a faraway city and be confined in a dungeon.

14 According to Blundell, there was a constant process of adaptation in the way myths were told: Agamemnon, for example, was killed by Aegistus, Clytemnestra's lover. However, "by the fifth century BC it is told that it was Clytemnestra, the wife herself, who killed Agamemnon" (1995, 16). A transformation of this sort has, of course, consequences in terms of the attitude toward women.

15 Chernin also adds that "Freud would always substitute a father for a mother when he was thinking about childhood" (1987, 92).

16 In the classical texts Electra's participation to avenge her father goes from not being an agent (Aeschylus, Sophocles), to having a very minor role and being a witness (Euripides).

17 In Sophocles, Electra waits for Orestes outside the palace while he commits the crime as Electra says: "Someone cries out inside. Do you hear?"; "Orestes, how have you fared?" and "Is the wretch dead?"(1957, 182–83). Euripides refers briefly to the episode, but it is not Electra the character that talks about the crime.

18 In *The Newly Born Woman*, Helene Cixous comments that as Clytemnestra knows that death is about to visit her "she skirts it and flees it: she knows that death, as life can flow from any unsuspected opening" (1995, 79).

19 M. Nourbese Phillip, in her creative essay "A Genealogy of Resistance," remembers the father in similar terms: "The only memory was the daily ritual: my father bringing light to the home" (1997, 9).

20 See Sue Blundel, *Women in Ancient Greece*.

21 Robert Graves clarifies the reasons why Clytemnestra had almost no cause to love Agamemnon: among other actions, he had killed both her former husband Tantalus and the infant at her breast; he married her by force and went away to a seemingly-endless war and allowed the sacrifice of Iphigenia at Aulis.

22 Graves is again useful here as he states that "at first Clytemnestra rejected [Aegistu's] advances because Agamemnon had instructed his court to watch on her and report to him in writing any sign of infidelity" (1969, 414).

23 This symbolic reconciliation has an indirect relationship with Angel's biography as the author discusses the dynamic of tension, silence, love and hate that dominated the relationship with her mother (see García Pinto 1988, 37).

24 *The Oxford Study Bible*. Revised English Bible with the Apocripha.

25 Besides, the Old Testament states: "God created man in his own image, in the image of God he created him; male and female he created them" (Gen. 1:27–28).

26 However, the epigraph with which *Las andariegas* opens draws attention to the ocean as the boundless mother of all, not to a diminished mother. Eve identifies with nature as she, according to Ostriker, is associated with "gardens, sacred trees and oracular snakes" (1993, 37); she is also portrayed as speaking to the serpent, a feature that also appears in *Les Guerilleres* by Wittig.

27 There is also a play written by Salvador Novo, entitled *Cuauhtémoc*, in which Tecuichpo has a minor role as Cuauhtémoc's wife. *La otra conquista* [*The Other Conquest*] (1998), a film directed by Salvador Carrasco, also includes a segment on Tecuichpo's role in the conquest of Mexico.

28 His purpose was to correct a work entitled *The History of the Conquest of Mexico*, by Francisco López de Gómara. This book is also important as it contains a number of details on Doña Marina or La Malinche: her origins, her status, and her role as a translator for Cortés.

29 As this is an Internet article, pagination is lacking. The translation is mine.

30 Throughout the journey to Tenochtitlan, Cortés mentions receiving women as presents and slaves.

Redefining Identities in Elena Garro's "La culpa es de los tlaxcaltecas"

Elizabeth Montes Garcés, University of Calgary

"La culpa es de los tlaxcaltecas" ["It's the fault of the Tlaxcaltecas"] is a well-known short story by the Mexican writer Elena Garro. The work was first published in 1964 as part of the collection entitled *La semana de colores*. The short story recreates Laura Aldama's marital and identity crises when she takes a trip with her mother-in-law to Guanajuato and finds herself stranded on Lake Cuitzeo. While her mother-in-law (Margarita) leaves to look for help, Laura meets her cousin, an individual who happened to be her husband in a previous existence as an Aztec woman at the moment when the Aztec civilization is being crushed by Hernán Cortés's army. From that moment on, Laura accepts the invitations of her *primo marido* ("Indian cousin/husband") and leaps three times into her previous existence as an Aztec woman in Tenochtitlan to witness the destruction of the city and to seek a new future for herself. Travelling and displacement[1] in time and space become, then, key issues in the protagonist's evaluation of the current life she lives with her husband (a well-established businessman from Mexico City with connections to the highest sectors of society, as he has dealings with the president of Mexico) and her past existence near her indigenous companion (an Aztec Indian). Through movement in space and time the protagonist of "La culpa es de los tlaxcaltecas" gains agency and actively resists and redefines dominant cultural patterns regarding men and women. All of these operations offer a new definition of male and female subjectivity that recovers the memories and accomplishments of the pre-Columbian civilizations and empowers women to be the link between the present and the past.

Several critics have analyzed Garro's short story from the poststructural, mythological, and feminist perspectives. Perhaps the most interesting to cite in this study are Cynthia Duncan's "'La culpa es de los tlaxcaltecas': A Revaluation of Mexico's Past Through Myth" (1985) and Sandra Messinger Cypess's "The Malinche Paradigm as Subtext" (1991). Duncan's article deals with the guilt Mexicans face due to the way in which they sided with their Spanish conquerors and rejected their indigenous ancestors. Her thesis is that "Myth ... allows the Mexican to reconcile some of the conflicts innate in his double heritage through the restructuring of objective reality in mythic terms" (106). The myth refers to the glorious past of the Aztec civilization as a means of coming to terms with the current reality of being a nation of mixed origin. In spite of her convincing argument, Duncan does not make any reference to the role La Malinche played in the development of the guilt feeling.

On the contrary, Sandra M. Cypess is perhaps the only critic who acknowledges the importance of the Malinche paradigm in Garro's "La culpa." The critic establishes a close link between Malinche and Laura Aldama because both figures possess the ability to switch identities according to the cultures they are immersed in and both pursue two marital relationships at the same time. That is precisely the reason why both women are perceived as traitors. However, Cypess (1991, 166) emphasizes that Laura "attempts to position herself as a subject and not an object"; from that perspective she is able to evaluate her husband's behaviour and make the conscious decision to recuperate the Indian civilization from its ruins. I concur with Cypess' reading of the short story, but I would like to take it one step further to underline the way in which Laura gains agency and offers women and men a new role in Mexican society by revaluating and re-appropriating the ancient Aztec tradition still present in indigenous dances.

In *Bodies that Matter*, Judith Butler (1993) claims that there is a difference between sex and gender. The first is prior to language and is "installed at a prelinguistic site to which there is no direct access" while gender "consists of the social meanings that sex assumes" (5). Those social meanings are subject to construction and require a process in which there is an attempt to appropriate and at the same time to contest the boundaries of what Butler calls "the regulatory law" (12). This appropriation requires "performativity," which is "always a reiteration of a norm or a set of norms" (12) achieved through constant repetition of the conventions of authority. Butler also suggests that "[i]f there is agency, it is to be found, paradoxically, in the possibilities opened up in and by that constraint appropriation of the regulatory law" (12): there is a constant negotiation with the set of imposed behavioural patterns.

Laura Aldama, the protagonist of "La culpa es de los tlaxcaltecas," has done her share of accepting and following the conventions that are expected from an upper-class woman. She is depicted in Garro's short story as a traditional upper-class housewife married to Pablo, a businessman from Mexico City. Following the Spanish and Catholic tradition – and in clear reference to the biblical text – Laura's husband name is Paul, like the apostle. In her household, her husband Pablo is the maximum authority and her role is to be his subordinate, obeying his orders without hesitation. Therefore, Laura's life is one of idleness and anticipation, since she is on a constant search for new meaning in her life. However, Laura gains agency by positioning herself in control of a discourse to reaffirm and challenge the norms that regulate her social and historical role as a woman in Mexican society.

The *récit* ["story"] begins with the conversation between Laura and her Indian maid Nacha in the kitchen after Laura's return from Tenochtitlan to her modern house in Mexico City. Laura has disappeared for several weeks and her husband Pablo has left the house since he has lost faith in the police's ability to find his wife. As she talks, Laura gains control of discourse, and as a sympathetic listener, Nacha becomes her narratee,[2] and recalls the details of her time leaps into ancient Tenochtitlan and her three encounters with her *primo marido* ["Indian cousin/husband"] in her past existence.

The reiterative pattern of Laura's encounters with her *primo marido*, as well as the constant reference to the short story's leitmotif, "la culpa es de los tlaxcaltecas" ["it's the fault of the Tlaxcaltecas"][3], act as reminders of the insistence of the past to make its mark on the present and the importance of Malinche's subtext in Garro's short story. The first encounter between Laura and her *primo marido* takes place during a trip Laura takes to Guanajuato in the company of Margarita, her mother-in-law. The car breaks down in the middle of the bridge on Lake Cuitzeo, where Laura agrees to wait while Margarita gets help. Once she is left alone, an Indian fellow with an open injury on his shoulder approaches her. Laura recognizes him as her cousin and husband in her past life in Tenochtitlan. From this point on, she begins to evaluate her former existence as a woman in ancient Mexico and her present life as an obedient and submissive housewife in modern Mexico. The way Laura describes the bridge makes the reader aware that Laura positions herself not only as a link between the present and the past, but also as a key figure to redefine the future of the nation. She says, "Y yo me quedé en la mitad del puente blanco, que atraviesa el lago seco, con fondo de lajas blancas." (Garro 1994a, 88) ["I stayed in the middle of the white bridge that crosses the dried lake with a bottom of white stones"]. It is quite obvious by these remarks that Laura, just like her ancestor La Malinche, is in between two cultures, and she is taking that opportunity to gain agency to determine her own future and that of her husband.

To carry out the project of redefining the new role of women and men in Mexican society, it is necessary for Laura to confront again the norms and myths that have surrounded women and men in Mexico. One of these myths has to do with the figure of Malinche. Historically, Malinche was the name given to Cortés' indigenous translator and mistress. Malinche has been blamed for the defeat of the Aztecs because she joined forces with the Tlaxcaltecas and with Cortés against them. That is the reason why she has been considered a traitor. In Garro's short story, Laura constantly repeats "La culpa es de los tlaxcaltecas" when she encounters her *primo marido* – meaning that she is not the only one that is supposed to carry the blame, even though she has been forced to play the role of the guilty party over and over again.

The ancient world into which Laura leaps in her encounters with her Indian husband is the city of Tenochtitlan on the verge of its destruction. The constant reference Laura makes to the Tlaxcaltecas' betrayal refers the reader to the La Malinche subtext. The Tlaxcaltecas were one of the fiercest enemies of the Aztecs at the time of Cortés's arrival in Mexico in 1521. Their cooperation with the Spanish as well as Malinche's allegiance with Cortés is cited by Octavio Paz in *El laberinto de la soledad* as the main cause of the Aztec civilization's downfall. According to Paz, due to Malinche's misbehaviour, Mexicans became the sons of *la chingada*, or the product of a violation of the Aztec culture and its women.

Betrayal and guilt are the key elements that characterize Malinche in Paz's essay and also become Laura's defining traits amongst her relatives and servants at her Mexico City house. When Laura returns to Mexico City with her mother-in-law, Pablo learns that the Indian who his wife met in Lake Cuitzeo had followed her to her house. He imagines that his wife has had an affair with him. He reacts violently, insulting her and slapping her face without even listening to her account of the story. Therefore, it is obvious that, in Garro's view, in contemporary Mexican society women embody feelings of guilt inherited from their cultural ancestor, Malinche, and are prone to suffering physical abuse by their husbands because women symbolize the stain of betrayal.

However, the text takes a twist that sets the reader on the path of finding a new way to define feminine and masculine roles in Mexican society. In control of her discourse Laura makes the following comments to Nacha regarding her husband Pablo's violent reaction towards her: "Sus gestos son feroces y su conducta es tan incoherente como sus palabras. Yo no tengo la culpa de que aceptara la derrota y la olvidara" (Garro 1994a, 96) ["His looks are savage and his conduct is as incoherent as his words. It is not my fault that he accepted defeat and forgot about it"]. She criticizes her husband's reaction and places the blame on him for selling himself to the enemy by imitating their violent behaviour and forgetting his ancestors and his culture. According to Laura, Pablo's physical appearance reminded her of that other Indian husband of hers: "Yo me enamoré de Pablo en una carretera, durante un minuto en el cual me recordó a alguien conocido, a quien yo no recordaba" (96) ["I fell in love with Pablo on a highway during one minute in which he reminded me of someone I knew, but whom I had forgotten"]. However, he had evolved into a body with no memory of the past and no respect for his roots, just like all the other men in Mexico City: "Inmediatamente volvía a ser absurdo, sin memoria como un cuerpo deshabitado y sólo repetía los gestos de todos los hombres de la ciudad de México" (96) ["Immediately he became absurd, without memory, and he only repeated the gestures of all the men of Mexico City"].

In contrast, Laura confesses that her Indian husband never gets upset with her and she commends him for his tenderness and his willingness to fight for their nation until the end of time. He is persistent in his constant pursuit of Laura and wants her to reassure him and give him the courage to continue his battle. Laura becomes his shield as she confesses to Nacha that, "Me agarró con su mano caliente, como agarraba a su escudo y me di cuenta de que no lo llevaba." (Garro 1994a, 91) ["He took hold of me with his warm hand, like he used to grab his shield and I realized that he wasn't carrying it"]. His comments also suggests that it is the end of a cycle and that they ought to be together; "Ya falta poco para que se acabe el tiempo y seamos uno solo ... por eso te andaba buscando" (92) ["It won't be long before time runs out and we are only one ... that's why I have come looking for you"]. Obviously, the contrast established between the behaviour of Pablo and the Indian husband reveals how male roles are reconfigured in the text. While Pablo displays an aggressive attitude towards his wife and wants to be in control of her destiny, the Indian husband shows enormous respect and admiration for his wife and looks for her support and companionship. Moreover, Pablo has no memory of his past and his culture, while the Indian husband is a constant reminder to Laura of her origin and her ancestors. His remark, "It won't be long before time runs out and we are only one," could be read in at least two different ways. It could mean that the sign of gender could be definitely erased so that the two characters will be able to find their new self and the new nation they are searching for, or it could refer to a total reinvention of the male and the female roles in a new society, one that re-appropriates masculine and feminine values buried in the indigenous past.

On the other hand, the Indian husband's way of conducting himself makes it obvious to the reader that more than one subtext is part of the story. That other subtext deals with ancient Indian mythology. In "The Royal Dynasty of Tenochtitlan," Susan Gillespie (1989) explains that the transfer of power amongst the Aztecs was "conceived as a repeating cycle." Each cycle was formed by a group of three kings linked to each other by brothers or nephews belonging to the same generation. According to Gillespie, "[t]he Tenochtitlan dynasty ... unfolds in a pattern of 1-3-1-3-1" (17). At the time of the conquest, Acamapichtli was the first of his generation, and Moctezuma the Elder and Moctezuma the Younger "were boundary figures making the transition between one cycle and the other" (153). For the Mexican, then, the conquest could be explained as part of the cycle: the Aztec defeat by the Spanish will be considered the end of a cycle. However, it also signals the beginning of a new cycle, because another Moctezuma will rise from the dead to regain control over his kingdom. Boundary figures like Moctezuma gained their power through the intervention of a female relative, usually a queen who "held the right to endow rulership" (18).

In "La culpa es de los tlaxcaltecas," Laura sees her role in contemporary Mexico as that of a woman that will legitimize the new rule. In his article "Montezuma's Daughter: The Role of La Malinche in Mesoamerican Dance," Max Harris (1996) claims that in many traditional dances in Mexico, New Mexico, and Guatemala, Malinche is depicted as a close relative of Montezuma's, often as his wife or his daughter. According to Aztec mythology, "women play a crucial role in the renewal of the cycle, the perpetuation of the dynasty, and the Mexican vision of the future. The Malinche of the danzas recalls one (or all) of these women" (153). In Garro's short story, Laura admits that she and her husband are first cousins; just as the Malinche figure of the dances, Laura has a close blood relationship with her spouse. However, In her conversation with her *primo marido*, she states that her husband "Quiso decirme que yo merecía la muerte y al mismo tiempo me dijo que mi muerte ocasionaría la suya" (Garro 1994a, 90) ["He tried to tell me that I deserved to die, and at the same time he told me that my death would bring about his own"], implying that, as Harris has suggested, she has the power to validate a man's position as a chief leader in Mexican society and that his existence depends entirely upon her.

Harris also argues that in traditional Mesoamerican dances Malinche not only represents the daughter or wife of Moctezuma but also a spiritual and powerful figure with close links to the goddesses of Aztec mythology, such as Toci, Tonatzin, Xochiquetzal, and Coatlicue (the mother-earth goddess, the beginning and the end of humanity). In "La danza de los matachines" a young girl dressed in white plays the role of La Malinche. The dance, which is performed by Hispanics and Native American Indians in several villages in New Mexico, represents the victory of Indian ghost warriors led by Moctezuma and Malinche against foreign invaders like Cortés and his soldiers. Initially, Cortés defeats Moctezuma and his forces, but his victory is short-lived since in the last act Moctezuma resurrects due to Malinche's spiritual power and manages to defeat his enemy. She is considered "the queen of the spirit realm" (Harris 1996, 153) since she can revive the ghost soldiers, purify them, and reunite them again to help Moctezuma accomplish his objective.

The second subtext to which "La culpa es de los tlaxcaltecas" makes reference must be precisely the one of the pre-Hispanic Indian legends still present in the traditional Mesoamerican dances. Just as the Malinche figure of "La danza de los matachines," Laura wears a white dress implying that she also possesses some kind of supernatural spiritual power. During her three encounters with her Indian husband, she is the only one that is able to see him and communicate with him, which confirms the fact that he is invisible to her husband Pablo and her mother-in-law. In Nacha's retelling of the story she comments that "La señora Margarita se quedó muy asombrada al oír lo del indio, porque ella no lo había visto, solo había visto la sangre como la podíamos ver todos" (Garro 1994a, 97) ["Margarita remained very surprised to hear of the incident of the Indian because she had not seen him in Lake Cuitzeo, she had only seen the blood that we could all see"]. Therefore, Laura indeed possesses supernatural powers. Her *primo marido* appears like a ghost and she is the only one that is able to understand his words and the circumstances he is facing. On the other hand, just like the Malinche figure in "La danza de los matachines," Laura offers help when she sees that her Indian husband is injured: "La sangre le seguía corriendo por el pecho. Saqué un pañuelo de mi bolso y sin una palabra, empecé a limpiársela" (90) ["The blood flowed onto his chest. I took out a handkerchief from my purse and without a word I began to wipe it off"]. By the same token, when she inquires about the other soldiers her Indian husband replies that, "los que salieron andan en las mismas tranzas que yo" (90) ["Those who came out alive are in the same situation as I am"]. Laura's Indian husband seeks her help and she exercises her healing powers to endow him and his fellow ghost soldiers with enough energy to go back to the battlefield.

Moreover, the stain on Laura's white dress is a constant reminder of the injury inflicted by the Spanish conquistadors on the body of the Mexican nation. During the three encounters between Laura and her Indian husband, Laura makes constant references to her Indian husband's open wound: "Tenía una cortada en la mano izquierda, los cabellos llenos de polvo, y por la herida del hombro le escurría una sangre tan roja que parecía negra" (Garro 1994a, 92) ["He had a cut on his left hand, his hair was full of dust, and from the wound on his shoulder dripped blood so red that it seemed black"]. Indeed, Laura's Indian husband survives the Spanish attack, but he is an injured and weak individual who is unable to regain his strength to fight back. Curiously enough, his injury is an open one that only Laura can heal because she has the power to do so according to ancient Aztec legends. By Laura's retelling of the story and the constant recreation of those events, Laura gains agency and accomplishes the transformation of the use of the sign of blame to the sign of healer of her Indian husband.

Cynthia Duncan (1985, 114) has analyzed the function of the third-person narrator in "La culpa es de los tlaxcaltecas." According to the critic:

A third person omniscient narrator, whose presence is scarcely felt throughout most of the tale, provides the external frame for the story. He establishes the context for the conversation which took place between Laura and Nacha at some unspecified time in the past, filtering, adding little details to set the mood.... The omniscient narrator's most important function, however, lies in the retelling of the tale, since both Laura and Nacha have since disappeared and cannot speak for themselves.

There is indeed a third-person narrative voice that sets the atmosphere for the tale and makes comments about Laura and Nacha's reactions. However, it is not his/her recollection of events that the reader is confronted with, because it is truly Laura who is in charge of retelling the tale. Nacha is Laura's listener or narratee because the story is addressed to her. Laura has control over her discourse and appeals to gain sympathy from Nacha, a woman and a direct descendent of the Aztecs, a group that she considers her own once she recovers her memory. Laura also forces the reader outside the fictional world to be placed in Nacha's shoes and involves the reader in the process of a critical reading of the social script and the myths that have shaped the role of women and men in Mexican society.

This process of reading critically, performed not only by the characters in the story, but also by readers outside the fictional world, implies Laura's constant confrontations between the ancient culture of the Aztecs and the contemporary mestizo culture of modern Mexico. This procedure corresponds closely with Judith Butler's mechanism of gaining agency through the use of the performative. According to Butler (1993, 95):

Performativity cannot be understood outside a process of iterability, a regularized and constrained repetition of norms.... This iterability implies that "performance" is not a singular "act" or event, but a ritualized production, a ritual reiterated under and through constraint, under and through the force of prohibition and taboo, with the threat of ostracism and even death controlling and compelling the shape of the production.

In spite of Pablo's violent reaction after learning that Laura had met with an Indian on the bridge of Lake Cuitzeo, she attempts to make contact with her *primo marido* once more. She puts on a white sweater to cover the stains on her dress and goes to Café de Tacuba[4] in search of her Indian husband. She is aware of the rule that she is supposed to obey Pablo's orders to not leave the house alone and that she will awaken his jealousy by again meeting the man she is interested in. Laura confesses to Nacha: "Cuando se enoja [Pablo], me prohíbe salir. ¡A tí te consta!" (Garro 1994a, 96) ["When he [Pablo] gets angry he doesn't let me go out. As you well know!"]. On the one hand, she is openly contesting the rule that a woman can only be devoted to one man in her life. She is operating under tremendous constraints and is even risking her own life: in Hispanic communities, infidelity in women is a highly reprehensible act that can be punished by death at the hands of the offended husband. On the other hand, by transforming herself into a protagonist instead of a passive entity eager to please the conqueror, she is openly re-appropriating history's means of production.

By actively seeking another encounter with her Indian husband, Laura is not only making evident the rules that regulate the female role in contemporary Mexican society, but also regaining the memories of ancient Tenochtitlan and its culture, which she had forgotten. When Laura leaps into the besieged city of Tenochtitlan in her Indian husband's company, she witnesses the destruction of the city and remembers how her relatives were killed and her father's house burned down.

Las piedras y los gritos volvieron a zumbar alrededor nuestro y yo sentí que algo ardía a mis espaldas.

– ¡No mires! – me dijo. Puso la rodilla en tierra y con los dedos apagó mi vestido que empezaba a arder.

– ¡Sácame de aquí! – le grité con todas mis fuerzas, porque me acordé de que estaba delante de la casa de mi papá, que la casa estaba en llamas, y que atrás de mí, estaban mis padres y mis hermanitos muertos. Todo lo vi retratado en sus ojos, mientras él estaba con la rodilla hincada en tierra apagando mi vestido. (Garro 1994a, 99)

> [The stones and cries began whizzing around us and I felt something burning behind me.
>
> "Don't look!" he told me.
>
> He knelt on one knee and with his fingers smothered my dress that had begun to burn.

"Take me away from here!" I shouted with all my might because I remembered that I was in front of my father's house, that the house was burning and that behind me my parents and my brothers and sisters lay dead. I saw everything reflected in his eyes while he had one knee on the ground smothering my dress.]

The fact that Laura's back is turned against this horrific scene and that she sees it reflected in her Indian husband's eyes transforms her companion into an agent who triggers Laura's memory of the past. Coming to grips with that tragic past is a painful experience that Laura can only confront with her Indian husband's help. However, Laura assumes her task with courage and determination because she has discovered that she has a crucial role to play in helping her fellow Mexicans to recover their roots and create a new future.

Nevertheless, there is a strong determination on the part of the members of the antagonistic culture to not allow her to accomplish her objective. When Laura returns to her other existence in Mexico City, she realizes that she has been missing for two days, which represents a clear violation of her duty as an upper middle-class Mexican wife. During her absence she has not contacted her husband and, as a result, the only conclusion that can be drawn on his part is that she has lost her mind. Pablo has her seen by their family doctor and she is confined to her room. To reinforce Pablo's perceptions, acting as a true representative of Spanish tradition, Margarita, Laura's mother-in-law, agrees when she says to Pablo: "Tu mujer está loca" (Garro 1994a, 103) ["Your wife is crazy"]. Once Pablo, Margarita, and the doctor agree that Laura suffers a mental depression, she becomes a prisoner in her own house. Laura's challenge of the norms of a "good wife" makes it obvious that if a woman does not comply with them she will be considered insane.

Laura's revaluation of her role as a woman in contemporary Mexican society continues when she requests that the doctor allow her access to a book on the conquest of Mexico. Pablo confesses to his mother: "–Mamá, Laura le pidió al doctor la *Historia* de Bernal Díaz del Castillo, dice que eso es lo único que le interesa" (Garro 1994a, 103) ["Mom, Laura asked the doctor for the *History* by Bernal Díaz del Castillo. She says that it's the only thing that interests her"]. Once again, the Malinche subtext is brought to the fore and becomes part of the story. Bernal Díaz del Castillo, an officer in Cortés's army, wrote his own account of the conquest of Mexico that he entitled *Verdadera Historia de la Conquista de la Nueva España*. Bernal Díaz wrote his account to counter the versions of the conquest published by Francisco López de Gómara, who had served as Cortés's secretary. In his book, Bernal Díaz del Castillo describes with enthusiasm the achievements of the Aztecs and the splendour of Tenochtitlan. He also describes the close collaboration between Cortés and Doña Marina (Malinche) and confesses his admiration for her talent as an interpreter. Laura devotes most of her time of confinement to reading Bernal Díaz's book in an attempt to recover her past and regain a true sense of the role that La Malinche played during the conquest of Mexico.

However, perhaps Laura's yearning for a true origin in books and chronicles of the conquest is an ill-fated activity. Fernanda Núñez Becerra, in her book *La Malinche: De la historia al mito* (2002), has traced the story of Malinche through several chronicles and novels from the Conquest on to the twentieth century.[5] In the conclusion of her study, the anthropologist suggests that there is an enormous corpus of texts associated with La Malinche. In spite of their abundance, none of these texts can be considered entirely accurate since their representation of Malinche is tainted by the medieval discursive practices common during the time of Bernal Díaz. Later, during the nineteenth century and even during the Mexican Revolution, her image was similarly influenced by interests invested in creating a new nation for the mestizo community.

Along those lines, Jean Franco, in her well-known book *Plotting Women: Gender and Representation in Mexico* (1989), contends that female writers of the sixties like Elena Garro and Rosario Castellanos attempt to inscribe women in national allegories. However, all their attempts fail because "ambitious women are expelled (or expel themselves) from the polis and thus fail to 'author' themselves or acquire a name for posterity" (145). In "La culpa es de los tlaxcaltecas," just as Franco suggests in her study, Laura "expels herself" from contemporary Mexico City. Nonetheless, in the process of vanishing Laura manages to undermine the principles that have created the modern nation. In truth, it is not possible for her to find her "own self" in the written representations. Instead she chooses to listen to the oral accounts still present in her culture. Perhaps that is the reason why Laura notices that her husband Pablo "no hablaba con palabras sino con letras" (Garro 1994a, 92) ["didn't speak with words but with letters"], meaning that she leans towards the oral culture instead of the one that relies on literacy and the value of the written word.

Laura's clear preference for the oral tradition explains why she embraces every opportunity to leap again in time and space to her other existence as a survivor in Tenochtitlan. That opportunity arrives during an outing to Chapultepec Park. Taking advantage of Margarita's distraction, Laura escapes to meet her Indian husband once more:

Andaba en esos tristes pensamientos cuando ... [s]u respiración se acercó a mis espaldas, luego ví sus pies desnudos delante de los míos ...

– ¿Qué te haces? – me dijo ...

– Te estaba esperando – contesté.

– Ya va a llegar el último día ...

Me pareció que su voz salía del fondo de los tiempos. (Garro 1994a, 104)

> [I was thinking these sad thoughts when ... I felt his breath on my back, then he was in front of me, I saw his bare feet in front of mine ...
> "What have you been up to? he said ...
> "I was waiting for you," I answered.
> "The last day is coming ..."
> It seemed to me that his voice came from the bottom of time.]

As Duncan points out in her article, Laura leaps into a mythical realm in which Western ways of measuring time do not exist. In this new era, Laura's role becomes the same as that assigned to Malinche in traditional Mesoamerican dances. Confronted with her husband's question "¿Qué te haces?", meaning "What have you been up to?", or even "What are you making of yourself?", she replies that she is waiting for him. She switches the role of the traitor assigned by history in favour of the role of a healer of her husband's wounds and her nation. She proceeds to clean again her Indian husband's wound: "Del hombro le seguía brotando sangre. Me llené de vergüenza, bajé los ojos, abrí mi bolso y saqué un pañuelito para limpiarle el pecho" (Garro 1994a, 104) ["Blood continued to flow from his shoulder. I was filled with shame, lowered my eyes, opened my purse and took out a handkerchief to wipe his chest"]. Once he has regained his strength he leaves again to continue fighting: "Me miró y se fue a combatir con la esperanza de evitar la derrota" (106) ["He looked at me and left to fight with the hope of avoiding defeat"].

Laura returns once again to her house in Mexico City to retell the story of her encounters with her Indian husband to Nacha, her Indian servant. The reader learns that Pablo has decided to take a vacation and has gone to Acapulco. Laura has succeeded in undermining Pablo's authority by leaving him. In an unexpected turn of events, Nacha sees Laura's Indian husband when he approaches the house: "Fue Nacha la que lo vio llegar y le abrió la ventana" (Garro 1994a, 107) ["It was Nacha who saw him coming and who opened the window"]. Through Laura's mediation, Nacha has also recovered her past and that is why she confesses to another maid, "Ya no me hallo en casa de los Aldama. Voy a buscarme otro destino." (108) ["I no longer feel at home in the Aldama house. I am going to look for a new fate"]. Just as Laura finds for herself another role as a healer and instigator of a new order, Nacha questions her role as a servant in the Aldama household. In the mestizo culture of postrevolutionary Mexico, Nacha has been erased from the picture of the nation. In fact, both women are now aware that in the mestizo community of modern Mexico they have been reduced to play a subordinate role – one that they are ready to defy at all costs.

Indeed, the defiance of the feminine role in "La culpa es de los tlaxcaltecas" goes further than we can ever imagine. As we have indicated earlier, all the ruling figures in the Aztec empire had structural equivalents amongst the gods and goddesses of Aztec mythology. In most rituals and dances, Malinche is often Moctezuma's wife or daughter, just as Huitzilopochtli is closely associated with Coatlicue, the Aztec mother-earth goddess. In his study of Mesoamerican dances, Max Harris (1996, 155) quotes Susan Gillespie to underline the fact that "sexual ambiguity (male inside, female outside) ... is an important aspect of the Aztec mother-earth deity" . He goes on to suggest "this partially explains the tendency to have a male dancer in female clothes represent Malinche" (155). Harris offers the case of Ochpaniztli as an example to prove his point: in this Aztec dance, a male dancer wears "the flayed skin of a scarified woman" in the dance, representing "the mother of the goddesses" (156).

During Laura's first encounter with her Indian husband, in the sand he draws two parallel lines that eventually join into a single line. In Laura's retelling of the story she describes it in these terms:

Agachó la cabeza y miró la tierra llena de piedras secas. Con una de ellas dibujó dos rayitas paralelas, que prolongó hasta que se juntaron y se hicieron una sola.

– Somos tú y yo – me dijo sin levantar la vista ...

Yo, Nachita, me quedé sin palabras.

– Ya falta poco para que se acabe el tiempo y seamos uno solo ... por eso te andaba buscando. (Garro 1994a, 92)

[He looked down at the ground covered with dried stones. With one of them he drew two parallel lines in the sand that he extended until they joined and became only one.

"This is you and I," he said without raising his eyes.

"I, Nachita, remained silent."

"It won't be long before time runs out and we become only one ... that's why I have come looking for you."]

Following the Aztec mythology, Laura and her Indian husband are going to be fused into one sexually ambiguous figure that possesses the powers of the ancient mother-earth goddess Coatlicue. Let us remember that once Laura and her Indian husband meet again, they have sex as a sign of a new beginning in the midst of Tenochtitlan's total desolation. As Coatlicue, Laura and her *primo marido* have the power to revive themselves from the ashes of destruction.

The sexual ambiguity that surrounds the figure of Laura towards the end of the story questions the very essence of gender. One of the last statements that Laura asserts before her final disappearance in the company of her Indian husband is "Faltaba poco para que nos fuéramos para siempre en uno solo" (Garro 1994a, 106) ["Little time remained before we would become one forever"]. Obviously her statement places under erasure the culturally acquired patterns of sexual difference.

In Butler's terms, by repeatedly addressing in her retelling of the story not only the norms that regulate her role as a middle-class wife in contemporary Mexican society, but also her duty as a healer and her authority to endow rulership in the Aztec community, Laura gains agency to question the positions that males and females have assumed in society. The new beginning and the new order that Laura fosters imply recognition of the Mexican nation's roots as well as a redefinition of the male and female roles in society. That new order favours understanding, compassion, and real fusion in opposition to violence and domination.

In "La culpa es de los tlaxcaltecas," Elena Garro manages to bring to the fore the very essence of the Mexican dilemma between the violence of the conquest and the injured mentality of the defeated, between a male dominated society and the submissiveness of the marginalized females and Indians. Laura Aldama, the protagonist of the short story, manages to come to grips with her traumatic past by retelling the story of her constant leaps in space and time into ancient Tenochtitlan. In doing so, she gains agency and divests of meaning the guilty attribute that has haunted her for centuries. She recovers the memories of Aztec mythology and endows herself with the healing power of her ancestors to restore her *primo marido* and her nation. Finally, she materializes a desire to initiate a new order in which gender differences are erased and equality between women and men can become real, so that peace and reconciliation between the present and the past can be achieved.

Works Cited

Butler, Judith. 1993. *Bodies that Matter: On the Discursive Limits of Sex*. New York: Routledge.

Cypess, Sandra. 1991. *La Malinche in Mexican Literature: From History to Myth*. Austin: Univ. of Texas Press.

Duncan, Cynthia. 1985. "La culpa es de los tlaxcaltecas": A Reevaluation of México's Past through Myth. *Crítica Hispánica* 7 (2): 105–20.

Díaz del Castillo, Bernal. 1983. *Historia verdadera de los sucesos de la conquista de la Nueva España*. Ed. Joaquín Ramírez Cabañas. Mexico: Porrúa.

Encarta. 2004. Aztecas. In *Encyclopedia Microsoft Encarta Online*. http://mx.encarta.msn.com.

Franco, Jean. On the Impossibility of Antigone and the Inevitability of La Malinche: Rewriting the National Allegory. In *Plotting Women: Gender and Representation in Mexico*, 129–46. New York: Columbia Univ. Press.

Garro, Elena. 1994a. La culpa es de los tlaxcaltecas. In *Cuentos mexicanos inolvidables*, ed. Edmundo Valadés, 87–108. Mexico: Asociación Nacional de Libreros.

———. 1994b. La culpa es de los tlaxcaltecas. Trans. Patricia Wahl. RIF/T Electronic Poetry Center, State Univ. of New York at Buffalo. http://wings.buffalo.edu/epc.

Gillespie, Susan D. 1989. *The Aztec Kings: The Construction of Rulership in Mexican History*. Tucson: Univ. of Arizona Press.

Harris, Max. 1996. Moctezuma's Daughter: The Role of La Malinche in Mesoamerican Dance. *Journal of American Folklore* 109 (432): 149–77.

Núñez Becerra, Fernanda. 2002. *La Malinche: de la historia al mito*. 2nd ed. México: Instituto Nacional de Antropología e Historia.

Paz, Octavio. 1987. *El laberinto de la soledad*. Mexico: Fondo de Cultura Económica.

Notes

1   In this context, *displacement* means a change of location and historical time in the life of Laura Aldama, protagonist of the short story.

2   "Narratee" is the term coined by Gerald Prince to refer to the listener of a character's story within the story. See Gerald Prince, "Introduction to the Study of the Narratee," *Reader-Response Criticism: From Formalism to Post-Structuralism*, ed. Jane P. Tompkins (Baltimore: Johns Hopkins University Press, 1986), 7–25.

3   All translated passages from "La culpa es de los tlaxcaltecas" are taken from the translation done by Patricia Wahl.

4   Café de Tacuba is a very traditional fine restaurant in downtown Mexico City. However, the name Tacuba is also important because it was the old name given to one of the Indian groups that inhabited Mexico City at the time of the Aztecs, and one of the causeways linking it to the shore. The Aztecs established alliances with the Tacuba and the Texcoco Indians to control the valley of central Mexico. The Tacuba Indians founded a city called Tlacopan. The Aztecs, the Texcoco, and the Tacuba Indians were defeated by Cortés and the Tlaxcaltecas during the conquest of Mexico in 1521. For more information on this topic, please access "Azteca."

5   According to Núñez Becerra, Bernal Díaz endows Malinche with fine qualities as a woman with noble origin because he intends to create an epic tale. True to the rules of medieval discursive practices, a noble knight (Cortés) will have an honorable lady at his side. Due to that fact, Bernal is quite prolific in his description of Doña Marina or Malinche (Núñez Becerra 2002, 34).

Miroslava by Alejandro Pelayo: Negotiated Adaptation and the (Trans)National Gendered Subject

Nayibe Bermúdez Barrios, University of Calgary

Miroslava, Alejandro Pelayo's 1992 cinematic adaptation of the 1989 short story of the same name by the Mexican journalist and writer Guadalupe Loaeza, centers thematically on the conflicts of Miroslava Stern, a female movie star of the "golden age" of Mexican cinema.[1]

The movie focuses on a privileged white woman who moves within certain circles of power. However, she still faces marginality due to the heterosexual matrix[2] and its limitations, and because of the rigid structures that separate public and private life. Miroslava, a Czech immigrant to Mexico, tries to bridge the gap between the public and the private through her work as a film star. Moreover, her character embodies aspects of the (trans)national as her position lies in the in-between intersection of two different cultures: the Mexican and the Czech. This position is marked by an attempt to keep her European origins and an effort to negotiate her insertion into Mexican life. Miroslava tries to adapt, but the terms in which her everyday life is represented place her search for belonging as a ceaseless return to the past as frozen time. Notwithstanding the fact that Miroslava tries to negotiate, the social confines in which she lives, as well as the restrictions imposed by textual strategies for her representation, curtail the possibility to expand the limits of her space and sentence her to failure.

My analysis pays special attention to the process of "adaptation" on two levels. The first level scrutinizes the process of "adaptation to life in Mexico" of the 1950s by the main character in the film, Miroslava Stern. The focus on Miroslava's character, her negotiations, and her conflicts highlight her difficulties in adapting to a Mexico that both attracts and rejects her. The second level examines Mexican filmmaker Alejandro Pelayo's actual "cinematic adaptation" of the Loaezian short story itself, and the filmmaking techniques he employs to do this. Pelayo's adaptation brings into play a number of decisions that echo and illustrate Miroslava's adaptation to life in Mexico. Due prominence is given to issues of gender made conspicuous in the film by the appearance of a voice-over originating in a male figure. This figure replaces the narrating agent of the short story and, ultimately, ends up displacing the protagonist not only from her own narrating space, but also from her central role in the narrative. From a narratological perspective, *Miroslava* establishes a distance between the object of representation and the source of that representation. The film uses the frame of a male voice as filter and center of authority to recreate the biography of the long forgotten movie star. This filter mediates between the audiences and the character to make more obvious than in Loaeza the self-referentiality of the strategies of representation. In the Loaezian narrative focalization fluctuates between Miroslava and an incorporeal narrating agency in a move that confers some authority on the character. However, in the movie the incorporeal agency is replaced by a male narrator. It is this adaptation decision that this essay considers in order to speculate about its implications both for the project of negotiation of the protagonist and the gender and genre issues that the film text itself has to negotiate. At both levels of adaptation, Pelayo's film lays an emphasis on the process of adaptation as a negotiated means to become a subject and a member of the nation.

Here negotiation is understood as a method of study of cultural productions whose meanings are constructed through the meeting of producers (institutional and individual), texts and audiences (Gledhill 1988, 7). From a sociological point of view, Christine Gledhill's proposal conceptualizes the cultural exchange as a process of production and reception that is realized on the basis of negotiation of meanings. My analysis proposes the textual study of the terms in which such a negotiation is produced and how it interconnects the various sociocultural issues that form part of the main character's daily life. Due to the narrative structure of the filmic text, I will interrogate negotiation especially with respect to representation and the narrative strategies used in order to determine if they construct a more liveable, less constrained space for the protagonist.

Miroslava is the focus of the narration because the film concentrates on the chronological mapping of her life via a voice-over originating in a narrator and, through this filter, by flashbacks "originating" in the character's conscience. The film is remarkable for its lack of action. The narrative part begins as Alex, the narrator, remembers the last afternoon he spent with Miroslava in a luxurious restaurant. As a character of the diegesis in the past, he notices she is sad and tries to "cheer" her up. After a while Miroslava goes home and starts, in turn, to reminisce about her past. Later in the film, Alex mentions that after realizing he failed to raise his friend's spirits, he tried to call her on the phone but he could not get through. The next day, on March 11, 1955, the body of Miroslava, who has committed suicide at the pinnacle of her fame, is found in her house.

Much like the short story, the film engages in the shifting of time planes. However, while the Loaezian narrative tries to postpone death through an emphasis on narrative pauses, as well as through Miroslava's gaze and her

A las 12:45 horas, del 11 de marzo de 1955, en el número 83 de las calles de Kepler, se encontró en la recamara principal, el cuerpo sin vida de la Sra. Miroslava Stern.

Figure 1. A sign open for interpretation: Miroslava (Arielle Dombasle) signi-fied as a writable and readable spectacularized dead body in *Miroslava*. Photo by Emmanuel Lubezki. *Photos are reprinted here with permission issued by Alma Rossbach and IMCINE, Mexico D.F.*

introspection during a well defined time frame of seven hours, the very initial frame in the movie focuses on death as dramatically and artistically represented in the beautiful but inert body of the movie star. Following this sequence, in which Miroslava's body is shot from above in a semifetal position, the film fluctuates between a past preceding the suicide, and the indeterminate present of narration. This oscillation notwithstanding, and due to the fact that the sequence mentioned is the very first of the movie, Miroslava's image as a dead body can be read as a sign open to interpretation and re-signification. As a matter of fact, in this first sequence, journalistic discourse is inscribed on the dead body of the woman as the news of her death is typed letter by letter over her image. The audience is presented with her body and with the slow typing of: "A las 12:45 horas, del día 11 de marzo de 1955, en el número 83 de las calles de Kepler, se encontró en la recámara principal, el cuerpo sin vida de la Sra. Miroslava Stern" ["On 11 March 1955, at 12:45 p.m., Ms. Miroslava Stern was found dead in the master bedroom at 83 Kepler Avenue"]. Much like the letter of the apparatus inscribed on the prisoner's body in Franz Kafka's "In the Penal Colony," the letter of the typewriter is imprinted on Miroslava's image. This act not only signals her imagined and constructed nature, but also effectively serves to pass sentence on her, albeit in a way less dramatic than in Kafka, as Miroslava, from a discursive point of view, is condemned to follow societal rules or face failure. The news posits the death of the famous and privileged star as the narrative enigma, and at the same time highlights the importance of the suicide for audiences fascinated by her stardom and public figure. Miroslava's constructed and commodified nature is further reinforced when Alex appropriates narrative discourse to recreate her life.

In addition to the change in narrative order, the film elaborates and transforms some details concerning the character, so that in contrast to the short story, Pelayo's Miroslava is not Jewish. As explained in the movie, Miroslava is not a Jew not only because her mother is not, but also because Dr. Stern, the only Jew in the family, is not her biological father. Considering that according to *Halakah*, the Jewish religious law, it is the mother who passes on ethnic identity, the movie's explanation seems redundant. However, the information about the adoption turns out to be essential to the protagonist's drama.

In the same way, and in contrast to Loaeza's narrative in which the cause of Miroslava's divorce is not mentioned, the film anchors this incident in her visualization of a sex act between Jesús Jaime and another man. If one takes into account Pelayo's comments on the book cover to the third edition of Loaeza's short story, *Miroslava* (1994), in which he cites rumours about Miroslava's engaging in lesbianism and international espionage, it is clear that the transference of sexual otherness to the husband conveys an attempt to displace and render (in)visible the protagonist's possible sexual difference.[3] However, the film's paratext, as cited on the book cover, returns the spectre of lesbianism to the movie, especially if one considers that it is homosexuality that works as an obstacle to Miroslava's insertion into the national text, specifically through her failure to procreate offspring, that is, new national subjects. In 1950s Mexico, roughly characterized by the critics of nationalism in its requirement of heterosexual and patriotic subjects, Miroslava's failure to reproduce, whether due to her own homoeroticism or that of her husband, brings sexuality to the fore as a major hurdle in the project of becoming an adapted subject. As the film tries to attenuate the spectre of ethnic otherness as a potential explanation for her problems in adapting, the possibility of sexual alterity comes back to the text to reveal insidious cultural subtexts of difference as exclusion.

Due to my emphasis on representation, I will only dwell on two of the mechanisms used by Miroslava to negotiate with her lived experience of exclusion. The first one is her incorporation into public life through her job as an actor. Her profession allows her to imagine a sense of community and belonging to the cinematic world of Mexican actors and moviemakers with whom she works. Concurrently, and as a second strategy, Miroslava envisions the institution of marriage as an opportunity to enter Mexican nationhood and to modify the contours of the purely private space that her late Czech mother always occupied. That is, Miroslava tries to expand the private space by experiencing an alternate subjective position still within the limits of family life and marriage, but also within the public realm. Miroslava does not try to radically change everything, but rather attempts only to alter the status quo so that she can have a liveable space. Her attempts, however, do cause many problems.

Miroslava comes from a traditional family. Through the rituals of everyday life, her father makes an investment in perpetuating Czech values and patterns of interaction. In a childhood sequence set shortly after arriving in Mexico, Miroslava studies Mexican geography but fails to properly pronounce some names. Even though her mother affirms that little Miroslava speaks Spanish better than she, Dr. Stern disapproves of such an attempt at adaptation and insists that the essence of homeland is in language. Thus at home they must all speak only Czech. The young Miroslava shifts easily from one language to the other but she prefers to speak Spanish. Her mother, in contrast to the oppressive ways of the father, promotes a connection with a Czech identity through songs. Of special importance is the one that Miroslava's grandmother liked and which is used in the film to connect young Miroslava with her. These family-enforced linguistic, cultural, and affective links are later cited and reinstated as a justification for Dr. Stern's opposition to his daughter's career.

The prohibition to go into the cinematic milieu is but an attempt at perpetuating the domestic as feminine space. When an adult Miroslava comes to the paternal house to introduce Jesús Jaime, to announce her engagement to him, and to share her success as a film star, her father calls her crazy for her desire to be in an environment that, according to him, is "sucio [y] depravado" ["dirty [and] immoral"]. As if this were not enough, Jesús Jaime sides with Dr. Stern by stating that Miroslava's career is just a "distraction" for her. Both the Czech father and the Mexican fiancé devalue Miroslava's work and undermine her effort to construct an intermediate adapted space by combining her own desire with her father's requirements for marriage and a family.

Miroslava's attempts at negotiating with the idea of the traditional family fail not only because of Jesús Jaime's lack of support, but also, as I have already mentioned, because of his closeted homosexuality and his compliance with the laws of a heterosexual matrix which does not accept difference.[4] The ensuing divorce deepens the family rift and also undermines the opportunity to legitimize Miroslava's Mexicanness through her erotic union with a Mexican. However, in spite of this traumatic experiential outcome and its negative implications for Miroslava's project of adaptation, Dr. Stern relentlessly pushes his ideas and interpellates his daughter to follow in her mother's footsteps in the following scenes by saying: "[H]ay cosas mejores [que el cine]: la familia, un marido, hijos" ["[T]here are better things [than a career in cinema]: a family, a husband, children"]. The paternal discourse turns public space into a dangerous and treacherous zone for women, and constructs the private domain as the desirable norm. This discursive positioning reinforces both compulsive heterosexuality and the heteronormative matrix at the expense of Miroslava's experience and suffering. Likewise, the representation of celibacy as an unhappy state and of stardom as an ephemeral and insubstantial experience leaves too little room for the protagonist to function outside of the institution of marriage, or beyond the limiting nationalist discourses of heteronormative procreation.

Miroslava experiences Dr. Stern's agenda for the subjective emplacement of the female as an emotional, anguished exertion. Such a feeling is caused not only by testing discourses that cannot satisfy her, but also through the experience of alternate positionings that enrage the men in her life. Miroslava's everyday life is signified in the film through narrative conventions that present her life in chronological order with an emphasis on her interpersonal relationships. This strategy brings to the fore daily processes for the transmission of practical knowledge and values. Following Tim Edensor's (2002, 19) notion of everyday life, the organizing of habits, assumptions, and routines within the family (that is, on a local level), brings about the institutionalization and solidification of bodies, which can then be subsumed under larger national orderings. However, as seen through Miroslava's example, her desire contradicts such designs.

In this respect, Teresa de Lauretis' (1999, 267) concept of "habit change or habit instability" proves useful for the analysis of Miroslava's identity crisis. This notion, which derives from Peirce's semiotics, names "a modification of a person's tendencies towards action, resulting from previous experiences or from previous exertions."[5] That is, a habit change "emphasizes the material, embodied component of desire as a psychic activity whose effects in the subject constitute a sort of knowledge of the body, what the body 'knows' or comes to know about its instinctual aims" (268). Because de Lauretis presents gender as a social form that can exert pressure on subjectivation, the notion of habit change is of paramount importance in studying the effects of everyday life in the body and the self's perception of it.[6] To paraphrase de Lauretis, and as seen from Miroslava's experiences, it is clear that her character suffers an emotional process of mediation or negotiation between her inner desires and the outer world. Miroslava's disposition to accept gender constraints in relation to her role in the domestic realm is destabilized by her successful performance of other subjective positions in the public domain, and by the felt and perceived disapproval she gets. As a consequence of this, the movie star feels the limbo of living exiled from family life and communication codes, both on the Mexican and the Czech sides of the equation. Furthermore, Miroslava starts to perceive herself and her body as unable to meet the gender cultural scripts of her historical context. This subjective positioning marks a habit change that is negative and destructive for her sense of belonging. In other words, Mioslava experiences her "gender instability" as a catastrophe and, powerless to renegotiate her inscription in the family and the nation, she sees the eradication of her body through suicide as the only way out.

Miroslava's problem, which as I will prove stems from the strategies of representation used, lies in the fact that her failed negotiation does not push her to regroup and to try to renegotiate. This is the paralyzing effect of subjective conceptualizations in which identity is thought of as a result and not as a process. No wonder the text fails to allow her the space to live and be perceived in her double (trans)cultural inscription of someone who, while trying to learn Spanish and other "Mexican" codes, also negotiates an investment in preserving her Czech language and roots in order to try to modify the accepted cultural scripts of nationality and gender.

The cinematic world, in spite of providing some satisfactions by constituting the means through which to make a way into the labour force, the public realm, and the larger Mexican community of spectators, is not exempt, as Miroslava soon realizes, from gender constraints and nationality issues. I will extend de Lauretis' sense of the body as a "gender symptom" to nationalism and will argue that, being also a social form, nationalism can and, in Miroslava's case, does exert pressure on her subjectivation.[7] Within a ten-year span, between 1946 and 1955, Miroslava shot a record of thirty-one films with well-known Mexican and foreign filmmakers and actors. In Pelayo's movie, Alex and Miroslava talk about her work with moviemaker Roberto Gavaldón and about Luis Buñuel's *Ensayo de un crimen* [*The*

Figure 2. Miroslava reflects about her cinematic work and her problematic double heritage in *Miroslava*. *Photo by Emmanuel Lubezki. Photos are reprinted here with permission issued by Alma Rossbach and IMCINE, Mexico D.F.*

Criminal Life of Archibaldo de la Cruz], her last filmic vehicle. In an economic manner, through pictures on Miroslava's walls, the film portrays this community that allowed Miroslava to become a member of the Mexican and international jet set. Miroslava appears alongside personalities such as Ernesto Alonso, Cantinflas, Dolores del Río, René Cardona, Gavaldón and Buñuel. From the space of her house, Miroslava looks at these pictures in a nostalgic way, while she spreads them on the floor and around her body as if to immerse herself anew in this environment.[8] However, in spite of her effort to join the cinema in order to be appreciated as an artist and a person, Miroslava is made to feel different even within her circle of co-workers. Discursive citations, such as "Miros-mango," used in publicity campaigns and by her audiences to signify her commodified status within the star system, also exoticize her Czech beauty and her foreignness. Miroslava is hurt by her representation as an exotic artifact to promote movies and to attract Mexican audiences. The idea that she interests the cinematic world only because of her looks anguishes her, as can be seen towards the end of the film in this comment:

Nunca me gusté en mis películas. Estoy cansada de que me hablen de mi físico, de "Miros-mango." Odio mi imagen. Estoy harta de la Miroslava, la del cine, la que no sabe realmente lo que quiere; la que no sabe si es realmente rubia o morena, la que siempre está buscando el amor. De ella principalmente es de la que me quiero despedir. Ella es la verdadera Miroslava, la que nadie conoce. La que me hace sufrir.

> [I hated myself in my movies. I am tired of them talking about my looks, of "Miros-mango." I hate my image. I am fed up with Miroslava, the one in the movies, the one who doesn't really know what she wants, the one who doesn't know if she's a brunette or a blonde, the one who is forever in search of love. She is the one I want to get rid of. She is the true Miroslava, the one no one knows. The one who makes me suffer.]

Miroslava, again, experiences her predicament as an overwhelming process of being "othered" and diminished in her corporeal self.[9] She feels that the mythification and exoticization of her filmic persona robs her of the opportunity to be accepted and taken as a human being. The perception of herself as an exscinded subject, as seen in the quote, is another instance of a habit change that leads her to question her position within the cultural text as an article of consumption. Taking into account the sociocultural context of the 1940s and 1950s, when many Mexican intellectuals, artists, writers, and filmmakers debated the question of *Mexicanidad* and construed *mestizaje* as a privileged sign of national identity, Miroslava's dilemma comes as no surprise. Her quandary resides in the fact that her "foreign" beauty is commercially exploited while at the same time it is used to deny her membership as a subject of the Mexican nation.[10] Besides being commodified, Miroslava feels the pressure caused by the discourses of nationalism and, as a result, experiences the unexpected and unsettling perception of herself as not Mexican. For a person who inhabits a doubly-inscribed cultural world, being denied both her personhood and her (trans)national identity is a blow too hard to take.

The dynamics at play within the process of adaptation transfer from the thematic level to the representational field through negotiated strategies that also fail to provide more room for manoeuvre to the protagonist. The film adaptation of the Loaezian short story, from a screenplay by Mexican writer and playwright Vicente Leñero, removes the narration from its contextual situation in *Primero las damas*. The informational network of associations between the stories in *Primero las damas*, which are used to promote a sense of suspense and unpredictability, is transformed in order to give rise to new expectations and relations in the cinematic adaptation of *Miroslava*. This new network realizes the type of intertextual negotiation and transformation that has come to be called adaptation (Stam 2000, 67).

The cinematically descriptive Loaezian text, so full of narrative pauses, finds its stylistic counterpart in Emmanuel Lubezki's breathtaking cinematography, which won the film a Silver Ariel.[11] For the analysis of form that I am undertaking, I will appropriate Robert Stam's (2000, 67) notion that film adaptation is a kind of multileveled negotiation of intertexts. Therefore, it is often productive to ask precisely what generic intertexts are invoked by the source text, and which by the filmic adaptation? Which generic signals are picked up in the adaptation, and which are ignored? To emphasize the multiple negotiations present in the process of film adaptation, Pelayo's *Miroslava* changes or omits details present in the short story, as already stated. The movie also cites intertexts and narrative devices that echo the documentary and journalistic modes of the Loaezian text and, in addition, takes up the specific cinematic genre known as "the woman's film."[12] These transformations are extremely useful for the examination of the ideological cultural subtexts at the basis of Pelayo's adaptation.

Intertextual negotiation with journalistic aspects of Loaeza's short story is made possible in the movie through the shifts in time. This oscillation allows for the introduction of journalistic and documentary discourses via the piece of news and the technique of voice-over. Returning to the initial sequence, the film opens with a very high shot in sepia colours of the young star's body as she lies on a large bed, exquisitely made-up and dressed in long and elegant garb. In other words, the lifeless body of the movie star occupies the full screen in its horizontal axis. Upon this static image, the piece of news already mentioned is typewritten letter after letter. In the same way as in the short story, journalistic discourse enters the film to emphasize double voice and the movie's negotiating abilities both with respect to the process of adaptation and the cinematic representation of Miroslava.

In addition, the chronicle aspects of Loaeza's narrative translate into the film through the voice-over narration in a strategy that replicates the documentary format. The narrative situation from an indeterminate present is introduced at the outset of the second sequence as the credits appear. This sequence registers a time shift with respect to the first one in which we see Miroslava's dead body. The second sequence opens with a shot of a door with a hand-held camera. The door is soon opened by a man who invites the newcomers in as he backs into the living room and sits down. The extreme movement of the camera irrupts into the closed space of the house to bring about a sense of intense subjective participation. This unstable point of view intensifies the feeling of immediacy and presence, leading the spectators to establish associations between the grammar used and the documentary genre.

A sense of "reality" is created through the camera's instability, together with the lighting, and a *mise en scène* that seems to be unprepared both in terms of being an "uninhabited" space and its relationship to the other elements of composition. In addition to that, the man in the frame, Alex Fimman, looks up directly into the camera. This stance renders "visible" both the camera and the people behind it, especially because Alex says: "Sí, aquí es, bienvenidos, pásenle, pásenle. Este ... está un poco abandonado esto como pueden ver; quería que conocieran la antigua casa del Doctor Stern. ¿Y ustedes se sientan? Ah, ¿no se sientan? Bueno, pues, cuando quieran háganme la primera pregunta" ["Come in, welcome, yes, this is the place. Hmmm ... I wanted you to see Dr. Stern's old house. No one lives here as you can see. Won't you take a seat? Oh, OK. Well, when you are ready, ask away"]. We know time has passed with respect to the first sequence because Alex describes the space of his enunciation as an abandoned place. That is, a place where no one goes anymore, or at least not very often. The conventions used here via the filming of a supposedly unprepared interview about the life of Miroslava as a subject of possible popular and national interest uses elements of the documentary genre. Moreover, the voice-over narration and the flashbacks draw attention to the authoritative voice of a narrator-witness who seems to have first-hand knowledge of the star's life. Alex portrays himself as a confidant and the putative father of Miroslava to substantiate his narration and his thoughts about the probable causes for the woman's suicide.

As I have suggested, the narrator's enunciation indicates the presence of several narratees, or extradiegetical addressees who are not characters within the diegesis, but who are interested in filming his version of the events surrounding Miroslava's life and death. The (in)visibility of these participants of the speech act, who are behind the camera, functions as a simulacrum both for the cinematic apparatus, and for the spectators targeted by narratives about the life of film stars. Alex, then, seems to be addressing a wide audience as he narrates a tragedy not only of national interest for everyone, but especially, due to its content, for women. Self-reflexivity, by underlying the camera's mediation, highlights, on the one

Figure 3. Self-referentiality and representation: Miroslava's friend and agent Alex Fimman (Claudio Brook) reinstates the patriarchal space (Dr. Stern's house) and the male voice as sources of narrative authority over the representation of the dead actor in *Miroslava*. *Photo by Emmanuel Lubezki. Photos are reprinted here with permission issued by Alma Rossbach and IMCINE, Mexico D.F.*

hand, the authority of the narrating self and, on the other, the power of the institution used as a vehicle for this narration. This, to cite Claudia Schaefer-Rodríguez (1991, 64), is part and parcel of the "rightness of rendering" of texts which package and organize narrative elements so that they ring true. It is hard not to notice, however, that the search for a stance of authority through the narrative's intermediaries and mediators effects a spatial displacement that is very significant for the dynamics of negotiation in its intersection with gender.

Even though Pelayo's movie recreates the same sense of spatial enclosure – rendered in Loaeza's narrative through the luxurious apartment of the young movie star – in the film the space of narration is relocated to the patriarchal space of Dr. Stern, Miroslava's father. Alex's time and enunciating location interrelates with Miroslava's past as she reminisces and prepares to commit suicide. However, the narrative situation rises in an indeterminate present and from a totally new space in which time seems to have reached stasis. The elements of the *mise en scène* in this new narrative location combine to create a sense of frozen time through decor covered in white sheets as if to keep the previous ordering of this place and to preserve it from inquisitive outside gazes. This feeling gets emphasized because, in spite of the fact that the film comes back to the narrating space eight times, the area that remains visible for the audience is drastically reduced to parts of the living room. Moreover, starting with the second framing of the narrative space, the only element onscreen is Alex, shown in a medium shot and bathed in bluish overtones against a dark backdrop. The contrastive use of lighting, as well as the evocation of the space in off, or out of camera shot, besides stressing Alex's voice and gaze, is successful in constructing the patriarchal space that remains there, but is invisible as a zone of restricted access. This has various implications. The displacement of Miroslava's space as the site of narration in the short story for the patriarchal space in the film results in the actual displacement of the protagonist's living body. Her corpse replaces this experiencing body, which is present throughout Loaeza's narrative, except for the final sentence. The dramatic change in focalization also underlines the patriarchal space, both literally and metaphorically, since the representation of Miroslava not only originates in the space of the father, but also derives from the point of view and discursive positioning of a male narrator.

This transformative adaptation manoeuvre seems to respond to issues related to negotiation with the cultural context of production of the film. From this perspective, the representation of such an unconventional female character as Miroslava, as conveyed through the rumours about lesbianism and espionage already mentioned, seems to "require" a traditional narrative structure as a means to alleviate any discomfort. By citing film conventions that privilege a male point of view, the film adaptation of *Miroslava* dramatizes restrictions and ideological negotiations.[13] These restrictions and negotiations seem to try to preserve the space of representation as sacred and patriarchal. Furthermore, the critical characterization of this movie as a "psychological drama" underlies the traditional field of representation where the female subject personifies the experiential body, while the male appropriates the analytical side of this dichotomy as a mind that can try to decipher and explain that body. Such film adaptation radically transforms Loaeza's short story and manages to personify the restrictions of the frozen and sacred patriarchal time and space. As shown, gender as a social form of pressure is actively implicated as a subtext for processes of ideological negotiations in changes to the source text.

In relation to the above, the film's self-referentiality, notwithstanding the citation of journalistic and documentary discourses of mimesis and truth validation, brings to the fore the artificiality of the terms of representation in order to disarticulate spectatorial expectations with regards to ontological knowledge about the protagonist. As I have already said, the film uses the frame of a male voice as a filter and source of authority to recreate Miroslava's biography. This filter mediates between the spectators and Miroslava to make obvious the self-consciousness of the strategies of representation and the creating act per se. Since *Miroslava* is a biographical film intent on exploring the psyche of the protagonist, it is reasonable to say that it tries to bring order into a chaotic array of situations and events that end with a suicide. This means that although there are very few verifiable facts, or precisely because of this, the movie engages in assigning some meaning to the "I" of Miroslava. By doing so, the film follows biographical narrative conventions similar to those that "dictate" the life patterns of film stars and famous public figures in some general manner. As a consequence, Pelayo's text falls in line with the need for affectivity that seems to be inherent in this type of textualization, especially because Miroslava's life is mapped within an order in which beauty, fame, and money are associated with loneliness, otherness, and lack of love.

The biographical intertext and the use of its conventions to achieve "rightness of rendering" is a gesture that draws attention to the importance of art as an intermediary between the self and representation. This means that the creative act can also function as an act of creation of the "I" as resulting from narrative models or life organization (Olney 1972, 18). The movie personifies this impulse in the figure of Alex, who literally occupies a chair not unlike those stereotypically used by filmmakers. From this privileged standpoint the narrator authorizes his narrative and creates its protagonist as a text that complies with a tragic biographic mode of narration of unhappiness and loneliness. Moreover, in the last intervention by the narrator, towards the end of the film, Alex replicates words attributed to Pelayo in the book cover of the short story's third edition. There Pelayo ponders the possible causes of the movie star's suicide and concludes, like the narrator in the movie, that: "Sólo ella nos lo podría decir, si viviera" ["Only she could tell us, if she were alive"]. This double-voiced discourse as an index of fusion between the director and Alex is an allusion to the principle of fusion between life and art. At the same time, this comment reveals the speculative and artistic nature of the creation produced both by the film director and by the film's narrator. As a result of this narra-

Figure 4. Miroslava's point of view is mediated through Alex' gaze in *Miroslava. Photo by Emmanuel Lubezki. Photos are reprinted here with permission issued by Alma Rossbach and IMCINE, Mexico D.F.*

tive excess, *Miroslava* establishes a clear distance between the object of representation and the source of that representation. But more than that, the importance of gender and its relationship with the status quo becomes apparent in this text due to adaptation decisions that choose to "restitute" a prominent location to the male voice and gaze.

Even though on occasion the flashback used to dramatize the past tries to bring Miroslava's gaze to the fore, the precariousness of her point of view is revealed through inconsistencies between the image and the soundtrack. While the images focus on the protagonist's life, the narrator's voice-over prevails as a guide for the spectators and as the interconnecting link between the fragmented experiences presented. The voice-over belongs to an elderly Fimman and his figure persistently turns the present of filming into a superimposition over the images of the past. In addition

Figure 5. The elderly woman Miroslava is looking at can only be seen by the spectators once Alex has become the focalizer in *Miroslava*. Photo by Emmanuel Lubezki. *Photos are reprinted here with permission issued by Alma Rossbach and IMCINE, Mexico D.F.*

to the politics of the voice, the dynamics of the gaze, as I have hinted at, plays an important role in destabilizing Miroslava's position as focalizer. It is very telling that in most scenes recreating her life through a flashback "emerging" from the character's memory, the woman's gaze seems lost and absent from her environment. By way of contrast, in the few instances when she notices her surroundings, spectators have no direct access to the objective reality that catches her attention. This reality tends to remain in off; that is, out of the frame. In the previously cited sequence in the restaurant, when the narrator is shown with Miroslava, it is through Alex that the film audience gains access to the object of the woman's gaze. Miroslava is staring at something outside the limits of the camera frame when Alex asks what she's looking at. The protagonist answers that she is looking at an elderly woman who reminds her of the grandmother left behind in

Figure 6. Background music and lack of diegetic noise cancel out Miroslava's perception of the present. *Photo by Emmanuel Lubezki. Photos are reprinted here with permission issued by Alma Rossbach and IMCINE, Mexico D.F.*

Czechoslovakia many years ago. However, it is only after the narrator's intervention when he sees her that the woman comes to be in the actual frame for a few seconds. Since the movie realizes a mnemonic journey from Miroslava's childhood to her experiences six months before her suicide, this mediation, or infiltration and filtration by the narrator, contributes to an association of the protagonist with a sense of "frozen" time; that is, with an eternal return to the past. If, to cite Tania Modleski (1987, 330), this idea of time is compared to the idea of historical time as a progression, it is evident why Miroslava can never insert herself into Mexican history as a proper national subject. Due to her representation as a melancholic being, Miroslava cannot transcend her nostalgia and is subjected to the eternal repetition of memories that haunt her.

Figure 7. Miroslava's gaze is postponed by her glasses and other reflective surfaces in order to render her inaccessible and to associate her with a return to the past as "frozen" time in *Miroslava. Photo by Emmanuel Lubezki. Photos are reprinted here with permission issued by Alma Rossbach and IMCINE, Mexico D.F.*

The postposition of the object of Miroslava's gaze implies a lack of control on the part of her character. The images of memory from the past seem to present us with the point of view of the protagonist, but the *mise en scène* and the transitions contradict or at least destabilize such presupposition by establishing a temporal fissure between the situations that are perceived and conveyed by the film and the ones that are lived by the main character. Such a gap is made clear, for example, in the sequence that follows the one after Miroslava's dinner with Alex. In this sequence, the movie star drives a convertible through the city of Mexico. It is remarkable that in spite of having the car roof open, neither Miroslava nor the spectators can hear the street noises or the other cars that pass her by. As a matter of fact, the background music and the protagonist's mirror glasses preclude the outside world and cancel out Miroslava's perception of the present as if she existed

Figure 8. Miroslava as spectacle, presented here through her car's windshield, is deprived of the possibility of expressing her inner thoughts and feelings in *Miroslava*. *Photo by Emmanuel Lubezki. Photos are reprinted here with permission issued by Alma Rossbach and IMCINE, Mexico D.F.*

in a hard to access and far away universe. What is definitively positioned to catch everyone's attention in this sequence is this woman's radiant beauty, accentuated through the combination of colours that adorn her attire, her bewitching violet scarf, and the flamboyant car she is driving.

In cinematic terms, Lubezki's cinematography and the transitions conspire to institute Miroslava's paradoxically displaced and alienated centrality. The transition to the next scene of the sequence, via a dark frame that seems to be a continuity of Miroslava's glasses, stresses the indeterminacy of who is controlling the gaze. The entry to the Czech space and time of childhood is facilitated by a pan, a slow descriptive camera movement that establishes the situation: the dark contour of the back of a standing figure who looks through a window, a tower bell, as well as the shadowy silhouette of a sitting person who sings in Czech. Then the

Figure 9. Frames and windows also contribute to create Miroslava's sense of alienation in *Miroslava. Photo by Emmanuel Lubezki. Photos are reprinted here with permission issued by Alma Rossbach and IMCINE, Mexico D.F.*

silhouette, close to the window, turns forty-five degrees and looks sideways at the singing person. Later we learn this person is the grandmother. The silhouette close to the window is Miroslava as a child. The grandmother tells her that soon they will all go to a far away and exotic country. However, the two, whose silhouettes seem cut out and glued to the window and the tower bell outside in the background, are separated by the inner frame of the window. Following this sequence, still in the past, we soon learn that the grandmother must stay in Czechoslovakia because Doctor Stern could only afford to buy passports for himself, his wife, and his daughter. As a result, Miroslava is forever separated from one of the persons she loves the most. The window/glass as a leitmotiv that alienates the character from her most immediate reality is introduced in this early sequence. Through visual means, Lubezki contributes to Miroslava's alienation in the same way as

Figure 10. Shades segment the body of Miroslava as her gaze emplaces her within a time frame and an affective space nostalgically associated with the past in *Miroslava. Photo by Emmanuel Lubezki. Photos are reprinted here with permission issued by Alma Rossbach and IMCINE, Mexico D.F.*

the narrator; the same is true of Ricardo, one of the characters in the film about whom I will speak shortly.

As indicated, the control of the gaze is exercised by the narrator, who organizes the narrative via a regressive impulse with the point of view defined as an obsession with the past. In this way the film solves the problem of who possesses control of the gaze. Miroslava can only see what Alex wants her and the spectators to see. A clearer example than the ones already mentioned appears in the scene in which Miroslava, once she has gotten home after dinner with Alex, sends her maid off on errands so as to prevent her from discovering her suicidal intent. As Chayo gets ready to leave, Miroslava goes upstairs to the master bedroom. Soon, through the window she sees the maid go. Via an interior voice-over that discloses her thoughts, Miroslava comments that Chayo is going to be very sad when she finds out about the suicide. However, Rosario remains invisible for the spectators who can only hear her leave through the sound effect of a metallic door being locked. It is noteworthy that in this shot Miroslava is looking through shades whose reflection from the outside sun cut and segment her body in multiple pieces. Again, this visual image signifies Miroslava's alienation. Even though in the film it is not clear if the two women are close or not, Miroslava's voice-over expresses concern for the pain Chayo is going to feel. However, the gaze attributed to the protagonist emplaces her within a time frame and an affective space that confines her compulsively and nostalgically to the past. Instead of seeing Chayo's real and present body, Miroslava "sees" with the audience a sequence from her teenage years which "materializes" from a picture that catches her attention and which is on a desk near the window. As seen in this sequence, Miroslava is not only shut away within her thoughts. She is also far away from Chayo and the present and hence she is not allowed to see or connect with her maid.

The dissolve from the picture dramatizes Miroslava's relationships with other people in the past. These relationships, however, are not very successful. In the long sequence that "materializes" from the picture on the desk, Miroslava unknowingly gets the role of *femme fatale* by becoming an object of desire to Ricardo, the boyfriend of her only and closest friend, Graciela. As she soon realizes, Ricardo wants to have the both of them. Young Miroslava harshly rejects Ricardo's objectification. She humiliates Ricardo when he comes to pick her up for a date by instructing her mother to say, within the young man's earshot, that she is not at home. Even though Graciela and Miroslava seemingly continue their friendship during the remainder of their adolescence and for some time after the actor's return from her studies in the United States, Graciela soon disappears from the film. Although no explanation is provided, it is easy to understand that her vanishing from Miroslava's life is due to Ricardo's refusal to let her see her friend. Ricardo is hurt by the rejection and he cannot seem to even bear hearing Miroslava's name. This becomes clear later in the same sequence when, some time after the conflict between Miroslava and Ricardo, Graciela tries to read to him a letter from her friend. Ricardo immediately gets mad and impatient. After that Miroslava only sees her friend once.

In this long sequence the film compulsively stresses Miroslava's inability to establish long-lasting connections with other women. Her failed relationship with Graciela, as well as her troublesome relation with the girls at the ballet studio she attends, gets sufficient narrative time to be of importance. In the studio Miroslava seems to be able to communicate only with Graciela as she is seen speaking solely with her. In this vibrant environment of young and energetic women, Miroslava is portrayed as immersed in memories that take her away from the present moment. The young woman uses the space of the studio as a pretext to remember the ballet practice her grandmother used to take her to in Czechoslovakia. The feeling of frozen time is intensified in this sequence by recourse to a match cut that portrays two analogous ballet classes taking place in different times. Another common link between the two spaces, which establishes a close connection with the past, is a shawl the grandmother gave to Miroslava. In the scene at the studio with Graciela, the other girls take the shawl and throw it at each other to play and make fun of Miroslava who seems to use it as a security blanket. The young woman gets enraged and promises to become violent next time the shawl is touched by the girls. Miroslava, thus, seems to be doomed to remain alone and engrossed in her memories of the past.

On the one hand, through the narrator's mediation as index of the gaze, the film emphasizes how the remembrance of things past stops the affective development of the main character. Miroslava is emplaced within a temporal, spatial, and emotional mindset that does not allow her to develop close links with other women. On the other hand, as seen through Ricardo's role, the long sequence described underlines how men get between Miroslava and the women in her life. Alex also manages to create a narrative in which the conditions for an affective connection with the present are ignored and undermined. Thus, the protagonist cannot seem to be able to see or relate with the women who surround her.

The genre limitations of the psychological drama revealed in the film through the emphasis on nostalgia and unfulfilled desires negotiate with their own restrictions regarding the type of help and support that Miroslava seems to need in order to survive. As is common in the "woman's film," Miroslava feels attracted by certain "feminine" attributes of Jesús Jaime, a character who is first introduced in the movie as the fiancé. He later becomes her husband in a wedding ceremony remarkable for the pronounced chiaroscuros and the blinding intensity of camera flashes that seem to signal Miroslava's inability to discern who Jesús Jaime really is. As Miroslava and her psychologist discuss her relationship with Jesús Jaime in a sequence that seems to have been made more to show off the camera work and the *mise en scène* than the protagonist's worries, the protagonist comments that she feels fascinated by her husband-to-be. This feeling is caused by such tender qualities as Jesús Jaime's gentleness, his softness, and his gracefulness. Miroslava also says she feels more desire for Jesús Jaime when he acts in an indifferent and possessive manner. This last comment seems to suggest, following the conventions of psychological dramas, that Miroslava is trying to substitute her husband for her aloof and distant father.

Figure 11. Medical discourse as enunciated by Doctor Roncal (Juan Carlos Colombo) combines with camera movement and attention to the excessively spacious and luxurious decor of the psychologist's office to dwarf Miroslava in *Miroslava. Photo by Emmanuel Lubezki. Photos are reprinted here with permission issued by Alma Rossbach and IMCINE, Mexico D.F.*

As a matter of fact, as a young woman, Miroslava felt she did not get enough attention from Dr. Stern. According to her, this was due to the fact that he was not her biological father. The narrative time devoted to Dr. Stern associates him with his medical practice and his violin. The father only manages to express his love for his daughter through gifts and travels. What is more, he does not seem to worry too much about Miroslava's first suicidal attempt when she was younger. Thus the protagonist resents her father's indifference and starts to look for other ways to validate her own self, especially through the cinema. However, her search for the father continues in her marriage. Such seems to be the psychological reading called for by the text. Alongside this reading, a more astute approach makes clear that the film manages to displace Miroslava's connections with other women by emplacing a male character endowed with "feminine" qualities.

Figure 12. A high angle shot of Roncal's office symmetrically works to remind spectators of the very first shot of the movie and to situate Miroslava as an alienated and tragic subject in *Miroslava*. *Photo by Emmanuel Lubezki. Photos are reprinted here with permission issued by Alma Rossbach and IMCINE, Mexico D.F.*

The film then moves on to prove how these traits are not enough to create a sense of security and happiness for the protagonist. Miroslava suffers terribly when she finds her husband with another man and realizes that his gentleness and softness, his indifference and control, are not a sign of strength and love, but rather signs of homosexuality and exclusion. By introducing the homosexual twist, the film seems to indicate on the one hand that the "feminine" is dangerous and, on the other, that the relationships with persons of the same sex are unnatural and undesirable.

Going back to the sequence with the psychologist, it appears that Miroslava's search for a sense of connection gets uttered within thematic limits that are not negotiable. Dr. Roncal diminishes Miroslava's complaints by citing in a condescending manner a clinical catalogue of distress, need for protection, and an inability to communicate. The psychologist uses

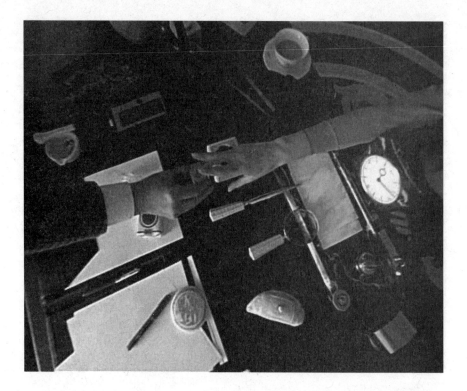

Figure 13. The framing of the pills and the zoom in foretells Miroslava's suicide and seals the disconnection between Roncal and the actor as their hands hardly touch in *Miroslava. Photo by Emmanuel Lubezki. Photos are reprinted here with permission issued by Alma Rossbach and IMCINE, Mexico D.F.*

medical discourse mechanically and fails to listen to what Miroslava is trying to say about her feelings. On the cinematic level, this sequence also emphasizes the idea of discursive limits and enclosure. Camera work in this sequence, through movement and attention to the excessively spacious and luxurious decor of the office, dwarfs Miroslava away. The first shot stylistically replicates the very first shot of the film in which the protagonist is seen from above to signify, even in death, her positioning as an article for manipulation and consumption. The sequence in Roncal's office starts off with a high angle shot that sets Miroslava's radical separation from the psychologist. This is achieved through proximic patterns and by framing between the two of them Roncal's enormous and imposing desk. Following this high angle shot, the camera penetrates the lower levels of the office with slow but perceptible movements that create the feeling that something

Figure 14. Miroslava behind glass doors at Roncal's office: the film's politics of fragmentation of the female body cite a traditional cinematographic gaze that constructs Miroslava as unsolvable enigma in *Miroslava*. *Photo by Emmanuel Lubezki. Photos are reprinted here with permission issued by Alma Rossbach and IMCINE, Mexico D.F*

ominous is about to happen. This is completed with a sudden zoom-in onto two hands as Roncal gives barbiturates to the protagonist. The framing of the pills seals the disconnection between the two characters whose hands hardly touch. Soon the spectators find out the results of Roncal's distanced stance as Miroslava uses the drugs to commit suicide. Just like the narrator, Dr. Stern, and Jesús Jaime, the analyst is unable to "cheer" the woman up.

The citation of a cold and detached medical discourse goes hand in hand with the citation of a traditional cinematographic gaze with its politics of fragmentation of the female body. In this same sequence with Dr. Roncal, there is a moment when Miroslava goes to the off space of the frame even though her voice can still be heard. A few seconds later the camera recaptures her reflection on the enormous glass doors of the office in a shot that seems to place her behind the doors, as if exiled from the office, and

Figure 15. Miroslava is disassociated from Mexican symbols such as the Virgin of Guadalupe in *Miroslava. Photo by Emmanuel Lubezki. Photos are reprinted here with permission issued by Alma Rossbach and IMCINE, Mexico D.F.*

divided in two by the door frame. Miroslava's representation in this medical space fragments, divides, and empties the main character of meaning and transforms her into a vessel that can be filled with interpretations and can be explained medically as the psychologist does. This sequence summarizes the film's representation politics with Miroslava as an unsolvable enigma whose body occupies at the same time a location of presence and absence. This means that Miroslava is obliterated and silenced even before she commits suicide.

In *Miroslava* the negotiation with gender constraints interferes with the creation of an expanded or liveable space for Miroslava both at the thematic and the representational levels. The intertexts manage to place the young movie star on the periphery by emphasizing a felt ambiguity about who the protagonist of the narrative actually is. This protagonist could either be

Alex through his narrative control or the cinematic apparatus as a creator of meaning. In this sense, the movie confines Miroslava to a blinded, excluded, and displaced position.

Above I have said that such an emplacement requires the "restitution" of patriarchal space as a site where narration originates. This is used as a means to attenuate the potential anomaly of the character. However, the truth is that the citation of all the other spaces where the main character functions realizes the dreaded anomaly. Miroslava feels at ease in luxurious restaurants, in the film studios, in the street, and at the movies. The film further tries to negotiate with this image by associating her with flowers. The flowers conspicuously appear everywhere with the protagonist, especially during her teenage years and her adulthood. Such an association seeks to assuage Miroslava's implied boldness by trying to attach to her a sense of fragility, transience, and vulnerability that further construes her failure to adapt and be happy as her own undoing.

Thus, it is no surprise that, in contrast to the short story, in none of the film spaces are there objects that could be identified as symbols of Mexicanness, with the exception of small statuettes of the Virgin of Guadalupe strategically placed in the film studios. Sometimes they are in the background as the main character walks by. However, Miroslava's back is always turned to them and she does not seem to be aware of these signs.[14] In contrast to other film icons, which at times were used by Mexican cinema to embody Mexicanness through religious associations, Miroslava is not only distanced from Catholicism, but also conspicuously exiled from her possible Jewishness. This seeming lack of values can explain her incapacity to construct solid links that could prepare her to assume her functions as a citizen and as a reproducer of the nation. Seemingly, the easiness with which she moves in the public space signals that the actor is more worried about herself and her career than about complying with the social requirement of constructing a family to strengthen the local paternal space and the wider patriarchal space of the nation. As a result, Miroslava seems doomed to commit suicide. In fact, she seems to be sentenced to obliteration without due process, much like the prisoner in Kafka's short story who, like Miroslava, is not given the chance to defend himself. Miroslava dies because the discursive and affective positions available for her in the 1950s do not tolerate alternate gender and sexual desires. Indeed, the conditions of a hegemonic nationalism cannot fathom her embodying (trans)national attributes. The protagonist is punished for her questioning of the discourses that society and its different institutions, among them cinema, try to imprint on her body.

Miroslava is excluded from the terms of her own representation and is, in contrast, subjected to a cinematographic stylistics that positions her as an artifact for consumption and as a subject for male analysis. The homogeneous and hegemonic concepts about nationalism in 1950s Mexico, and the idea of patriarchal space as frozen and sacred time in which categories such as gender and national identity are conceived as fixed or essentialized constructs, create the conditions for the character to give up her negotiation and stop her adaptation process. *Miroslava* proves that "without the space for the renewal of the imagination and the concomitant re-imagining of who one is and who one seeks to become, we are unable to get effectively the project of becoming a person off the ground" (Cornell 1995, 5). Without the minimal conditions for individuation, Pelayo's Miroslava is doomed to fail to constitute her personhood and, thus, has to commit suicide.

Works Cited

Ayala Blanco, Jorge. 1986. *La condición del cine mexicano: 1973–1985*. Mexico: Posada.
———. 1979. *La aventura del cine mexicano*. 2nd ed. Mexico: Era.
Cornell, Drucilla. 1995. *The Imaginary Domain: Abortion, Pornography, and Sexual Harassment*. Routledge: New York.
De Lauretis, Teresa. 1999. Gender Symptoms, or, Peeing Like a Man. *Social Semiotics* 9 (2): 257–70.
Doane, Mary Ann. 1987. "The Woman's Film": Possession and Address. In *Home Is Where the Heart Is: Studies in Melodrama and the Woman's Film*, ed. Christine Gledhill, 283–98. London: British Film Institute Publishing.
Edensor, Tim. 2002. *National Identity, Popular Culture and Everyday Life*. New York: Berg Editorial Offices.
García Riera, Emilio. 1963. *El cine mexicano*. Mexico: Era.
———. 1969–78. *Historia documental del cine mexicano*. 9 Volumes. Mexico: Era.
———. 1986. *Historia del cine mexicano*. Mexico: Secretaría de Educación Pública.
Gledhill, Christine, ed. 1987. *Home Is Where the Heart Is: Studies in Melodrama and the Woman's Film*. London: British Film Institute Publishing.
——— 1988. Pleasurable Negotiations. In *Female Spectators: Looking at Film and Television*, ed. E. Deidre Pribram, 66–98. New York: Verso.
Hershfield, Joanne. 1999. Race and Ethnicity in the Classical Cinema. In *Mexico's Cinema: A Century of Film and Filmmakers*, ed. Joanne Hershfield and David R. Maciel, 81–100. Wilmington: Scholarly Resources Books.
———. 1996. *Mexican Cinema/Mexican Woman: 1940–1950*. Tucson: Univ. of Arizona Press.
Kafka, Franz. 1995. In the Penal Colony. In *The Metamorphosis, In the Penal Colony, and Other Stories*, 140–67. Trans. Willa and Edwin Muir. New York: Schocken.
Kaplan, Ann. E. 1987. Mothering, Feminism and Representation: The Maternal in Melodrama and the Woman's Film 1910–1940. In *Home Is Where the Heart Is: Studies in Melodrama and the Woman's Film*, ed. Christine Gledhill, 113–37. London: British Film Institute Publishing.
LaPlace, Maria. 1987. Producing and Consuming the Woman's Film: Discursive Struggle in *Now, Voyager*. In *Home Is Where the Heart Is: Studies in Melodrama and*

the Woman's Film, ed. Christine Gledhill, 138–96. London: British Film Institute
Publishing.

Leñero, Vicente. 1995. *Miroslava*. Mexico: Plaza y Janes.

———. 2000. *Les années sidérales d'Arielle*. *Techniserv*. http://www.arielledombasle.net/.

Loaeza, Guadalupe. 1994. *Miroslava*. 3rd ed. Mexico: Alianza.

Maza, Maximiliano. 2004. Biography for Miroslava Stern. *International Movie Database (IMDb)*. http://us.imdb.com/name/nm0827797/bio.

Modleski, Tania. 1987. Time and Desire in the Woman's Film. In *Home Is Where the Heart Is: Studies in Melodrama and the Woman's Film*, ed. Christine Gledhill, 326–38. London: British Film Institute Publishing.

Monsiváis, Carlos. 1994. Preface, Miroslava: De la tragedia como perdurabilidad. In *Miroslava*, by Guadalupe Loaeza, 11–16. Mexico: Alianza.

———. 1998. El fin de la diosa arrodillada. In *Miradas de mujer: Encuentro de cineastas y videoastas mexicanas y chicanas*, ed. Norma Iglesias Prieto and Rosa Linda Fragoso, 163–66. Tijuana, Mexico: Colegio de la Frontera Norte; Davis: Chicana/Latina Research Center, Univ. of California Press.

Mora, Carl J. 1982. *Mexican Cinema: Reflections of a Society: 1896–1988*. Los Angeles: Univ. of California Press.

Naremore, James, ed. 2000. *Film Adaptation*. New Jersey: Rutgers Univ. Press.

Olney, James. 1972. A Theory of Autobiography. In *Metaphors of Self: the Meaning of Autobiography*, 2–50. Princeton Univ. Press.

Ramírez Berg, Charles. 1992. *Cinema of Solitude: A Critical Study of Mexican Film, 1967–1983*. Austin, TX: Univ. of Texas Press.

Ramon, David. 1993. Lectura de las imágenes propuestas por el cine mexicano de los años treinta a la fecha. In *80 años de cine mexicano*, ed. Aurelio de los Reyes, David Ramon, Maria Luisa Amador and Rodolfo Rivera, 93–120. Mexico: Univ. Nacional Autónoma de Mexico.

Ruy-Sánchez, Alberto. 1995. Approaches to the Problem of Mexican Identity. In *Identities in North America: The Search for Community*, ed. Robert L. Earle and John D Wirth, 40–55. Palo Alto, CA: Stanford Univ. Press.

Schaefer-Rodríguez, Claudia. 1991. Embedded Agendas: The Literary Journalism of Cristina Pacheco and Guadalupe Loaeza. *Latin America Literary Review* 19 (38): 62–76.

Sefchovich, Sara. 1987. *México: país de ideas, país de novelas. Una sociología de la literatura mexicana*. Mexico: Grijalbo.

Stam, Robert. 2000. The Dialogics of Adaptation. In *Film Adaptation*, ed. James Naremore, 54–76. New Jersey: Rutgers Univ. Press.

Films

¡A volar joven! Directed by Miguel Delgado. Clasa-Mohme, 1946.

Bodas trágicas. Directed by Gilberto Martínez Solares. CLASA Films Mundiales, 1946.

Ensayo de un crimen [*The Criminal Life of Archibaldo de la Cruz*]. Directed by Luis Buñuel. Alianza Cinematográfica, 1955.

Escuela de vagabundos. Directed by Rogelio A. González. Laguna Films, 1954.

Las tres perfectas casadas. Directed by Roberto Gavaldón. Filmex, 1952.

María Candelaria. Directed by Emilio Fernández. Films Mundiales, 1943.
Miroslava. Directed by Alejandro Pelayo. Instituto Mexicano de Cinematografía, 1992.

Notes

1   Miroslava is a historical subject about whom there seems to be little verifiable informa-
    tion. Loaeza does not reveal in her short story what her historical sources are. Some
    family pictures of the movie star that appear as paratext to the third edition also are cited
    without a note about their origin. Among the books devoted to the study of Mexican
    cinema in general, and to the analysis of the golden age of Mexican cinema in particular
    (1936–56), Miroslava is hardly mentioned, except when she is listed in the technical
    information about the movies she made. As a rule, when she is mentioned, her name
    appears linked to Luis Buñuel and other filmmakers. See Mora (1982, 93), Ayala Blanco
    (1986, 445), and García Riera (1969–78, passim). In *La aventura del cine mexicano*, Ayala
    Blanco compares her briefly to Ninón Sevilla, who starred in the "cine de cabareteras,"
    a Mexican genre of films set in a cabaret (1979, 143). Miroslava's erasure from the pages
    of Mexican cinema history is made conspicuous by her exclusion from studies such as
    80 años de cine mexicano by Aurelio de los Reyes et al.; Charles Ramírez Berg's *Cinema
    of Solitude* (1992) and Joanne Hershfield's *Mexican Cinema/Mexican Woman* (1999).
    Even Carlos Monsiváis, whose preface to the third edition of Loaeza's short story was
    reprinted in 1998 in *Miradas de mujer: Encuentro de cineastas y videoastas mexicanas
    y chicanas* under the title "El fin de la diosa arrodillada," chooses to exclude all previ-
    ous references to Miroslava (163–66). The systematic exclusion of Miroslava could be
    explained as a result of the traditionally negative criticism given to melodrama, a mode
    that could describe many of her movies. However, it is also possible that her suicide
    and her perceived otherness might also play a role. Cultural critics such as Monsiváis
    make explicit comments about Miroslava's foreign accent, thus appropriating a role as
    implicit agent of immigration and denying her a membership in the Mexican nation.
    Even though I have only been able to see three of her films: *¡A volar joven!* (Miguel
    Delgado, 1946), *Escuela de vagabundos* (Rogelio A. González, 1954) and *Ensayo de un
    crimen* (Luis Buñel, 1955), these movies span several years of the career of the star and I
    did not notice anything particularly foreign in her speech. Miroslava's slow diction in *¡A
    volar joven!* could be explained by the qualities of the character she plays. In the other
    two films, Miroslava speaks with the accent of an educated middle-class Mexican.

    Interestingly enough, Arielle Dombasle, the French actor who plays the role of Miroslava
    in Pelayo's movie, expresses herself correctly although with a touch of affectation
    that makes her speech sound artificial. Even if this could be attributed to a "faithful"
    interpretation of Miroslava's character, the ambiguity remains due to Dombasle's own
    migratory experience and her own speech patterns. Even though she now lives in France
    and is identified as French, she was born in Norwich, Connecticut and spent all of her
    childhood in Mexico, until the age of eighteen. For a brief biographical note and a filmog-
    raphy of this actor, consult the Internet site *Les années sidérales d'Arielle*. For a brief
    biography of Miroslava Stern online see Mazimiliano Maza, "Biography for Miroslava
    Stern." Maza's comments coincide with those of Monsiváis and Loaeza.

    Probably due to Pelayos' film, Miroslava has acquired the status of cult figure among
    lovers of Mexican golden age cinema. This mythification attests to Miroslava's use as
    a sign open to interpretation and re-signification. Lately she is deemed to be a kind
    of Mexican "Marilyn Monroe." See *Estrellas del cine mexicano* online. Several of the
    pictures in Loaeza's 1994 edition of the short story suggest this parallel.

2   The term "heterosexual matrix" refers to gender restrictions according to biology and
    to the taboo of homosexuality as prohibition.

3   This paratextual comment can also be read as a possible strategy for marketing, both for the film and the short story, by inciting the voyeuristic imagination of readers and spectators.

4   I say Jesús Jaime is homosexual – and not bisexual – because in the film he never sleeps with Miroslava. The closet continues to be a reality for women in the nineties, the period in which the film was produced. This is reflected in the movie, as indicated, through the attempt to erase Miroslava's possible otherness as hinted at by Pelayo.

5   See de Lauretis (1999). Combining a semiotic and Freudian point of view, de Lauretis establishes a distinction between the "objectified body," that is, its image or representation, and the "living body," that is, the body that feels and is felt (263). According to this author, the social representations of the body discipline the living body, thus implanting gender/sex in the body that *feels* (original emphasis, 264).

6   Subjectivation refers to the process of configuration of subjectivity as the body bears the inscription of different social forms, such as gender, social class, ethnicity, race, nationalism and the like.

7   De Lauretis (1999, 264) writes that "the body is a gender symptom in that it bears the inscription of gender and speaks it back through the subject's very senses, through the perceptual apparatus that constitutes the bodily ego."

8   In volume 5 of *Historia documental*, Emilio García Riera cites information about the public and artistic life of Miroslava Stern. This information shows her commitment and active participation both on an artistic and political level. Riera states that in 1953 Miroslava supported Cantinflas during a dispute of the actors' guild union. Also, in 1954 Miroslava won an Ariel for best supporting actor in her role in *Las tres perfectas casadas* (1952) by Roberto Gavaldón (García Riera, 128, 130).

9   The idea of "habit change" is related to the socio-cultural positioning of the subject, which is not necessarily fixed. As a matter of fact, de Lauretis (1999, 267) states "that sociocultural positioning is often unstable or variable over time, with life contingencies and, at the very least, with age." Miroslava's anguish over the questioning and indeterminacy of her citizenship increases during her adulthood.

10 Thinkers such as Samuel Ramos and Octavio Paz go back to Indo-Hispanic origins to construct the idea of a national essence (Hershfield 1996; Ruy-Sánchez 1995; Sefchovich 1987). The same is done during the golden age of Mexican cinema by filmmakers such as Emilio "El Indio" Fernández, who in *María Candelaria* (1943) personifies the values of the Mexican nation in an indigenous woman. For a summary of the cultural battles between ideas about the nation anchored in *indigenismo*, *mestizaje* or *hispanismo* during the post-revolutionary era, see Hershfield (1999, 82–92).

11 The Ariel is the Mexican equivalent to the Oscar.

12 For many critics this cinema distinguishes itself for its use of a female protagonist, for a feminine point of view, and for the use of the melodramatic mode that usually centers on the traditionally "feminine" space of the family, as well as for its interest in the domestic, the romantic, the emotional, the repressive and the hysterical (LaPlace 1987, 139; Kaplan 1987, 126; Modleski 1987, 331). Mary Ann Doane points out, however, that as an index of subjectivity, in this type of film the female point of view is untenable (1987, 290). The resulting fluctuation reflects itself in the narrative structure as the classical Hollywood "woman's film" combines different genres and narrative modes – melodrama, *film noir*, the gothic or horror film – in a mixture that finds unity in the female audience it addresses (Doane 1987, 284). Doane's descriptions of this filmic mode of the 1930s and 1940s in Hollywood cinema are useful as they help to contextualize Pelayo's movie within a film tradition that is thematically and technically obvious in his text. In *Miroslava*, as in the "woman's film," the female protagonist is the focus of narration as she is associated with psychological instability and symptoms of repression that seem to connect her with

hysteria, illness, and finally suicide. These characteristics provide a pretext for the male investigation, or rather analysis of the psyche of the protagonist. Ultimately, it is this attempt to privilege the male point of view which makes more obvious the problem of the protagonist's incognoscibility.

13   This adaptation decision could also be a reference to the patriarchal modes of narrating in the 1940s and the 1950s, among which one finds the genre of melodrama. In attention to this context, the narrating voice would have to be male. I am indebted to several of my students for this alternative interpretation, which further stresses the connection between time and space.

14   The first time she is seen in a film studio, when getting ready to shoot *Ensayo de un crimen*, Miroslava passes by a statuette of the virgin that she seems not to notice. The same happens towards the middle of the film, when Miroslava is shown singing and rehearsing for yet another shoot. In the background to the right there is another statuette of the virgin of Guadalupe that Miroslava never looks at.

5 LITERATURE AND GLOBALIZATION

The Latin American Intellectual Redefining Identity:
Nestor García Canclini's *Latinoamericanos
buscando lugar en este siglo*

Rita De Grandis, University of British Columbia

"Hay golpes en la vida"
Hay golpes en la vida ...
E inconscientes
En el filo de lo que ya no se puede
   predecir,
Te escuchamos:
Escapa,
Me dijo,
*Que la ruina fue una trampa que nos
   tendieron*
Para imaginar la unidad en lo disperso
      (Luis Torres, *El exilio y las ruinas*)

"A 'ña María, con cariño"
Que vengan todos a verla-que ya está
   aquí
Que vengan todos a celebrar-que ya
   está aquí
....
ha llegado sola y solita
camina que te camina
largos senderos de lunas
y soles que se le olvidan
....
      (Nela Río, *El espacio de la luz*)[1]

América Latina en su literatura (*América*) first appeared in 1972, published as part of a UNESCO project under the coordination of César Fernández Moreno.[2] A collection of essays on literature and languages, it illustrated the theoretical trends of the time.[3] This publishing initiative resulted from Resolution 3.325, adopted at the fourteenth General Conference of UNESCO, held in Paris in 1966. Among its contributors were "the most lucid critics from Latin America,"[4] such as Fernando Alegría, Roberto Fernández Retamar, Adolfo Prieto, Antonio Cândido, and several representative writers of the time such as Mario Benedetti, Juan José Saer, José Lezama Lima, and Severo Sarduy.

In his introduction, the editor, Fernández Moreno, posed the question: "What is Latin America?" He took as a point of departure Hegel's ideas about America; that is, America as the continent of the future in opposition to the Old World of Europe and America as divided by the struggle between North and South. For Fernández Moreno, a century-and-a-half had elapsed since Hegel's notions concerning this hemisphere appeared, and what for Hegel was the future is now the present; what was Nature is now History.[5] According to Fernández Moreno, Hegel's distinction between North and South America reveals a crucial difference: the north holds the most powerful nation of the world, while the south, under a different and newer name, is a continent that represents "one of the most dynamic ideas of the present world;" a region intellectually vital in cultural and artistic expression, political ideas, and philosophical questions (Fernández Moreno 1972, 5). However, he proposed that the essays that comprise *América* demonstrate the inadequacy of the term *"Latin America,"* because of this term's spurious links to the "Roman Empire" given the African and pre-Columbian Indigenous presence, as well as the influence of Latin America's multiculturalism on other cultures. Fernández Moreno offered *América* as an illustration and showcase of the cultural diversity that Latin America encompasses, and of the politico-ideological underpinnings of *Latin America* as a geopolitical term. He claimed that this collective endeavor aimed to enlighten the world and, most specifically, Latin Americans themselves about this cultural diversity. For this reason, a series of meetings were held by UNESCO in different Latin American countries, affording an opportunity for an increased exchange among intellectuals, writers, and essayists committed to this idea of Latin America.

Those present at the Lima meeting set up the intellectual agenda of the project: namely, to consider the terms in which Latin America is a unitary entity though composed of separate, distinct nation-states and cultures; to encourage this perception among the meeting participants and to promote the goal of the UNESCO project. This goal included the study of the diversity of the cultural, ethnic, and political experiences that constitute Latin America. Undoubtedly, this region has an undeniable cultural impact on the rest of the world, as the continuous presence of America in travel writing and European literatures attests.[6] Another item on the agenda was to increase the self-awareness of Latin American writers and essayists with respect to the shared and rich cultural properties of the region. Only Latin

Americans were invited to participate in the meeting, which also planned to consider the contemporary character of the region with references to the past only when necessary, in order to focus on the then current conflicts within Latin American nations and the external conflicts that affect this region.

In summary, the objective was not to study the cultures of Latin America but rather to examine how Latin America manifested itself *in* or *through* its cultural expressions. With that purpose in mind, the collaborators worked as if they were "psychoanalysts," delving into the most intense manifestations of the unconscious as revealed through Latin-American cultural and artistic expression. In so doing, the UNESCO project attempted to interpret the entity then known as "Latin America" with intellectual precision.

At the same time as the UNESCO project, Fernández Moreno (1972, 17–18) declared that

… tenemos una clara intuición de esta región que va imponiendo en el mundo sus productos culturales, sus hombres, sus mitos…. Esta obra colectiva ayudará a la toma de conciencia de los latinoamericanos sobre la real originalidad y posible unidad de la región que integran…. Se trata de una empresa que, como todas las que importan a los hombres, parte de una ignorancia esperanzada y se dirige hacia un conocimiento anhelado. ¿Qué es América Latina? Lo único seguro que de ella sabemos, por ahora, es que es nuestra.

> [… we have a clear intuition that this region was becoming known to the world through its cultural products, stereotypes, and myths…. The collaborative work undertaken will help Latin America to become aware of its real originality and its possible unity as a region…. It is an enterprise, like all those that matter, that starts from a hopeful conviction and moves towards a quest for knowledge about what Latin America is. The only certainty that we have so far is that it is ours.]

With this statement of intent and the use of the first person plural "we," Fernández Moreno concluded his introductory remarks, expressing a sense of pride for the cultures of Latin America. He also insisted that the bewilderment of the colonial enterprise for both the Spaniards and the Indigenous peoples gave rise to the creativity of this continent, which is expressed in a dynamic culture of synthesis that resulted from the amalgamation of the autochthonous cultures combined with the European and the African contributions.

Latinoamericanos buscando lugar en este siglo (*Latinoamericanos*) by Néstor García Canclini was published in 2002 and it was awarded the Luis Cardoza y Aragón[7] Foundation Essay Prize in October 2001. The essay coincidentally begins with a question similar to Fernández Moreno's of thirty years before. Notably, García Canclini's interrogation in evoking the earlier question of Fernández Moreno addresses a different historical, socio-political, economic and cultural context. Fernández Moreno's "What is Latin America?" emerged in response to the concerns of Latin-American intellectuals of the left and the cultural agenda of the late 1960s and early 1970s.[8] This time saw the climax of the international socialist utopian projects and national revolutionary movements that evoked the *patria grande* of Bolívar.[9] In contrast, *Latinoamericanos* emerges from the decline of such utopian projects and their associated radical intellectual models alongside the rise of so-called global capitalism and neo-liberal democracies during the last two decades of the twentieth century. Furthermore, any discussion or concern with Latin American identity and its relationship with the rest of the world requires attention to questions or phenomena that were not relevant, present, or at the centre of attention during the time when Fernández Moreno assembled his volume. *Latinoamericanos* draws in a synoptic way from much of the cultural phenomena treated in *América*. García Canclini attempts to evaluate the last two decades of the twentieth century, assessing the benefits and disadvantages of globalization and positing again the question of Latin American identity, inducing the reader to make connections between these two last decades and the previous ones to which *América* bears witness. Likewise, he addresses the role of the intellectual, prefiguring a function of someone deeply connected with the history and concerns of his region. Hence, linking *América Latina en su literatura* and *Latinoamericanos buscando lugar en este siglo* allows us to highlight, among other issues, the centrality of the question of identity in both works, the importance attributed to culture as Latin America's most vital asset and dynamic contribution to the world, and the social function of the cultural essay genre as a means of understanding Latin America. Both works speak of the richness and creativity of Latin American cultures and aim at reaching a transnational community of writers, artists, and intellectuals committed to the social and cultural realities of their nations. García Canclini follows the tradition of the essay as a critical form par excellence that links art and theory.[10] In Latin America, the essay genre arose as an urgent response to a threat of danger, particularly during the periods of independence and early nation building. To say something on the political, ethnic, racial, or cultural challenges of Latin America became a pressing, compelling act for the essayist, who took it upon himself/herself to use the versatility of the essay and its multiple possibilities to intervene in affairs so dear to his/her country. We may ask, then, in the beginning of this new century, what is the urgency that triggers *Latinoamericanos*? What is its challenge? The challenge is globalization. Globalization has become the urgent, pressing issue to contend with, and in *Latinoamericanos* García Canclini poses the following questions: "What does it mean to be a Latin American?" (2002, 12); "What is left of Latin American narratives?" (17); "Who wants to be a Latin American?" (23); and "What does one understand today by *Latinity*?" (68).[11]

By positing these questions, the essayist attempts to capture the ambivalence, uncertainties, and contradictions of Latin America within the context of global capitalism. He describes how the region operates with its cultural products, the massive migration phenomenon in the past two decades of the twentieth century, and the increase in external debt. In earlier works, like *La globalización imaginada* (García Canclini 1999) and "La épica de la globalización y el melodrama de la interculturalidad" (García Canclini 2000), he analyzes globalization with field work carried out on the US-Mexican border,[12] whereas in *Latinoamericanos* his focus is more on arguing for strategies and policies that would protect the local market of cultural goods. He suggests first and foremost the rethinking of the role of the state, so that it can be conceptualized as an entity with a regulatory function, capable of intervening and providing policies for promoting Latin American cultural industries in the global market. He maintains that Latin America will not be able to envisage a better future unless a shift occurs in the conception of the role of the state. He criticizes conceptions based on the Manichean opposition between the state and private enterprises that certain intellectuals hold, arguing that such positions do not contribute to supporting Latin American cultural production. He further advocates a new role for the state, in which it would act as a place of articulation between governments, private initiatives, and other sectors of civil society. To design cultural and market policies for cultural goods in the midst of transnational forms of privatization would require a new role of the state, as well as a redefinition of the market and its relationship with cultural creativity. Even though state intervention to control artistic creativity was very much opposed by progressive intellectuals in previous decades, for García Canclini the time has come to reevaluate this position, since the culture industry (music, videos, radio, and Internet) has become crucially important as a social and political actor (García Canclini 2002, 67–68). In sum, his working hypothesis is that Latin America's main tension is between the promises of global cosmopolitanism and the loss of national projects (50).

After two decades of globalization, Latin America no longer experiences the illusions of the early 1980s: its democracies remained fragile throughout the 1990s and the beginning of the new century and are haunted by the prospect of the 2005 Free Trade Agreement for the Americas (FTAA; known in Spanish as Acuerdo de Libre Comercio de las Américas or ALCA) proposal by the US for free trade in the Americas. Throughout the 1980s Latin America tried to become globalized with great asymmetries that increased social inequalities, giving rise to a crisis of the national political models which, along with the modernization projects from previous decades, started to explode. As a result, new autonomist alternatives emerged, such as the Land Movement in Brazil, the Zapatistas in Mexico, and regional ethnic groups in Chile, Ecuador, and Guatemala. Furthermore, new legal initiatives have been begun, favoring indigenous autonomies in Brazil (1988), Colombia (1991) and Ecuador (1998), revealing a progress in politics of identity affirmation (García Canclini 2002, 41). Within this context, the forces of transnational capital through the new FTAA agreement represent another major threat to the economic and social development of the region. This gives rise to the possibility of overriding previous regional pacts, such as MERCOSUR between Brazil, Argentina, and Uruguay, and of decisions being made outside the region that will undeniably affect the continent. An example of this is the current U.S. intervention in the war in Colombia (57). García Canclini alerts the reader to be suspicious of this new "Alliance for Progress" with the Giant from the North, although he expresses a sense of its inevitability at the same time. Thus, the essayist suggests that rather than rejecting it, it is imperative to be prepared; in order to do so, scientific studies are needed so that when the moment to sign the FTAA arrives, Latin Americans will be in a better condition to sign than Mexico was in 1994, when the NAFTA agreement was established. Likewise, it is important to disseminate the results of these studies as widely as possible in order to generate more social participation, since a more democratic interaction between government and civil society will allow for more productive outcomes (33).

This mode of argumentation that is more engaging of the public than it is analytical allows the writer to reach a larger audience and address more politically the issues at stake for Latin Americans. In so doing, Néstor García Canclini has distanced himself from the scientific or purely analytical essay style of his previous works,[13] and has leaned towards a more journalistic style, offering a general cultural-political commentary on Latin America's current challenges with globalization. His essay, a relatively short work, compresses some already known facts on globalization, oscillates between critical distance and adherence, and focuses on cultural issues that derive from his general assumptions on mass culture, specifically, on consumption and the culture industry.[14]

In *Latinoamericanos*, the autobiographical characteristic of the essay genre becomes explicit not only in the use of the first person, as illustrated by the inclusion of a personal conversation with a taxi driver in Buenos Aires in 2001 (García Canclini 2002, 15), but also in his references to his generational experience and his literary and artistic taste, both past and present. In tune with the massive migration and diasporas that have characterized the continent, the essayist defines himself as an intellectual who lives between Mexico and Argentina. He expresses the difficulties of trying to study Latin America as a unity since any attempt to compare the two distinctive nations (Mexico and Argentina) implies an emphasis on their differences more than on their commonalties. Therefore, he claims that to embark on such a pursuit requires another struggle with the question of what Latin America is. This is a question that predecessors like Alfonso Reyes (1889–1959) and Arnaldo Orfila (1897–1998) have already attempted (García Canclini 2002, 12).[15] However, García Canclini does not engage in what these predecessors have achieved; their contributions are assumed as given. Rather, these men are portrayed as exemplary intellectuals who influenced the cultural development of Latin America in definite ways: Alfonso Reyes, in the realm of literature and Arnaldo Orfila, in the publishing industry. Reyes and Orfila captured the cultural, political, philosophical, and literary vibrations of their time and devoted their lives to the cultural development of the continent as a totality. In so doing, García Canclini describes his own function as someone who expects to continue their task and embrace the region's concerns and possibilities. Thus, the maintenance of the tradition of these predecessors requires acknowledging the region's richness in cultural expression as well as its possibilities of cultural and social thought. To embark on this task presupposes the redefinition of ideas and notions used in the past along with a history of shared studies, diasporas and migrations in the region, cinema and literature, *telenovelas* and tango, bolero, and rock. He contends that it is urgent to consider seriously the profits of these cultural products which are comparable to those of oil, tourism, and basic food commodities: Latin American culture industries represent a source of capital worth taking account of if intellectuals are to be concerned with the social and cultural welfare of their fellow people.

Within this new context, *Latinoamericanos* pleads for governmental policies to protect its national culture industries, as Latin America offers incredible cultural riches in music, television, cinema, and literature. The question to ask is not whether García Canclini supports the regulation of cultural production by the state, but rather what would be entailed in government policies to protect culture? He insists on highlighting the asymmetries within globalization, which have generated not only inequality in the distribution of economic benefits, but have also deepened the historical irregularity in communication relationships and in public intervention at national and transnational levels. Although the phenomenon of massive migration of the last decades of the twentieth century is primarily the result of a lack of employment, it is also the consequence of a lack of education and of cultural development. García Canclini thus argues for government-backed provisions that would protect and stimulate local culture industries, as Spain has done with its film, television, and publishing industries.[16] In fact, the region's ministries of culture must promote "our" cultural capital among the Hispanic communities in the United States and Europe. This does not mean that the state creates culture, but that it is indispensable for generating policies to stimulate and regulate cultural production and consumption as much as for providing access to these policies without discrimination (García Canclini 2002, 71).

In this return to the support of the role of the state, one recognizes a major characteristic of Latin American populist movements, in which the state and the intellectual mediated and regulated the needs of the people. As argued by specialists on populism, in national populist governments the state is the key institution of social and political organization. Thus, García Canclini's claim for a stronger participation of the state in cultural matters comes from a long historical tradition of national-populist ideology in Latin America. Certainly, this position builds on past memories and on the lasting symbolic force that populism still has despite the passage of time and the drastic transformations experienced by Latin American societies on their way to a less painful modernity.

In this line of argumentation on the role of the state, the essayist returns to the periodically devalued and re-evaluated question of Latin American identity to remind the reader of certain aspects of its conceptual pilgrimage. In order to characterize the stage of the present process, he recalls how identity was conceptualized in ontological and political terms in the nineteenth century; part of the ideological agendas of populism and nationalism used it to integrate and "resolve" differences. Even when anthropologists and intellectuals pleaded for ethnic and local identities, the ethnic question was organized around a national culture. For example, works by José Carlos Mariátegui and José María Arguedas advocated for ethnic identities within a national project.[17] In the current situation, Latin American identity is predicated on concepts of diversity and resistance to homogenization,[18] as a heterogeneous cultural space beyond its territory and its languages. It includes other localities, mainly the Latinos in the US, which constitute the second largest minority in that country,[19] as well as other linguistic combinations such as Spanglish. For the essayist, Latin American identity under the global order configures also a space or network of Latin-derived languages associated with academic and publishing circuits, gastronomy, tourism, and communications – all of which attract high economic investment. "Latin Americanness" modulates itself with different emphases, according to historical and current influences from Europe, America, and Asia, and according to other ethnic and new political configurations.[20] In doing so, García Canclini returns to his conception of hybridity as historically identifiable stages of cultural development to characterize the Anglo-American Latino stage with its culture and language. Beyond these de-territorialized configurations, he warns the reader not to forget that these mixtures – far from being a celebration of diversity – entail deeply uneven power relations. Having said this, no new insights on an already well-established view of Latin American identity under the effects of globalization on the continent are presented. The essayist suggests (García Canclini 2002, 107–8) instead a return to the idea of a transnational community united by cultural ties and common concerns, reasserting the view that culture will, as has always been the case, salvage Latin America:

Es preciso escribir esta palabra – lo mismo que *latinoamericano* – con modestas minúsculas. Contra las Alianzas Militares y Políticas que en estos tiempos guerreros se inflaman de mayúsculas, y también para diferenciarnos de tantas palabras que se gastaron al solemnizarse en épicas pasadas, lo *latinoamericano* puede crecer si se nutre de intercambios solidarios y abiertos, renovados y renovables.... Buscar otro lugar. No encontrar, a veces, más que promesas.... Imaginar la cultura como ese relato, la inminencia de lo que todavía no ocurrió, el derrumbe que tal vez aún puede evitarse. Contar la experiencia posible de los otros. Contar con los otros.

[It is necessary to write this word – just like *latinoamericano* – with modest lower-case letters. One must do this against the political and military alliances that in these war-like times are written in upper case and also to distance ourselves from so many words that were wasted in the solemnity of past epics; the *lationamericano* [Latin American] can grow if it nourishes itself from new solidarities that are open, renewed, and renewable.... One has to continue to seek, even though sometimes it implies not finding, or finding only promises.... It is possible to imagine culture as the narrative of that which still has not happened, or of the collapse that might be avoidable. It is possible to tell the stories of the others' experience. And to be one with the others.]

With this call for solidarity and unity through shared experience and culture, the essayist returns to the affective and empathic "we," which seeks to commit the reader, as does Fernández Moreno's "Latin America[n] is ours." The two writers recommend not the opposition of globalization but rather its reconceptualization, and in so doing García Canclini predicts that Latin America will have a more equitable share in the global market.

The call for rallying forces behind the claims conveyed by the essay implies a departure from the scientific essay, a leap outside a strictly "academic" reason to engage rather in a political debate, even in a war of ideas, which the changeable and polemical characteristics of the genre permit. From this vantage point perhaps *Latinoamericanos* should be read as a personal account, even as a testimony of the trajectory of the essayist himself, whose community is undergoing a painful transition. He responds with subjectivity, reflecting on the issues with certain creativity, flexibility, and fragmentation. His appeal to responsibility and calls for historical memory, as mentioned above, draws from the paradigm of the Latin American radical intellectual movement of the 1960s and 1970s, from which García Canclini comes, expressing the will to represent the collective interests of Latin Americans and to speak on behalf of the experience of his people. *Latinoamericanos* could be analyzed and argued on the basis of epistemological and methodological questions, but it could also be read as an opportunity to work through the controversies that it raises, or as an illustration of the essayist's intellectual development. If we read *Latinoamericanos* more as a testimonial or autobiographical narrative, then this essay creates different expectations. In García Canclini's long trajectory, the attempt to bridge the gap between an elitist perception of culture and a more democratic adherence to mass culture has lead him to embody a new intellectual function within global capitalism: a role of cultural advocate or consultant, as if the academic intellectual had become a commercial functionary of the new symbolic capital.[21] He believes that if the possibilities for political intervention were otherwise, it would be feasible to articulate an inter-American network of spheres of knowledge that would benefit not only artists, consumers, and intellectuals of Latin America, but also those who reside in the US and Canada. He elicits sympathy for the region and suggests that, rather than meeting with researchers from the North in two congresses per year, the institutions that organize these events should provide funding for North/South joint-research ventures and promote independent research on the cultural funding policies of foreign banks in regard to Latin America. If that were to happen, it would be possible to intervene more directly and positively on matters that will affect the next generation of Latin Americans. He is wary of globalization's alleged negative effects, such as massive impoverishment, social exclusion, and war (García Canclini 2002, 57).

We may ask, then: How should we evaluate such a cultural and ideological critique? It would seem as if Eco's apocalyptic or integrated discourse on mass culture has found the intellectual in a paradoxical position.[22] His later studies on mass culture and consumption are a clear indication of García Canclini's departure from earlier dependency theory's critique of mass culture, a position that clearly identifies him with an integrated perspective on mass culture. Based on Pierre Bourdieu and Umberto Eco, it is a view that suggests that cultural creation be articulated also in the circulation and reception of symbolic products. In addition, García Canclini offers the notion of an active "producer" and "receptor," capable of making use of strategies of distancing and critique such as parody and irony, as done in his famous description of the devils of Ocumicho (García Canclini 1995).[23] However, *Latinoamericanos* does not continue defending or abandoning these ideas, but rather argues for preventing the social and cultural exclusion predicated on the basis of the conditions of production and consumption in the market of symbolic practices. Therefore, it is necessary to consider the importance of social policies that affect the consumption and reception of cultural products, since the commercialization of symbolic goods produces segregation between those who have the economic means to access them and those who do not (García Canclini 2002, 68).

Given this change of focus and style, the essay has opened the possibility of reaching a transnational audience, of advising a community of intellectuals of the dangers and possibilities of globalization, and of inviting the exit of the "lettered city" in order to form a network of solidarity beyond the political and symbolic limits of the Latin American nations. Does it matter that the essay circulates in a form like a pamphlet for advocacy on cultural policy for Latin America? A call to an ideological battle has thereby forfeited a claim to the rigor of a scientific pursuit. In this sense, the slippage from scientific argumentation or epistemological considerations to a more ethical and autobiographical penchant, along with his performance of self-authorization to speak on behalf of Latin –Americans, expose the reader to a different truth and intellectual duty. The essay, as a symbolic gesture, joins antiglobalization gatherings, such as the Porto Alegre Summit, and is a participant in the "large conversation we [Latin-

Americans] are having with the world" (García Canclini 2002, 107). Latin America becomes, once again, a highly-charged locality from which to speak as figures like José Martí did in *Nuestra América*, or Pablo Neruda in his *Canto general*; *Latinoamericanos* has mobilized all this cultural capital and cultural memory at the crossroad of a crisis of globalization at the turn of the century.

The essay's efficacy and persuasion, but also its danger and limitations, arise from its reliance on the image of the essayist himself, which draws from the prominent public function Latin American intellectuals have had in their societies, serving as the local agents of the continent's ongoing ideological battles. As Jorge Castañeda (1993, 180) contends, "[t]hey have bridged the multiple chasms opening wide between the rest of the world and Latin-American political and economic elites." *Latinoamericanos* allows the reader to follow the evolution of García Canclini's thought on Latin American modernity in its transcultural intertextuality, particularly in dialogue with the critical paradigms of postmodernity, cultural studies, and postcolonial studies.

At this juncture, it appears that finally the subaltern is no longer a theoretical concern, but rather has disappeared entirely from the critical discourse. Although its disappearance has been announced,[24] the subaltern surely does persist. In *Latinoamericanos*, García Canclini speaks of the millions of underpaid Latinos in the improvised music industry maquiladoras in Miami and throughout Latin America.[25] He argues that popular cultures can no longer be discerned in terms of affirmation or subaltern resistance, but rather as practices in which subordinated groups dispute and negotiate social meaning. The prosperity or poverty of subaltern groups depends in part on the trends that govern globalization, which in turn are based on exclusion and unequal power relations. The well being of these groups also depends on the creativity with which they confront something or someone and how well they manage to exercise certain controls over the products and messages within the circuits of the culture industry. That is why García Canclini argues for improvements in working and creative conditions in the culture industry and in uniting forces with the disposed. The radical intellectual has moved to an arena of cultural brokerage; he has packaged a cultural and historical memory upon which to draw and, thanks to his privilege as an intellectual, he has become the spokesperson on behalf of the experience of his people and from within his region and continent. This harking back – this eternal return to the same – is once again the way to inscribe the new colonial, dependent, marginal, or peripheral situation in which the intellectual acts as mediator. The dominant ideology of neo-liberalism seems to have cornered the intellectual into pleading for a more equitable political economy within the culture industry. This strategic position, endowed with certain academic power, provides authority and legitimacy to advocate for policies that would protect the artistic production of Latin America in the global market. There are specific goals to promote on behalf of Latin America: budget increases for education and research, protective policies for the Latin American culture industry, and promotion policies for local artistic production in cinema and television. Certainly, the essay genre is most apt for this type of discursive and social intervention.

What, then, are some of the consequences for the intellectual when he finds himself assuming a role as an intermediary between the state and the culture industry? As mentioned, these consequences touch upon García Canclini's approach to mass culture. There is a clear consensus on the evolution of the analysis of the culture industry, as demonstrated by arguments of dependency theory.[26] Mass culture is no longer viewed as an evil of ideology,[27] but rather as a democratizing tool that breaks down an elitist view of culture (Stolovich and Mourelle qtd. in García Canclini 2002, 59):

Libros y discos se venden en supermercados y grandes tiendas, las obras teatrales y la música clásica y popular encuentran espectadores en la televisión. Aunque este pasaje a los espacios y circuitos masivos, asociado a ventas y modas fugaces, provoca sospechas sobre la calidad cultural de la comunicación masiva, más escritores y músicos pueden vivir de su trabajo. Al mismo tiempo, públicos no habituados a los templos estéticos acceden a obras de su país y de muchos otros. *La cultura da trabajo* es el título de un libro publicado en Uruguay sobre las funciones económicas de los bienes culturales. (García Canclini, 59)

[Books and CDs are sold in supermarkets and big stores; theatre plays and classical and popular music find spectators in television. Although this movement of mass consumption is associated with sales and fleeting fashions, and provokes doubts about its cultural quality, more writers and musicians are able to live from their work. At the same time, audiences not used to high culture now have access to works from their own countries or from abroad. *Culture Offers Work* is the title of a book [by Stolovich and Mourelle and] published in Uruguay about the economic value of culture.]

García Canclini's confidence in the culture industry seems, however, to have reached a point where culture is analyzed solely as a commodity, whereas in the 1960s and 1970s, his concern was distinctively otherwise. Latin American cultures meant avant-garde experimentation and innovation, singularity and diversity, all of which transcended the reification of realism and the stereotypes associated with Latin America. Thus, what is the fate of the intellectual who departs from the Adornian conception of the universalizing view of the intellectual, and of the aesthetic, ethical, and epistemological values that this intellectual articulates and represents? How can this intellectual still formulate a critical perspective on the logic of the market and on the illusions of dominant ideologies? This dilemma persists.

Over the long period of his career, García Canclini has traversed several intellectual arenas, from his earlier works on the avant-garde in the 1970s (as mentioned above) to his current studies on mass culture and consumption. He has taken up Rama's dictum that the radical intellectual should move beyond the "lettered city" and transcend the modernist distinctions between high and low art. But, in doing so, a progressive process of abandonment of a more theoretical and scientific critique of globalization has taken place, producing rather a consultant or advisor in cultural matters. Such a position results from the diminishing importance of the role of the intellectual from public discourse and is heightened by the privatization of culture. Furthermore, this stance derives from the intellectual movement in which García Canclini has been engaged since the 1980s, which has been defined by some as populist,[28] since populism seems to be a constitutive element of cultural studies. Others ironically refer to this position as demagogic because it entails departing from canonical literatures, for example, and embracing forms from popular culture.[29] Considering that the populist or demagogic position renders the intellectual weak or short-handed vis-à-vis his ability to perform a radical critical function, the question of how to articulate a critique that will not be stated purely in the realm of the universal and conceptual still remains open to challenge. Will it entail primarily a critique of academia and an abandonment of the ivory tower of radicalism in theory?[30] How can cultural studies contribute to a radical cultural critique of globalization and academia from within? Can theory/philosophy contribute not only to the interpretation of reality but also to its transformation, as Marx envisioned?

Finally, the intellectual formation and transformations of Néstor García Canclini over several decades show the dilemmas that this type of intellectual confronts when attempting to exercise a socially engaged critique of globalization from an integrated perspective on mass culture. That is why *Latinoamericanos*, this prize-winning essay, is precariously "scientific" and "academic"; it appears grounded more in affection, shared experience, and empathy for the dispossessed, the migrant, and the artist. In contrast, the essays in Fernández Moreno's *América* emanated from the distinction between high and mass culture, and primarily analyzed how literature played a fundamental role in the definition of identity. The essays of this collective volume illustrated the role of the literary intelligentsia of the time as the critical consciousness of society. If the influence of the mass media was acknowledged, it was conceptualized particularly in relation to literature and avant-garde techniques of experimentation, and argued on the irreducible condition of these two realms.[31] Likewise, *América* was aimed at a specific audience of literary critics, ones who favoured the printed word for the exploration of Latin American identity and its modernity, whereas *Latinoamericanos* reaches wider interests, including other cultural manifestations like music, popular culture, and film.

García Canclini's fluid style amalgamates common knowledge on globalization and Latin America, and moves freely on different disciplinary domains while remaining grounded in the tradition of the essay of interpretation of Latin American identity. The use of *América* as a point of departure and counterpoint for parallelisms and differences allows us to grasp some of the main issues in the discussion of the cultural essay on identity. What binds the two works is, of course, the quest for Latin American identity through its cultural manifestations. Both works are based on the idea of reclaiming a place of importance and dignity in the world for Latin American cultural manifestations and the conviction that Latin American culture is the most dynamic aspect and capital of Latin America. Further, the two works share a conception of the social function of art and literature as a means of understanding Latin America: they make a call to a transnational community of writers, artists, cultural producers, and intellectuals, and they do this in spite of the dispersion which has afflicted the region for many decades, first under the Cold War paradigm, and now under globalization. Paralleling these aspects highlights the figure of the intellectual who calls for a symbolic unity around Latin America. Even though "Latin America" is too large and diverse to be a rigorous category of analysis, it still constitutes a frame of reference for understanding the histories and cultures of an entire world region.

What differentiates the two works at a fundamental level is the shift from a conception of modernity, founded on ideas of high and low culture, to a postmodern one, which attempts to dissolve such binarism in the pursuit of a more pluralistic function of culture that includes mass culture. This more inclusive conception argues that television, cinema, and other forms of the culture industry, along with new digital technologies, have democratized culture. This has led to the breaking down of limits between "high" and "low" and fostered new hybridizations, which enrich an already highly heterogeneous culture.

Also worthy of mention is that García Canclini's culturalist trajectory cannot result, as Roberto Follari claims, from his imitation of the methodologies and agendas of U.S. academia. García Canclini's path is forged in a long tradition that has used the cultural essay at the intersections of culture, politics, anthropology, and sociology of culture, as practiced in the Latin American intellectual milieu by thinkers such as Fernando Ortiz and Angel Rama. Rama's *Lettered City* (1984), in which culture (principally writing) is related to the rise of the urban intelligentsia in Latin America, is a particular example of this. For him, urbanism and the role of the state constitute a central nexus from which lettered culture has sprung in Latin America since the colonial period. In other critical essays, Rama opens up the literary object to incorporate sub-genres of popular and mass culture like the *feuilleton*, as in his study of *gauchos malos* like Juan Moreira, and of the popular theatre of the Podestá brothers in Argentina, or the sub-regional cultures and literatures of the Andean region. García Canclini follows Rama's path and takes up the nexus of urbanization along with popular and mass culture to develop his own framework to account for what lies outside the prestige of "lettered" culture. As Rama did, García Canclini often offers panoramic historical and cultural views and generalizations to make sense of large and complex aspects of collective experience. This tradition is, needless to say, deeply rooted in a dialectical relation with the "Other," be it Empire/Colony, North/South or Centre/Periphery.[32]

Latinoamericanos, as its title indicates, inscribes once again the trope of the quest for an identity that is in constant transformation and under threat. The modernization and modernity that globalization has brought about at the turn of the century has mixed extreme poverty with rapid technological development. This has rendered the present and future confusing and impossible to predict in the absence of a social discourse to bind the intellectual to society. García Canclini's text attempts to fill this void and, despite its contradictions and limitations, uses the essay as a critical practice of public vocation. The essay thus becomes a social medium, a piece of writing in progress, posing questions and seeking answers; the essayist not yet ready to abandon the conceptual realm has combined the theoretical perspective with a pleasure for writing. Most importantly of all, he has taken on the task of narrating the experience of his people at the new crossroads of their perilous and peripheral modernity.

Our own reflection straddles García Canclini's perspective over a span of time that underwent profound changes in history and culture, leaving an imprint on his intellectual trajectory. In a movement similar to García Canclini's, in dialogue with some of his critics, we have striven to situate our own insights beyond deadening binarisms and attempted not to lose the empathic dimension of critical inquiry when engaged with issues that involve discrimination, exclusion, and struggles for self-determination.

Works Cited

Adorno, Theodor W. 1991. *The Culture Industry*. London: Routledge.

Beasley-Murray, Jon. 2000. Towards an Unpopular Cultural Studies: The Perspective of the Multitude. In *Cultura Popular: Studies in Spanish and Latin American Popular Culture*, ed. Shelley Godsland and Anne M. White, 27–45. Oxford: Peter Lang.

Beverley, John. 2003. La persistencia de lo subalterno. *Revista Iberoamericana* 69 (203): 335–42.

Bravo, Ana and Javier Ardúriz. 2000. *El ensayo o la seducción de lo posible*. Buenos Aires: Kapeluz.

———. 2003. Embajadas de la fuga y pensadores académicos. *Revista Iberoamericana* 203 (April–June):355–60.

Castañeda, Jorge G. 1993. *Utopia Unarmed: The Latin American Left After the Cold War*. New York: Vintage Books.

De la Campa, Román. 2000. On Border Artists and Transculturation: The Politics of Postmodern Performances and Latin America. In *Unforeseeable Americas: Questioning Hybridity in the Americas*, ed. Rita De Grandis and Zilà Bernd, 56–84. Atlanta: Rodopi.

De Grandis, Rita. 1998. The Néstor García Canclini Exchange. *Canadian Journal of Latin American and Caribbean Studies* 23 (46): 109–16.

———. 2004. A propos de " Gourmets multiculturels: Jouir du patrimoine des autres" de Néstor García Canclini. In *Proceedings of the International Conference "Aesthetics and Cultural Recycling, 26–28 April 2001, Université de Montréal*, Ed. Walter Moser.

Devés Valdés, Eduardo. 2002. Estudios culturales y pensamiento latinoamericano. *Cuadernos hispanoamericanos* 627:15–21.

Fernández Moreno, César (coord.). 1972. *América Latina en su literatura*. Mexico: Siglo XXI.

Follari, Roberto A. 2002. *Teorías débiles: Para una crítica de la deconstrucción y de los estudios culturales*. Rosario, Argentina: Homo Sapiens.

Franco, Jean. 2002. *The Decline and Fall of the Lettered City*. Cambridge, MA: Harvard Univ. Press.

García Canclini, Néstor. 1993. *Transforming Modernity: Popular Culture in Mexico*. Trans. Lidia Lozano. Austin, TX: Univ. of Texas Press.

———. 1995a. *Consumidores y ciudadanos: Conflictos multiculturales de la globalización*. Mexico: Grijalbo.

———. 1995b. *Hybrid Cultures*. Trans. Christopher Chiappari and Silvia López. Minneapolis: Univ. of Minnesota Press.

———. 1999. *La globalización imaginada*. Buenos Aires: Paidós.

———. 2000. La épica de la globalización y el melodrama de la interculturalidad. In *Nuevas Perspectivas desde/sobre América Latina: El desafío de estudios culturales*, ed. Mabel Moraña, 31–42. Santiago, Chile: Cuarto Propio.

———. 2002. *Latinoamericanos buscando lugar en este siglo*. Buenos Aires: Paidós.

Gilman, Claudia. 2003. *Entre la pluma y el fusil: Debates y dilemas del escritor revolucionario en América Latina*. Buenos Aires: Siglo XXI.

Giudici, Alberto. 2002. *Arte y política en los '60*. 2nd ed. Buenos Aires: Palais de Glace.

Huntington, Samuel P. 2004. *Who Are We? The Challenges to America's National Identity*. New York: Simon & Schuster.

Dorfman, Ariel & Armand Mattelart. 1975. *How to Read Donald Duck*. New York: International General.

Monsiváis, Carlos. 1998. Arnaldo Orfila ante la gratitud de los lectores? II y última. *La Jornada*, 17 January 1998. http:www.jornada.unam.mx/1998/ene98/980117/monsi. html(accessed 23 August 2004).

O'Connor, Alan. 2003. Consumers and Citizens: On Néstor García Canclini. *Pretexts: Literary and Cultural Studies* 12 (1): 103–20.

Paz-Soldán, Edmundo, and Debra Castillo, eds. 2001. *Latin American Literature and Mass Media*. New York: Garland.

Rama, Angel. 1982. *Transculturación narrativa en América Latina*. Mexico: Siglo XXI.

———. 1984. *La ciudad letrada*. Hanover, NH: Ediciones del Norte.

Río, Nela. 2004. *El espacio de la luz/The Space of Light*. Ed. and trans. Elizabeth Gamble Miller. Fredericton, NB: Broken Jaw.

Sarlo, Beatriz. 1994. El relativismo absoluto o como el mercado y la sociología reflexionan sobre estética. *Punto de vista* 48 (April): 27–31.

Stoll, David. 1999. *Rigoberta Menchú and the Story of All Poor Guatemalans*. Boulder, CO: Westview.

Torres, Luis A. 2003. *El exilio y las ruinas*. Santiago, Chile: RIL.

Trigo, Abril. 2000. Shifting Paradigms: From Transculturation to Hybridity: A Theoretical Critique. In *Unforeseeable Americas: Questioning Hybridity in the Americas*, ed. Rita De Grandis and Zilà Bernd, 85–111. Atlanta: Rodopi.

———. 2003. Review, *The Exhaustion of Difference: The Politics of Latin American Cultural Studies*, by Alberto Moreiras. *Revista Iberoamericana* 205 (Oct.–Dec): 1024–28.

Notes

1   I acknowledge these two Latin American-Canadian poets and include a sample of their poetic expression because it evokes the phenomenon of deterritorialization and cultural identity this study reflects upon; also because the authors' turn toward the poetic form resymbolizes their homelands – Chile and Argentina – in an attempt to bridge the dislocations provoked by the new adopted land –Canada. They participated in the special session entitled "Emigration, Exile: Towards a New Hybrid Identity," in which this work was first presented and discussed at the XL Conference of the Canadian Association of Hispanists, celebrated at the University of Manitoba, 29 May to 1 June 2004. The epigraph, as a paratext that appeals to the reader, situates our own reflection in close relationship with the work of the imagination, of which the essay is one of its genres. The proximity of the poetic and the critical brings together the objective and the subjective. In García Canclini's *Latinoamericanos buscando su lugar en este siglo*, the essayist moves away from the more objective realm of inquiry which characterises his previous work to the sphere of essay writing, binding the conceptual with his personal and intellectual experience.

2   César Fernández Moreno, poet and critic, son of the celebrated poet Baldomero Fernández Moreno. Between 1961 and 1964 he resided in Habana, Cuba, and then moved to France where he held the position of director of Unesco for Latin America and the Caribbean, between 1972 and 1978. He coordinated and wrote the Introduction of *América Latina*

en su literatura, a collaborative work of great resonance at the time, which assembled the most relevant literary, linguistic and cultural trends of the 1960s.

3   The approaches and themes include the transformations of literature in light of avant-garde movements and the crisis of realism. Of note is the famous essay "El barroco y neobarroco," by Severo Sarduy, which was to exert a long-lasting influence on all subsequent thinking about identity and modernity in Latin America, as demonstrated in the essays by Julio Ramos, Irlemar Chiampi, Mario Santí, and Roberto González Echevarría. Other themes included the presence of Latin American literature in other literatures, the linguistic plurality of these Latin American literatures, and the influence of the Amerindian languages of this continent. Themes of a more socio-cultural perspective are included, such as the renowned works "Literature and underdevelopment," by Antonio Cândido, a major essay on dependency theory applied to literary and cultural criticism; "The Conflict of Generations," by Adolfo Prieto, on the role of the intellectual and the differences between the European and the Latin American intellectual; and "La literatura y los nuevos lenguajes," by Juan José Saer, dealing with the impact and influence of media culture and its presence in avant-garde literature. *América Latina en su literatura* remains one of the most significant compendia of trends, critics and writers from a transnational Latin-American community of that decade.

4   As with subsequent translations, this one is mine.

5   Latin American philosophers and essayists have criticized Hegel's considerations on America as Eurocentric, amongst other things, because for Hegel American civilizations (particularly those in Mexico and Peru) were not fully developed; therefore, they should not be considered as part of the development of world history. America was a natural continent, its people rather inferior and with a tendency to disappear when in contact with people from higher civilizations. Hence, these American civilizations were excluded from "History, Reason and the Spirit," and not yet ready to assume a role in history. Estuardo Nuñez, in "Lo latinoamericano en otras literaturas," analyzes this aspect of Hegel's ideas, pointing to the fact that by 1825, Hegel already had a clear perception of the distinction between North and South America and under the influence of the travelers' readings from the eighteenth century, Hegel considered the American continent immature, weak and inferior in strength and capability in regard to Europe. According to Hegel, Americans lived like children and the Spirit was absent. However, in 1837, in his posthumously published *Lectures on the Philosophy of History*, Hegel conceptualized America as the continent of the future (Fernández Moreno 1972, 93–120).

6   "Lo latinoamericano en otras literaturas," by Estuardo Núñez is entirely devoted to how the New World has been portrayed in other literatures since the Conquest (Fernández Moreno 1972, 93–120).

7   Luis Cardoza y Aragón (1901–92) was a poet, essayist, storyteller and art critic. Born in Guatemala, during his youth he traveled and lived in France where he published his first work (*Luna Park*, 1932). In 1944 he returned to Guatemala and worked for the reformist government that had overthrown Jorge Ubico. In 1945, he founded and directed *Revista Guatemala* and The Guatemalan Movement for Peace as well as the House of Culture. During the administration of President Juan José Arévalo, he was ambassador in Norway, Sweden, and France. Later on, and due to the political history of the country, he lived in Mexico in exile until his death in 1992. As Jorge Castañeda contends, he was until his death perhaps Latin America's foremost art critic. During the time he was forced to leave Guatemala for exile in Mexico in 1954, "he served as mentor, foster parent, and source of consolation to two generations of Guatemalan dissidents and revolutionaries" (Castañeda 1993, 91). The jury of the Luis Cardoza y Aragón Prize included Rigoberta Menchú, a symbol of indigenous struggle and spokesperson whose testimony has inspired so much debate in the 1980s and 1990s due to the veracity of her testimony (see Stoll 1999).

8   About the problem of the chronological limits of these two decades, much has been discussed. Oscar Terán's *Nuestros años sesentas* (1991) is a fundamental work for the Argentine intellectual field. There is a resurgence of interest in these decades: there is particularly a consensus for Latin America in circumscribing a cultural-ideological unit around the end of the 1960s and the beginning of the 1970s, which corresponds to the time frame of the UNESCO project mentioned. See Claudia Gilman (2003). The resurgence of interest in the 1960s is also evident in art exhibits throughout Latin America. In October/November 2002, in Chile, *Las Condes* Cultural Foundation organized a major exhibition around the 1960s. In September/October 2002, in Argentina, the *Palais de Glace* organized an exhibition entitled *Arte y política en los '60*. Also in November/December 2003, MALBA (Museo Arte Latinoamericano de Buenos Aires) exhibited the works of, among others, Jorge de la Vega, a painter of the generation of the 1960s.

9   Jorge G. Castañeda explains that Latin American leftist intellectuals have been traditionally powerful because they have been chosen by governments and the rest of the world as interlocutors. For example, they helped to conceptualize the populist regimes of the 1930s and 1940s. Although they never dictated policies, they exerted great influence in preserving their accomplishments in the memory of future generations. In the 1960s, as the Cuban Revolution became isolated, intellectuals came largely to substitute for governments and embassies. Every Latin American intellectual "worthy of his pen, canvas, or songbook made the journey to Havana at one point or another" (Castañeda 1993, 184). As Gabriel García Márquez affirmed:

> The definition of a Latin American left intellectual became the unconditional defense of Cuba. And the Cubans, through their own mechanisms, determined who complied with its solidarity, and who did not, taking advantage of the situation that prevailed for many intellectuals in their countries. The second-tier intellectuals, without opportunities in their own lands, found a way of acquiring power: by becoming the paladins of solidarity. Entire pilgrimages of second-rate intellectuals wended their way to Havana with the purpose of displacing the front-line intellectuals from their positions of leadership. (Castañeda 1993, 184–185)

10   The essay "The Centaur of Genres," as understood by Ana Bravo and Javier Adúriz, is a critical form closer to theory in its pursuit of truth and its use of concepts, and linked to rhetoric in its persuasive intent. Furthermore, the essayist has a view of his/her own, a strabismic gaze, as Sartre would say, which allows him/her to see what others don't. Because of this intensely personal viewpoint, the essay manifests a singular style (Bravo and Adúriz 2000).

11   Other questions that García Canclini (2000) raises are: "how should the economic and cultural integration of Latin American societies be regarded within the re-composition of the global market?" (68); "can we continue to talk about Latin America or have we entered a postnational era?" (30); and "under the trans-nationalization of cultural markets, what would the profits be for Latin-American countries?" (30).

12   In *La globalización imaginada*, he considers globalization a key concept and develops it using a trans-/interdisciplinary methodology based on notions and concepts from various fields of knowledge, such as the social sciences, the humanities and economics. For example, he uses the concept of metaphor, claiming that it has more explanatory power than conceptual tools from the social sciences. At the same time, he has moved from his concept of hybridity to one of cultural recycling. He has done this to describe more accurately the status of the series of artwork installations exhibited on the San Diego-Tijuana border by the avant-garde group *In-Site*. We indicated that the incorporation of new notions such as metaphor and cultural recycling into his methodology suffers

a certain conceptual precariousness, particularly when compared and contrasted with the concept of hybridity, which is more developed. Metaphor and cultural recycling are effective as descriptive instruments, but these terms appear to be used interchangeably. The question remains: To what extent does his general approach to a sociology of culture become impregnated, whether consciously or not, with the ideology of the reproduction of capitalist values, even as this perspective attempts to dislodge those values? For a full analysis of this critique (see de Grandis, 2004).

13   This can be seen particularly in regard to *Transforming Modernity: Popular Cultures in Mexico* (Casa de las Américas 1981 Prize), and of *Hybrid Cultures* (Latin American Studies Association 1990 Book Award).

14   Interestingly, Alan O'Connor also considers that García Canclini's earlier works were much more progressive than his later work. He affirms that García Canclini's *La producción simbólica* (1979), published by the leftist publisher Siglo Veintiuno and much of which was later reformulated in his *Hybrid Cultures* (1990), "decidedly" belonged to the radical use of the theory (of thinkers such as Althusser, Bourdieu, Marx, Lukacs, Freud, and Lenin) that occurred in the 1970s (O'Connor 2003, 104).

15   Alfonso Reyes was a Mexican humanist, poet, diplomat, translator and essayist whose intellectual curiosity made him one of the most prolific Latin American writers in the twentieth century. In Fernández Moreno's *América* the works of Alfonso Reyes are mentioned in most of the essays of the volume; for example, Guillermo Sucre in "La nueva crítica" mentions the important role of Alfonso Reyes in the development of literary criticism. For Reyes criticism was inherent to Man's nature and was an act of creation that carried with it a poetics that looked for the revelation of a critical gaze (Fernández Moreno 1972, 259). Arnaldo Orfila was an Argentinean who settled in Mexico and became a key figure in the development of the left-oriented publishing industry. He was first the director of Fondo de Cultura Económica between 1948 and 1958, and later of Siglo XXI Editores, producing a decisive cultural transformation in the direction of the editorial perspective of these companies. He promoted the most representative trends of the Cuban Revolution, the Boom writers, dependency theory, and the theology of liberation. As Carlos Monsiváis affirms, Orfila was a supporter of revolutionary movements, disseminated orthodox, critical and heterodox perspectives that will have a lasting influence in the formation of the intellectual generations of Latin America. In his half-century of work as editor, Orfila was an actor and a witness of first rank in the cultural life of Latin America, which was determined by the culture of the book and also by the scarcity of the culture of the book. Orfila believed in the intelligence of the reader. He died in Mexico at the age of 101.

16   Spanish publishers have a greater rate of production and distribution than Mexican or Argentinean publishing houses. The economic power and the distribution of the Spanish publishing industry has made it possible to reach a large transnational readership with not only the celebrated "Boom" writers (Cortázar, Fuentes, García Márquez, Vargas Llosa), but also with lesser-known authors. Interestingly, these companies limit the publication and circulation of Latin-American writers in their own countries because only a percentage (70 per cent) of what is published in Spain gets to Latin America; in contrast, only 3 per cent of what is published in Latin America reaches Spain. Furthermore, Latin America seems to provide fiction but not theory. For instance, the publication of social or cultural thought seems to be only of domestic interest in the countries that generate this type of knowledge, but seems to lack interest for a wider readership. A common Ibero-American cultural space of production and circulation is carried out in a very asymmetrical manner (García Canclini 2002, 49–50).

17   García Canclini does not mention nor analyze any particular work by either José Carlos Mariátegui or José María Arguedas; rather, he brings them to the fore for the general

thrust of his argument. His intent is to draw a comparison taking into consideration a rethinking of the national question within globalization.

18 Eduardo Devés Valdés, while examining cultural studies in relation to what he calls "pensamiento latinoamericano," argues that identity and modernity are two of its major topics, and that García Canclini's work embraces both of them. This is also central to Nelly Richard's critical practice. Devés Valdés concludes that the conceptual map of Latin American thought within cultural studies has oscillated between a critique of modernity/modernization and a valorization of identities. Although these two aspects of a tradition of Latin American thought are not exclusive of cultural studies, they have had a great part in its development (Devés Valdés 2002, 15–21).

19 In *Who Are We? The Challenges to America's National Identity*, Samuel P. Huntington (2004) affirms that in the two years between 2000 and 2002, the Hispanic population in the United States had increased by almost 10 per cent and had become larger than the Afro-American.

20 In addition to external influences, the continent has continued to experience new ethnic-political configurations internally, such as those of the government of Ecuador under the presidency of Lucio Edwin Gutiérrez Borbúa and the government of Venezuela under the Hugo Chávez regime. These politicians, by their ethnic makeup (*mestizo* from indigenous and black ancestries), break from the former principally white-European tradition of political leadership. Gutiérrez Borbúa (b. 1957) is a soldier and politician. He was a colonel who became president of Ecuador in 2003. Having participated in a military coup that overthrew the previous government, he acceded to the presidency by election and with the strong support of the indigenous communities. Hugo Chávez was also a soldier who participated in a military movement in 1994 that resulted in the overthrow of President Pérez. Chávez was elected in 1998, re-elected (or, as they say in Venezuela, "re-legitimated") in 2000; he will govern until 2006. Even Argentina, under the Menem (of Lebanese heritage) Administration points to the postmodern turn towards increasingly heterogeneous ethnicities; this turn could be further nuanced or developed in terms of class or region. Examples of such figures would be Labour Party leader Lula, who became president in Brazil, and Nestor Kirchner, a premier of the remote southern and non-influential province of Santa Cruz, who became president in Argentina.

21 Interestingly and coincidentally, Alan O'Connor also notices, particularly in *Consumers and Citizens*, a conservative turn in García Canclini's approach. The work was published in Spanish in 1995.

22 As is well known, he and Jesús Martín Barbero are among the most influential critics of this period to take up Angel Rama's predicament about the need of the writer and critic to go beyond the elitist culture. Their intellectual projects re-evaluated the Frankfurt School/Adornian theory of mass culture and the culture industry, as articulated in dependency theory in the 1960s and 1970s. Edmundo Paz-Soldán and Debra Castillo argue that, in an interview from the early 1980s and in addition to his earlier formulations, Rama suggested the need to go beyond the lettered city because "both the writer and the critic belong to the street and not to the university cloisters. Their real world is the world of society; it is the world of communication" (qtd. in Paz-Soldán and Castillo 2001, 7).

23 The devils of Ocumicho in the region of Michoacán became one of the most successful ceramic products in all of Mexico in the 1980s. Through the humorous elements imprinted on them, García Canclini argues that these parodying tactics allowed the communities to symbolize their intercultural conflicts and gave them an imaginary resolution. Although relatively recent (1960s), these objects provided an economic explanation and related to two ancient myths. In the 1960s, the lack of rain made some nearby *ejido* peasants take over some of the more fertile soil. As a consequence, the inhabitants of Ocumicho had to expand their pottery production and increase their sales

to compensate for what they had lost in the countryside. Added to this explanation are two myths; one refers to the devil, which was an important figure in pre-Cortés beliefs of the region as well as during the colonial period. The second myth refers to Marcelino, an orphan and homosexual child whose grandmother trained as a ceramist and who began making "beautiful figures." At first he made angels, and then, following an encounter with the devil in a ravine, devils. Seeing that his sales increased considerably and that he was invited to handicraft fairs in Mexico City and New York, his neighbors learned and perfected the technique, reproducing and altering the images even after Marcelino died. Then different members of the community give diverse emphases to the story and update it when telling these accounts (1995, 158–61).

24　At LASA 2001, John Beverley made public the dissolution of the Subaltern Studies Group, which had been formed and announced at LASA 1994 in Atlanta. He notes that, paradoxically, since the Subaltern Studies Group dissolved, the subaltern seems to appear everywhere in academic discourse. It confronts the intellectual with the task of affirming why the project continues, and why the intellectual is doing this (Beverley 2003, 335–36).

25　He explains that, despite the fact of the enormous local contribution to the music industry, this industry has not helped to improve the economic positions of Latin American societies. As shown by George Yúdice, due to the use of cheap labor in short-term contracts and the very low-cost of production, these culture industries have become *maquiladoras*, whether in the U.S. or in Latin American countries. The underpaid are the *Latinos* and members of other ethnic groups (García Canclini 2002, 59). In "The García Canclini Exchange" (Grandis, forthcoming), García Canclini's hybridity theory places more importance on processes of cultural reproduction rather than on the subaltern. For him culture production is more about hybridity than subalternity. He is more interested in analyzing culture in terms of reproduction and/or resistance; in fact, his conception of culture oscillates between these two poles, reproduction on one side and resistance on the other. When referring to the role of the subaltern, the subaltern is not as central as the processes of hybridization one is engaged in. O'Connor also points to this ambivalence, suggesting that García Canclini's analysis of popular culture makes use of Bourdieu's sense of reproduction of dominant culture and Gramsci's role of culture as resistance.

26　Jean Franco notes that Armand Mattelart and Ariel Dorfman's *How to Read Donald Duck* (1971) was a highly influential study because it showed the subliminal messages encoded in Disney comics and their insidious influence. For Latin American critics, in the 1960s and '70s, the "free flow of information" predicated by the U.S. was perceived suspiciously because the superiority of the U.S. media demonstrated that this flow was unidirectional: from North to South. Nevertheless, this position progressively gave way to a more-nuanced evaluation of the media and new forms of cultural literacy. In Latin America, García Canclini and Jesús Martín Barbero carried on this new perspective (Franco 2002, 188).

Jean Franco contends that the publication in translation of *How to Read Donald Duck* was prohibited in the U.S. and cites in reference Frank Kermode's *Not Entitled* (1995). (See endnote 43, Franco 2002, 284) However, we discovered an English translation published in the U.S. in 1975 by David Kunzle, with an introduction by the authors in exile, and since then several reprints.

27　As when Adorno affirms that the culture industry intentionally integrates the consumer from above;

> to the detriment of both it forces together the spheres of high and low art.... The seriousness of high art is destroyed in speculation about its efficacy; the seriousness of the lower perishes with the civilizational constraints imposed on the rebellious resistance inherent within it as long as social control was not yet total. (Adorno 1991, 85)

28   Jon Beasley-Murray notes that the populism of cultural studies on globalization means a democratization of culture because it pays attention to oral histories, to testimonies of ordinary people, and to women; all of which are conceptualized as "the people." However, this recuperative effort falls short because it substitutes a concept of culture for an analysis of power, and so tends to downplay the importance of ideology (Beasley-Murray 2000, 29). Moreover, in the abundance of literature on populism in Latin America, the key role played by the incorporation of the intellectual as one of the main categories of society brought into the political sphere of populism is well known, though their role in the left goes well beyond populism. Another aspect in which populism is at stake is in regard to mass culture, the most powerful rival of print culture. Critics like Beatriz Sarlo call "cultural populism" the type of socio-cultural criticism that reduces all artistic expression to a question of function and considers that the market is the ideal space of pluralism. Although she agrees with doing away with the hierarchy of high/low culture, she does not agree with a farewell to the lack of discrimination, because to not consider questions of value leads to an implicit collaboration with neoliberalism and takes away the oppositional function of art (Sarlo 1994).

29   Those involved in the Latin American Subaltern Group, such as Beverley, understand the democratization of culture as a displacement from the sphere of high culture, which in turn entails a move from the canon of national literatures to a more popular, heterogeneous and multifaceted subject which identifies itself as the subaltern (Beverley 2003, 336).

30   Abril Trigo, in reviewing Alberto Moreiras's *The Exhaustion of Difference: The Politics of Latin American Cultural Studies* points to the limitations of post-structuralist, Derridean criticism because it forecloses all possibility to its own criticism. For Trigo, the emphasis that Moreiras places on the cognitive priority of thinking in his rhetorics, argumentation and discursive logic is what requires critical analysis because it produces a continuous return on itself, lacking any exteriority (Trigo 2003, 1024–28). In the same vein, Román de la Campa warns of a radical position consisting of a theory that manifests itself mainly though a powerful verbose apparatus (de la Campa 2003, 359).

31   This is the case in Juan José Saer's "La literatura y los nuevos lenguajes." For Saer, mass culture, although a stimulus for fantasy, is the mortal enemy of literature. If one takes into consideration the power of the media, its extent and the uses made by powerful groups, it will be evident to what extent a literature that mediates mass culture may disappear and become no more than a covering ideology. In Latin America, the literature of the twentieth century has been written in a parallel process to the creation of mass society and mass culture: writers are closely linked to mass culture because of their origin and formation. Even though they may keep an ambivalent relation with mass culture, the writers may sometimes presuppose, without a precise ideological basis, a total rejection of it. This ambivalence usually results from the fact that many intellectuals who work in the media to make ends meet make reference to mass communication only to express their contempt, for mass media presents a society frozen in its false universality (Fernández Moreno 1972, 301–16).

32   Abril Trigo (2000) studies García Canclini's hybridity paradigm in relation to Rama's transculturation theory, and Román de la Campa (2000) compares it with Fernando Ortiz's *Contrapunteo cubano del tabaco y del azúcar*. I examine García Canclini's cultural recycling within the transculturation paradigm of both Ortiz and Rama (de Grandis, 2004).

Sirena Wears Her Sadness Like a Beautiful Dress: Literature and Globalization in Latin America

Catherine Den Tandt, Independent Scholar

The limits and termination of literature, not its restitution, are today the project of a Latin American cultural or literary politics and a key component of any intervention into the neoliberal market. – Brett Levinson, *The Ends of Literature*

Since the early 1990s, many of the key debates involving culture have revolved around the question of globalization and global capitalism. It is hardly possible to open a journal, read the program of an upcoming conference, or glance through the cultural section of a daily newspaper without finding some reference to culture and globalization. These discussions seem to move in two seemingly disconnected directions. The first can be described as an old-fashioned, almost preglobalized response to the perceived pressures of globalization on local, national cultures. Academics, journalists, and politicians involved in this project are not opposed to globalization, or to the neo-liberal economic policies that sustain it. They merely argue that culture should not be considered a commodity like any other and that cultural expression (meaning "national culture") must remain outside the purview of trade agreements that otherwise ensure the free circulation of goods throughout the world (see, for example, Grant and Wood 2004). This vision is "old-fashioned" because, even though it admits that culture is an industry, it perceives culture as fundamentally separate from the market, and its proponents call on national governments to protect their cultural patrimony through legislation and activism before international organizations such as UNESCO.

Apparently disconnected from the protectionist/nationalist stance I have just described, but equally present in academic publications and the media, is the notion, put forth by practitioners of cultural studies, that political and cultural hegemonies no longer congregate in and around the (national) state. In this view, and here I am loosely quoting/translating Colombian social scientist Santiago Castro Gómez, power has become transnational and, as such, capital no longer has national connotations. The social is thus configured by post-national and post-traditional relations empowered by new information technologies. Accordingly, the cultural industries have become one of the most or perhaps the most important force of production of contemporary capitalism. That which is produced and marketed today is no longer nature (labour) converted into "exchange value," as it was for

Marx, but rather information and entertainment. Rather than "produce packaged articles," the new economy "packages information articulated as merchandise" and the production and reproduction of capital now depend on the control that corporations exercise on images and representations (Castro Gómez 2003, 349). In the discussions of culture and globalization that subscribe to the analysis I have just summarized, culture drives and supports the market.

While these two views of culture and globalization (protectionist/ nationalist vs. culture/market) appear disconnected or even contradictory, I argued in an earlier conference version of this paper ("Inversiones culturales") that they are actually quite compatible. This would explain why, in Quebec, where I lived for six years, the left-leaning nationalist/ separatist party, the Parti Québécois, and the generally neo-liberal Parti Libéral du Québec both follow the same protectionist/nationalist agenda in the area of culture. What I want to note for the purposes of the following discussion on Latin American literature and globalization, however, is that in all this talk of culture and globalization, one rarely finds a mention of literature.

Certainly, studies such as Peter S. Grant and Chris Wood's *Blockbusters and Trade Wars* (2004), or the economic history *Creative Industries: Contracts Between Art and Commerce* (Caves 2001), which trace the growing centralization of the culture industries as well as the increasingly powerful function of cultural "gatekeepers," include some discussion of the book industry, of convergence in publishing as well as in film, television, music, and broadcasting. But most of their attention goes to the latter four areas of cultural production and, to a lesser extent, to the print media. Literature as an institution and the publishing of literary books are treated in much less detail. Discussions about literature in the debates on culture and globalization in cultural studies or globalization studies are often absent altogether. Numerous anthologies on culture and globalization either fail to mention literature at all or mention it only briefly (see, for example, Appadurai 2000; Tomlinson 1999; Jameson and Miyoshi 1998; Lowe and Lloyd 1997; Wilson and Dissanayake 1996). Given the importance that cultural studies has placed on the exploration of identity, the key role that literature has played with regard to questions of identity, and the fact that many cultural studies practitioners are literary critics, this seems surprising.

In fact, there is, at least on the surface, a fairly simple reason for this absence of discussion about literature in cultural studies. Critics of globalized culture no longer consider literature to be an adequate or valuable instrument for the study of contemporary society. *Globalization: The*

Reader, published in 2000 by Routledge, for example, does not include literature in its list of "principal agents" of globalized culture, citing pop music, television, cinema, and tourism instead (Beynon and Dunkerley 2000, 18). In her discussion of globalization and intellectual property rights, Caren Irr (2001, 774) points out the following:

To date, most theories of globalization have granted a prominent role to nonliterary culture or "media" (along with information technology, finance capital, reorganization of labour, declining sovereignty of nation states, and other elements) when they describe contemporary developments.... But in few of these discussions of globalization does the literary medium figure centrally; film, food, music, and fashion have been more common topics.

Irr notes that while some attention to literature as a mode of representation can still be found in discussions of postcolonial identities, one rarely "finds scholarship bringing a broadly defined materialist account of policy together with reflection on the economics of literature in particular" (774).

There are several reasons why cultural studies has abandoned literature as a means of understanding and analyzing contemporary culture. Literature, especially in the case of Latin America and the Caribbean, as critics such as Angel Rama, Doris Sommer, Antonio Benítez-Rojo, Edouard Glissant, and J. Michael Dash have established, functioned throughout the nation-building process and up to the end of the twentieth century as an elite discourse, always assumed by intellectuals, writers and critics alike, to play a central role in the elaboration of societal models, in the construction and promotion of regional and national identities. Today, the role and function of literature seem to have changed, or are perceived to have changed, in part because, as cultural studies critics explain it, the very nature of culture and identity in advanced capitalism has changed.

Again, according to Castro Gómez (2003, 349), culture has become a repertoire of signs and symbols, technically produced according to particular interests, which are then diffused throughout the planet by the information media. This symbolic universe, disconnected from tradition, begins to define the way millions of people around the globe feel, think, desire, and imagine their identities (349). Because the reproduction of capital has taken on "rasgos decididamente 'culturales'" (350) ("features that are decidedly 'cultural'")[1] in the new economy, "culture" has become the linchpin that connects social structures with the subjects that produce them (351). Literature is now only one element in this vast repertoire of signs and symbols and, as a vehicle of identity, it competes badly with other forms of mass consumer culture such as popular music, film, television, and consumerism itself.

As Román de la Campa makes clear in his account of Latin American cultural studies, the shift away from elite discourse (away from literature) throughout the 1980s and 1990s allowed for the democratization of contemporary cultural discourse, as well as for a better understanding of our contemporary world, especially in Latin America (see La Campa 1999). As Brett Levinson (2001, 2) remarks: "The death of literature ... evidently signals the descent of high or bourgeois culture and the opening to new works, an emerging class of formerly suppressed creators or subjects, and authentically democratic pluralisms." At the same time, however, literature's fall has made it a marginal "cultural player":

[L]iterature, which once occupied a privileged position within the institutions of civil society, and therefore within the state itself, must now battle for that rank and legitimacy with other forms of creation, above all, mass and popular culture. What we call cultural studies is hence born, at least, in part, from literature's ruin: not because literature has been liquidated but because alternative cultural labor [sic] now vies with literature for the role that was once played, or that was imagined to be played ... by literature exclusively. (Levinson 2001, 2)

Literature would seem to be only peripherally involved in the process of identity formation, and therefore not an important site for discussions about identity in the context of globalization. It has been supplanted or replaced both as object of study and as elite philosophical discourse by popular mass culture and its scientific/philosophical discourse, cultural studies.

In Latin America, critics of contemporary culture such as Néstor García Canclini tell us over and over again that the work of identity construction today, like globalization itself, is a kind of mobile "performance," a dance that brings together transnational capital, political and cultural democracy, and an infinite number of identitarian choices and options (see, for example, García Canclini 1995, 2001). Together with other critics such as George Yúdice, García Canclini sees these new forms (or newly recognized forms) of identity construction within postnational globalization in an optimistic light, as the site of new opportunities for traditionally marginalized groups. As I myself wrote in an essay on Caribbean literature (Den Tandt 1999) some years ago, literature in this new context is an impoverished medium, clumsy in a world dominated by electronic and visual media, elitist, and unable to fully respond to the needs and demands of cultural capital and its citizen consumers.

At the same time, much of contemporary literature in the Latin American and Hispanic Caribbean contexts seems effectively to have abandoned the project of identity, at least as it was previously conceived in colonized or postcolonial spaces; that is, as a project to construct subjectivities grounded in geographic territories and landscapes, language, race, and nation. The most successful articulation of identity as project was clearly the nation but, in fact, literature has been central to a series of important paradigms of identity in Latin America and the Caribbean. In the perception of writers and intellectuals, literature was considered to be a dominant component for the construction of a public sphere. And yet, in her introduction to an anthology of new Puerto Rican literature, writer Mayra Santos Febres (1997, 19) declares that the primary "graphic" of her generation is the anonymous and uniform urban space of the city, rather than the nation. Santos Febres comments that the speakers in these texts "no son colectivos y, si pertenecen a algún grupo por razones sociológicas azarosas, no se asumen como miembros de ninguna colectividad. Si son homosexuales, negros, mujeres o trabajadores, lo son por obra del azar y no por condición determinante y suficiente para la fragua de una identidad" (*Mal[h]ab[l]ar* 19) ["are not part of a collective, and if they belong to some group by pure sociological chance, they do not take up their collective identities. If they are homosexual, black, women or workers, it is by chance and not according to any determining condition sufficient for the forging of an identity"].

The critic José Eduardo González (2001, 187) cites Chilean writer Alberto Fuguet saying something similar when he writes of "nuestros escritores hispanoamericanos que escriben en español, pero que no se sienten representantes de alguna ideología y ni siquiera de sus propios países" ["our Latin American authors who write in Spanish but who don't feel that they represent any particular ideology or even their own countries"]. For their part, Debra Castillo and Edmundo Paz-Soldán (2001, 11) refer to a group of "hyper media-conscious young writers" like Fuguet and the Peruvian Jaime Bayly as "the alienated Latin American youth whose idea of MaCondo is probably something more like an apartment in Miami than a godforsaken town in northern Colombia." Even more than "anti-national," this literature tends to simply disregard questions of place altogether, as well as any sense of a collective project (political, racial, gendered, national, etc.).

One striking example of such literature is Pedro Juan Gutiérrez's 1999 *El rey de La Habana*, a novel with a stark and often brutal representation of urban life in Havana that has very little to do with any recognizable form of previous Cuban or Caribbean literature. Although the hypermarginalized characters in the book are admirable, even heroic, in their ability to survive and make lives (so to speak) for themselves in the middle of a devastating urban environment that just happens to be Havana, Cuba, the novel provides no way out, aesthetically, politically, or philosophically; nor does it comment on its own desperate representation of contemporary life. In novels like Colombian Jorge Franco Ramos's *Rosario Tijeras* (2000), and Mexican Xavier Velasco's *Diablo Guardián* (2003), the characters lead lives of violence and substance abuse, relying solely on each other; they are unable and unwilling to integrate into a mainstream existence whose institutions (family, police, government, religion) are all quite normally, yet grotesquely, corrupt, regardless of ideological bent or political affiliation.

The alienation from society evident in these texts, where bonds of affiliation and loyalty exist only between individual, equally marginalized characters, is partially explained by writer Pedro Antonio Valdez (2000, 109) in his discussion of new short fiction from the Dominican Republic: "Enmarcados en un país 'abierto al mundo,' puesto en cuatro para recibir la penetración del neoliberalismo ... no es extraño que los cuentistas más recientes presenten en sus textos a un ciudadano perdido en el detritus del mundo, identificado con los objetos y el onirismo que los dueños del mundo nos rentan a alto precio" ["Framed by a country 'open to the world,' on all fours waiting to be penetrated by neo-liberalism ... it is hardly surprising that these newest writers introduce in their texts a citizen lost in the detritus of the world, identified with the objects and the dreams rented to us at high prices by the owners of the world"]. For Valdez, this literature is a direct response to Latin America's state of crisis in the neo-liberal era. Disillusion in the face of greater poverty and insecurity, rather than the prosperity promised by the engineers of free trade and globalization, is thus reflected in the region's literature. As Eduardo González (2001, 185) notes, one finds a kind of pessimism or disenchantment that recognizes that the thing called democracy is also the result of greater capitalist penetration in Latin America.

At the same time, however, González reads the alienation evident in the new literature as the response of the Latin American *letrado* ("man of letters") who, stripped of his traditional authority in globalized culture, reacts in the face of market-based postnationalism (185–87). The reaction of the dis-authorized *letrado* differs radically from the optimism of cultural studies and its practitioners. Toppled from his throne and profoundly disaffected, the *letrado* feels removed from the 'myths' of national culture (González 2001, 186), distanced from a society that, meanwhile, is dancing the dance of identity in more propitious settings such as film, television, and popular music.

These are, in a sense, two quite different explanations for the alienation (from the nation, collective identity, and political projects) present in this literature. The first, with some fine-tuning to explain the Cuban scenario, implies that literature in fact continues to reflect local socio-political realities, a kind of mimetic response to the crisis of neo-liberalism, while the second focuses more on the (sour) reaction of the disenfranchised writer. While both of these explanations provide a plausible and satisfactory reading of recent Latin American literature, they only partially address the issues at stake in this discussion. This is because they fail to exploit fully the fact that this literature "has abandoned the project of identity." We have seen, from cultural studies, that representation, and therefore identity, is the linchpin of globalized capital. In globalization, the ability to create, manipulate, and market identity is synonymous with power. Having abandoned the project of identity (to film, popular music, television, and consumerism), this literature has rendered itself powerless, and in doing so "it has shown itself to be fully responsive to globalization," doing exactly what is expected of it. Any discussion of "alienation" must take into account the highly nuanced position of literature within globalized culture. In fact, Latin American literature fits right in. It either produces identities for sale through historical nostalgia (Rosario Ferré's *Eccentric Neighbourhoods* (1998) and *House of the Lagoon* (1995) are examples of what Chris Bongie (2002) has called, in another context, the "postcolonial middlebrow") or it simply abandons the very project (identity) that made it "literature."

This is why Brett Levinson (2001, 27) speaks of the "death of literature" in the era of globalization. He defines literariness as "the condition of novel articulations (the 'in the name of' that makes a political affirmation possible), hence of novel communities and communal projects which would craft those senses." Later on, he says, "If there is no literature, then there is no politics, no activity, no activism, no 'in the name of'" (155). I would add that, conversely, if there is no politics, activity, or activism, then there is no literature. The new literature I am referring to here (which Levinson would argue can no longer be called literature) rejects its own "literariness," because it rejects its own "myth-making function."

I want to argue, by reading examples of recent fiction from Latin America, that the refusal to participate in the "myth-making function" makes these texts fully complicit with globalization (they behave as expected). At the same time, however, precisely because they "no longer matter," they offer a number of observations about the ways in which globalization and global capital function. This is more than the mimetic reflection of the neo-liberal crisis in Latin America and more than the sour grapes of the *letrado*, although both of these aspects are involved in this process. Literature is, in a sense, the "outsider who is inside," and because of this, literary texts may be able to make precisely the kind of observations that are at risk in cultural studies, which always faces the danger of forgetting that capitalism in globalized times acquires a symbolic dimension (Castro Gómez 2003, 352). In other words, because cultural studies analyzes the ways in which contemporary imaginaries are produced, distributed, and consumed by eliminating the distance between itself (as "science") and "common sense" (351), it always risks becoming just another object of consumption. The book of fiction, of course, is always already an object of consumption. It has finally admitted this completely, which is why it is "dead" and also why attempts to address the question of aesthetic or artistic value today (Sarlo 1994; Bongie 2003) are fraught with tension. Paradoxically, it is this very "death" of literature that makes it an insider and an outsider at the same time. Santiago Castro Gómez, whose defense and explanation of cultural studies I have quoted extensively, shows us that we cannot return to the traditional social sciences and humanities to gather knowledge about our contemporary world. As separate and discrete methods of social analysis, they are no longer sufficient to address culture today. He argues that cultural studies is the necessary knowledge form of globalization, and I agree. Nonetheless, I want to suggest that the literary text, precisely because it has lost its "literariness" and is no longer involved in the construction of collective identities, may be a particularly appropriate place to seek greater understanding of the philosophical and political workings of globalization and global capitalism themselves.

   In the section that follows, I would like to begin tracing the ways in which one example of this new literature, Mayra Santos Febres's *Sirena Selena vestida de pena* (2000), talks to us about globalization. I want to introduce my reading of the novel with a discussion of Brett Levinson's *The Ends of Literature* (2001), a book of criticism I have found very useful throughout this study. Levinson's book is key for Latin American studies because it sidesteps the cultural studies/traditional (literary) studies divide that has dominated the field in recent years and allows us to think about literature and globalization in new ways. Levinson declares literature "dead" in a very particular philosophical, political, and social context. He traces literature's fall as "public topos," as an artefact that "lends itself to the construction of the private or exclusive individual: ground and telos of both bourgeois society and the modern state" (21). The question he asks is, of course, "Where do we go from here?" As Levinson points out, the promise of cultural studies, which is the promise of a postmodern politics (the deconstruction of the hegemonic subject and the empowerment of previously marginalized subjectivities), and in Latin America, the promise of postdictatorship and democracy (the splintering of the public sphere to make way for new social movements), has not been fulfilled, giving way, instead, to an almost completed neo-liberalism (5). As such, the period of "transition" (from totalitarianism and dictatorship, from the hegemony of literature), which is represented by postmodern fragmentary thought and praxis, has also lost its political legitimacy. We are now experiencing, according to Levinson, a "transition from transition," with signifies the decline of both ventures of postmodernity: the exhaustion of totalitarianism as well as its debunking, meaning "fragmentation as open labyrinth or project" (7). In this "transition from transition," the greatest dangers are the risk of a return to "statist thinking" or a kind of endless repetition of transition itself (6–7).

Levinson concludes his introduction with the following question:

What to do, what to write, when the differences between the literary and the cultural, between the state-form and the poststate, between totality and fragmentation slip away and lose legitimacy – yet, when any effort to make a transition beyond them, to pronounce their conclusion, cannot help but violently (or silently) resurrect and reestablish their ineffective corpses? (2001, 9)

Rather than answer his question, Levinson shows how boom and postboom texts (up to 1991) from Latin America announce or foreshadow the cultural, political, and economic "transition" of which he speaks. For Levinson, the boom "should be understood as the last great literary movement of the West and as the expression and thematization of the end of that movement" (28). However, he insists that literature, although dead, must remain part of a "post-transition" politics (when and if such a politics can be articulated) because transition itself requires the death of literature over and over again: "Transition, then, is a question not of turning to literature/literariness, or of shutting it down, but of never ceasing to turn from/to literature as that closure" (54). It is no coincidence that the chapter where this is most clearly explicated is his chapter on Rigoberta Menchú's testimonial novel *Me llamo Rigoberta Menchú y así me nació la conciencia* (1985), which is, of course, the key text of "transition," showing both the death of literature and its constant rebirth, only to die again. In his discussion of the testimonial genre, Levinson says: "Needed for a contemporary cultural politics is another word, an alternative name (an alternative to 'literature') for the thing called literature, as well as for the role of the 'literary,' one that would index the limit of literature's function, and hence mourn it" (2001, 155).

What I would like to suggest in my reading of the Santos Febres novel is that the newest fiction emerging from Latin America (beginning, more or less, in the early 1990s) may, paradoxically, announce itself as this "alternative to literature." One of the most compelling "antiliterary" traits of this new literature is that it no longer takes itself quite so seriously. The writers themselves, and this is clearly evident in their fiction, do not show much interest in defining their craft as "high" or "low" art. As Edmundo Paz-Soldán notes in a discussion of Alberto Fuguet's *Por favor, rebobinar* (1994), this generation of writers is distrustful of ideological positions and promises of social liberation, comfortable in the world of "fast food and fast culture," and seriously concerned with the laws of the market (Paz-Soldán 2002, 43). Mayra Santos Febres makes the point even more clearly: "Ahora con esta novela estoy de lleno en la economía global donde hay que atacar todos los mercados. Así que poesía, cuento, novela, de todo. Hay que pagar la luz y el agua" (García Cuevas and Vicens 2000, 79) ["Now, with this novel, I am fully within the global economy where we have to attack all markets. So poetry, the short story, the novel, everything. One has to pay the bills"].

This is not to say that these writers (or their texts) show no interest in literary value. On the contrary, they recognize that "value" has itself become integral to the market, something Angel Rama would foretell in a 1982 article on boom literature ("El boom en perspectiva"), wherein he commented that contemporary mass readership was becoming increasingly sophisticated, turning "value" into a primary category of mass consumption (Sosnowski and Martínez 1985). Beatriz Sarlo's well-known attempt to revive the category of "aesthetic value" in the context of a "disinterested artist" in *Escenas de la vida posmoderna* (1994) fails to take the marketability of value into account (although he also argues for a return to "literary value," Chris Bongie's discussion (2003) of value in the context of postcolonial literature is, in this sense, far more nuanced because it begins by affirming this very marketability). None of the new writers make this mistake, especially not Mayra Santos Febres, and this is one of the overarching points I want to make in my reading of *Sirena Selena*.

Secondly, Levinson notes (2001, 28) that literature, from its inception as an institution in modernity, has been "the cultural agent of either revolution or conservation, or of both." Furthermore, he claims that "It [literature] comes to a close [dies] when we can no longer discriminate between the two" (28). Most of what follows is thus an attempt to show, beginning with an article by Rita Felski (1996) on transsexuality and postmodern thought, and then moving through a series of articles which appeared in a special 2003 issue of *Centro Journal* (published by the Center for Puerto Rican Studies) devoted to the novel that *Sirena Selena*, although a novel of counterdiscourse and "hypermarginalizations," makes it very difficult to talk about "transgression" in the postmodern sense of the word ("fragmentation as open labyrinth or project" in Levinson's terms).

In his introduction to the *Centro Journal* articles, editor Alberto Sandóval Sánchez comments: "These critical readings and practices at times intersect, overlap, complement, or even contradict each other. No one has a final reading" (2003, 7). While it is hardly unusual to find different and even contradicting readings of a text, there is a remarkable lack of consensus regarding the novel's "political message" or lack thereof evident in these articles (read against each other, and even within individual articles). The most coherent reading of the novel, and one that I will argue speaks most clearly to Levinson's notion of "transition" as a kind of self-perpetuating political and philosophical trap, is given by the author herself in an interview included in the series of critical articles in the special issue. This makes me wonder if the new Latin American writers, under so much more pressure to produce texts for the new economy, do not understand their challenge far better than we critics working in time-lapsed universities.

Towards the end of my essay, I introduce Antonio Negri and Michael Hardt's *Empire*, a well-commented book published in 2000 that argues, much like Levinson in the Latin American context, that globalized capitalism has effectively consumed the transformative potential of postmodern transgression and difference, turning it into its own, most powerful tool for the production and reproduction of capital. I try to show that *Sirena Selena* illustrates, dramatizes, and otherwise "exposes" the relationship that exists between culture and power. It does so in a Caribbean context (which is the context of the *Centro Journal* essays), but also in a Latin American context and beyond.

While I certainly do not argue that *Sirena Selena* provides an answer to Levinson's rightfully anguished question ("Where do we go from here?"), I think that it does expose the problem more clearly than Levinson himself does, and less romantically than Hardt and Negri. In other words, the novel takes us one step beyond the critical text, as opposed to the other way around. We may not yet be able to catch a glimpse of a "post-transition" cultural politics, but I do think that Levinson is correct when he states that the interruption of the neo-liberal consensus will come through reading, rather than the "unconcealment" of "overexposed truths" (2001, 126), which is the tactic of "transition." What we read in *Sirena Selena* is a kind of "refusal of myth," a cultural text that acknowledges its own weakness or failure as an instrument of identity, thus forcing us to acknowledge the instrumentality of more powerful tools of representation such as film, popular music, or television. I suppose this is a form of "unmasking" or "unconcealment," except that, for the moment, it makes no claims to a better future.

Sirena Selena: A Caribbean (Latin American) Story for Our Times

Mayra Santos Febres is one of Puerto Rico's best-known authors. She has, along with Rosario Ferré, Olga Nolla, and Mayra Montero (also claimed as a Cuban writer), made the move to large publishers and an international audience. *Sirena Selena vestida de pena* is her first novel. She had previously published two books of poetry as well as two collections of short stories in the 1990s, along with a collection of stories in English translation. Mondadori published her second novel, a mystery called *Cualquier miércoles soy tuya*, in 2002.

Sirena Selena is the story of a transvestite bolero singer who travels with her manager, Miss Martha Divine, to the Dominican Republic where the young boy/girl can work underage. Martha had previously discovered the "boy" as he was collecting cans, high on drugs, in the streets of San Juan. Sirena's voice is fabulous and both are now hoping that a contract to perform in a large Santo Domingo hotel will be the beginning of a journey out of the Caribbean, towards fame and financial security in New York or some other First World city. By the end of the novel, Sirena has disappeared after the owner of the hotel, Hugo Graubel, falls in love with her. Martha must then start all over again with another young protégé.

In a 1996 article entitled "Fin de siècle, Fin de sexe: Transsexuality, Postmodernism, and the Death of History," Rita Felski notes the "pervasiveness of images of transsexuality within much postmodern and poststructuralist thought" (337), as well as the use of transgenderism as an "overarching metaphor ... to describe the dissolution of once stable polarities of male and female" (337). According to Felski, "gender emerges as a privileged symbolic field for the articulation of diverse fashionings of history and time within postmodern thought" (338). She continues: The "end of sex echoes and affirms the end of history, defined as the pathological legacy and symptom of the trajectory of Western modernity" (338). As such, "a hierarchical logic of binary identity and narrative totalization gives way to an altogether more ambiguous and indeterminate condition" (338). Finally, Felski comments that "this idea that history [and sex] [have] come to an end has become perhaps the most ubiquitous and least questioned commonplace of postmodern thought, even as particular expressions of this motif vary in register from the nostalgic [Jean Baudrillard] to the celebratory [Donna Haraway; Judith Butler]" (338). Felski's goal in her essay is to stand clearly on the side of the celebratory: "the questioning of sexual difference does not inevitably signal a waning of the historical imagination; rather, it may help to generate powerful new feminist stories of possible futures, fueling imaginative projections of new worlds and alternative genealogies" (346). As a feminist theorist, she also wants to maintain a fractured space within the general emptiness of postmodern time for significant social struggles, and thus for history [and sex]: "the histories being written by women or postcolonial peoples, to take just two examples ... seek to contest and transform our view of the past by discovering its exclusions, oppressions, and hidden triumphs, to rewrite and extend, rather than negate history [and sex]" (345).

I introduce my discussion of Mayra Santos Febres's novel with Felski's article because, in so many ways, *Sirena Selena* is the perfect story to read alongside the familiar theoretical and philosophical account of postmodernity given by Felski. In her novel about Sirena, the beautiful transvestite bolero singer, Santos Febres takes up the metaphor of transgenderism and performance to tell a story that is almost entirely devoid of history as a narrative of concrete events in the past as well as a progressive plan of action for the future. As Luis Felipe Díaz makes clear in his contribution to the *Centro Journal* special issue dedicated to the novel, *Sirena Selena* does far more than simply contest the dominant patriarchal, masculinist, and nationalist versions of history targeted by Puerto Rican and Caribbean literature of the 1970s and 1980s. Unlike the work of writers such as José Luis González, the early Rosario Ferré, Ana Lydia Vega, and Luis Rafael Sánchez, to name just a few of the important figures and influences of this period, *Sirena Selena* abandons the preoccupation with projects for social and political change ("la utopía del cambio político-social") and shows no signs of nostalgia or regret when faced with the disintegration of the Puerto Rican national "family" (Díaz 2003, 29).

The novel breaks with a tradition of Puerto Rican and Caribbean writing that places literature at the centre of Caribbean history, even in its most recent postmodern manifestations from the 1970s and 1980s. This is what Díaz is getting at, I think, when he tries to explain how the Santos Febres novel differs from its immediate predecessors, also known for writing "discontinuous" and "fragmented" fiction. The metaphors of transvestism and transgenderism in *Sirena Selena* are not simply another version of an established paradigm of Caribbean criticism that foregrounds hybridity and indeterminacy as formal and theoretical models for Caribbean writing and identity. One has only to think of J. Michael Dash's 1998 book, *The Other America: Caribbean Literature in a New World Context*, to get a sense of this reading of Caribbean literature and identity, which in turn reflects the seminal work of figures such as Edouard Glissant and Antonio Benítez-Rojo. Their key theoretical contributions to the study of Caribbean identity were both published in the 1980s (*Le discours antillais* [1981] and

La isla que se repite: el Caribe y la perspectiva posmoderna [1989]). In this tradition, literary manifestations of hybridity, indeterminacy, and *créolité* served as metaphors for a racial and cultural history of the Caribbean, and for a future of resistance and affirmation that was both cultural and juridical, as in the drive to nationhood and regional affirmation. In this critical and writerly approach, the postmodern nature of Caribbean cultural production served a wholly modernist project.

Sirena Selena does something different, much more in keeping with the discourses of the end of history and the end of sex described by Felski (1996). Although the novel identifies categories of oppression, such as race and gender, urban poverty and violence, class differences, homophobia, and unequal development in the Caribbean, it makes no attempt to analyze the past or engage the future. Various critics, quoting comments made by the author herself, point to the use of transvestism as a metaphor to describe the Caribbean, or even the Third World, under conditions of globalization: "América Latina: sus ciudades son travestís que se visten de Primer Mundo, adoptan los usos y las maneras que no les corresponden a fin de 'escapar' de su realidad y acercarse a lo que cada día se ve más lejos: el progreso y la civilización" (Santos Febres qtd. in Barradas 2003, 58) ["Latin America: her cities are transvestites dressed up to look like the First World, taking on gestures and habits that do not belong to them in order to try and 'escape' their reality and move closer to something that just gets further and further away: progress and civilization"]. It is extremely difficult, however, to take this reading any further. While certain critics (Barradas and Van Haesendonck, for example) manage to locate political allegories in the novel, their readings are strained. *Sirena Selena* identifies vastly unequal structures of power and oppression, but does nothing to encourage the belief that these structures can be transformed. The novel seems to suggest that they can only be negotiated by individuals intent on survival. As José Delgado Costa (2003, 76) concludes, the novel's message appears to be that in the New World Order, only the fittest survive: "sólo el cojonudo sobrevive."

Although the story is formally complex – each chapter represents the point of view of one character or another, at times presented through a third person narrator; at times in the first person; at times through a monologue or scripted performance; at times through dialogue with no intervening narrator; at times through stream of consciousness – Santos Febres's use of form and language is itself much more performance than prescription or project. Díaz (2003, 30) refers to Santos Febres's "relatos de tipo *light*" ("'light-fiction' stories") that demonstrate a heightened awareness of today's avid but fickle consumer who, of course, is far more easily interpellated through popular music than through the literary text. The book, in a sense, becomes a bolero; its *refrán* is the bolero itself. It is no coincidence that Santos Febres chose to foreground a genre whose evolution, as Carlos Monsiváis tells us in his 1997 essay on the history of the bolero, is inextricably linked to mass-media technologies and mass circulation. The publicity on the first reprint (2000) of the novel is a quotation from a literary star, Laura Esquivel, equating the book with popular (world/Latino) music: "¡Sirena es fantástica! Como Cesaria Évora, te cautivará; como Marc Anthony, te robará el corazón. Los premios Grammy tendrán que inventar una nueva categoría: Mejor Álbum de Ficción del Año" ["Sirena is fantastic! Like Cesaria Évora, she will captivate you; like Marc Anthony, she'll steal your heart. The Grammy awards will have to invent a new category: Best Fiction Recording of the Year"].

By structuring her book as music, Santos Febres evokes a well-known Caribbean and Puerto Rican literary tradition. One has only to think of *La Guaracha del Macho Camacho* by Luis Rafael Sánchez or Ana Lydia Vega's "Letra para salsa y tres soneos por encargo." In this novel, however, the promise of that earlier literature, heavily invested in the project of Caribbean identity, becomes as elusive as the love promised in the bolero. Carlos Monsiváis puts it this way:

[T]he bolero is what was once called "romantic" (when a culture still bothered to produce such labels), but [it] has suddenly become a deposit of the experiences of generations who, for all of three minutes (which you can play again and again), believe themselves to have wrought in words and melody what they sought in love and found in melancholy. (1997, 167)

The novel pays tribute to the *cursilería* or cheap sentimentalism of the bolero. This is the only nostalgia it allows itself – the nostalgia of illusion, mass produced and imminently useful. Monsiváis speaks to these aspects (useful mass illusion) of the bolero in his essay, describing the popular genre as the "autobiography of everyone and no one" (192), and the "only alternative at your disposal: everyday unreality" (177). Santos Febres's novel turns itself into a bolero, acknowledging its greater power as well as its "usefulness," not only for her characters as they make their way through the minefields of contemporary life, but also for her readers, who can respond far more easily to the music then they can to a literary tradition, and even for the writer, who knows that, above all, she must sell her novel.

In the book's conclusion, Sirena's manager, Miss Martha Divine, who, with Sirena's disappearance, has lost yet another opportunity to achieve financial security as well as a wholly female body, is on the stage again, talking to her audience of gay men and transvestites:

Ustedes sigan esperando su buena estrella. Ella está allá arriba, brillando en el firmamento, augurándoles un futuro de lujo y felicidad. Por eso les quiero cantar este numerito positivo y juguetón, para que nos dé ánimos de alcanzar nuestra estrella. La mía casi la veo a la punta de mis manos. Siento que la alcanzo. Les juro que hay días en que creo que con la punta de los dedos la puedo tocar. (Santos Febres 2000b, 266)

> Just keep on looking for your lucky star. It's up there, shining in the firmament, holding a future of luxury and happiness for you. That's why I want to sing you this positive, playful song, to give us the courage to catch our lucky stars. I can already see mine, just beyond my grasp. I can almost reach it. I swear there are days when I believe I can touch it with my fingertips. (Santos Febres 2000a, 214)

Hope lies in the repeated performance of desire for a new body, for fame and fortune, in the continued possibility of recreating oneself: "inventarse otro pasado, empaparse hasta las teclas y salir a ser otra, entre spotlights y hielo seco, vitrinas de guirnaldas y crystal, a estrenarse otra vez, recién nacida" (2000b, 31); "to invent a new past, dress ourselves up to the hilt, head out, and be someone new, among the spotlights and the dry ice, mirrors and strings of lights, to start out fresh, newly born" (2000a, 20–21). Love, always so available to assist in the production of modernist Latin American histories, especially national histories, as Doris Sommer showed in *Foundational Fictions* (1991), is, in the end, unattainable here. As Martha tells Selena, "Ay nena, tú reza por no enamorarte jamás.... Es malo el amor en esta vida. Para cualquiera es malo, pero para una loca, es la muerte" (2000b, 140); "Girlfriend, pray that you never fall in love.... Love is bad in this life. It's bad for everyone, but for a *loca*, it's death" (2000a, 110).

One of the most striking passages in the novel is the one that gestures most clearly towards a radical deconstruction of gender and fixed subjectivities. It occurs near the end, when Leocadio, the young boy whose story is told alongside that of Selena and who will, in the end, simply take her place in the dreams and desires of Martha and the audiences she places before him, dances in the arms of Migueles, his friend and protector:

Hay muchas maneras de mandar, muchas formas de ser hombre o ser mujer, una decide. A veces se puede ser ambas sin tener que dejar de ser lo uno ni lo otro. Dinero, el carrazo, los chavos para irse lejos, para entrar en las barras más bonitas, más llenas de luces. Eso le toca al hombre. Y si se baila y otro dirige entonces se es la mujer ... ¿Y si fue ella quien lo convence a bailar, quien lo atrae con su cara caliente y sus trampas? Entonces, ¿quién es el hombre, la mujer? (2000b, 258)

> There are many ways to rule, many things required to be *un hombre* or to be *una mujer*, for each person can decide for himself. Sometimes you can even be both, without having to choose one or the other. Money, a big car, the *billetes* to go far away, to go into the best bars, the ones with the most lights. That's what the man has. And if he dances and the other one leads, then he's *la mujer*.... But what if it was she who convinced him to dance, who brought him here with her hot face and her tricks? Then who is *el hombre*, who *la mujer*? (2000a, 208)

Leocadio's questioning continues on from here and makes up most of a short chapter in the novel. While it represents an almost complete deconstruction of gendered and sexual roles, a kind of beautiful striptease that gradually sheds the norms and conventions of gender and sexuality in contemporary society, its effect in the end is more sobering. This process of deconstruction leads, not to release and freedom, but rather to a realization that gender is entirely flexible but determined solely by power. Leocadio's goal is to turn himself into, dress himself up as, someone with a little power: "Yo soy de respeto y cuando crezca, me vestiré de más respeto y vendré a bailar aquí, adonde no hay fieras" (2000b, 259); "I am respectable and when I grow up, soon, I will dress respectably and I will come to dance here, where there are no wild animals, only men" (2000a, 209).

If this is the case, then taking advantage of one's hybridity, now the privileged marker of postmodern identities and postmodern economies rather than a metaphor of Caribbean history, is the only "strategy" available to these characters. This is something that Martha effectively suggests to her audience during one of her shows:

Brindemos porque las rusas sean comprensivas y nos entiendan como lo que somos, lo mejor de dos mundos, y que cuando aterrice la Brigada de Dragas en Defensa del Glamour, capítulo de Puerto Rico, nos acepten como sus mentoras y guías espirituales. Porque coaching van a necesitar las pobrecitas. Tantos años privados de todo, sin películas de Hollywood, sin *Vogue*, sin *Elle* traducidas al ruso.... Nos van a necesitar, así que brindemos por ellas. (2000b, 178)

A toast for the Russians [drag queens] to be compassionate and to understand us for what we are, the best of two worlds, and to the proposition that when the Drag Brigade in Defence of Glamour, Puerto Rico chapter, lands, they accept us as their mentors and spiritual guides. Because the poor things are going to need some coaching. So many years without everything, without Hollywood movies, without *Vogue*, without *Elle* translated into Russian.... They're going to need us, so we'll toast to them. (2000a, 140)

Puerto Ricans, and Puerto Rican drag queens in particular, understand fragmented and hybrid identities better than anyone else. This is cultural knowledge worth exploiting.

While *Sirena Selena* signals the end of history and the end of sex, it also presents some of those fractured moments of subjectivity that Felski seeks to recover or protect in the midst of postmodern freefall. After all, this is a novel written by a black Puerto Rican woman about gay men and transvestites in the Caribbean, largely set in the Dominican Republic (the most marginalized of the three Hispanic islands, with a heavily marginalized migrant population in Puerto Rico itself). There are numerous group identities at play here and numerous histories of repression and marginalization that come to the fore in the performance of this novel. However, the very preponderance of marginalities present in the novel and its circumstances (its characters, its setting, and the figure of the author) make them all, in a sense, interchangeable. I don't mean to suggest that these different categories of marginalization are trivialized, but rather that they lead to a kind of "hypermarginalization," as I discuss in the first section of my paper. I think this is what Arturo Sandoval Sánchez means as well when he describes Santos Febres's work as a "total immersion in abjection" (2003, 9).

Despite this, the marginalizations performed in and by the novel remain in constant dialogue with the center. The book was published in Spain (by Grijalbo Mondadori, now part of the Random House Group) and has circulated widely since its initial appearance, hence the quote from Laura Esquivel. By June 2002, thirteen thousand copies had been sold in Spain alone and the novel has been translated into several languages, including English. Santos Febres has become a new star in the world of Hispanic fiction, following the tendency of the culture industries in general to let fewer artists through the gates but to market them aggressively once they are through (see Caves 2000, for an economic history of the culture industries today, including publishing). The postmodern blurs the distinction between center and periphery, and a book marketed like *Sirena Selena* moves in and out of both spaces, making it the perfect novel for our (globalized) times.

In this sense, Michael Hardt and Antonio Negri's 2000 book *Empire* becomes far more interesting for a reading of *Sirena Selena* than the Felski analysis of postmodernism that I discussed earlier on. Hardt and Negri smash Felski's attempt to read postmodernity as a "liberating icon rather than a nightmarish catastrophe" (1996,341). Even the emergence of fractured subjectivities within the postmodern narrative is presented by them as a strategy of new power structures that thrive on contingency and difference, as opposed to the old modernist binaries which were threatened by movement and fluidity: "[I]t certainly appears that the postmodernist and postcolonialist theorists who advocate a politics of difference, fluidity, and hybridity in order to challenge the binarisms and essentialism of modern sovereignty have been outflanked by the strategies of power" (Hardt and Negri 2000, 138). In other words, we have moved to a new distribution of global power that Hardt and Negri call "Empire" and define in the following way:

Empire establishes no territorial center of power and does not rely on fixed boundaries or barriers. It is a *decentered* and *deterritorializing* apparatus of rule that progressively incorporates the entire global realm within its open, expanding frontiers. Empire manages hybrid identities, flexible hierarchies, and plural exchanges through modulating networks of command. (xii, original emphasis)

What optimistic postmodernists have called "transgressive" is, for Hardt and Negri, complicit with a system of global command that moves hand in hand with global capital and the needs of "freer and freer" markets.

Even the alternative subjectivities (of women, postcolonial subjects, gays and lesbians, African-Americans, women of colour) that the critique of modernity made possible (although, as the Felski article shows, they were never completely reconciled within a postmodern framework) are tainted because

[m]arketing itself is a practice based on differences, and the more differences that are given, the more marketing strategies can develop. Ever more hybrid and differentiated populations present a proliferating number of "target markets" that can each be addressed by specific marketing strategies.... Every difference is an opportunity. (Hardt and Negri 2000, 152)

The link between marketing strategies and postmodern thought is nowhere more clearly outlined than in Thomas Frank's *One Market Under God*, a history of the economy of the 1990s that shows quite convincingly that the underlying ideology of account planning is almost identical to that of cultural studies, which is the critical practice that emerges in the context of postmodernity and globalization, and one that privileges consumption as a space for resistance and agency. As Hardt and Negri maintain, "postmodernist thinking – with its emphasis on concepts such as difference and multiplicity, its celebration of fetishism and simulacra, its continual fascination with the new and with fashion – is an excellent description of the ideal capitalist schemes of commodity consumption ..." (152).

Difference, multiplicity, fetishism, and simulacra: these are the terms of Mayra Santos Febres's novel, and without a doubt they can lead critics to claim that the novel opens up a space for the construction of new subjectivities that resist the borders and frontiers of repressive regimes, be they nationalist, gendered, sexual, or racial. Such is the case for Jossianna Arroyo (2003, 49), for whom the transvestite is a "relational character" who is "emptied" of significance yet, at the same time, serves as a kind of axis (*eje*) for the circulation of multiple signifiers and discourses. This corresponds to the critic's notion of "cultural drag," which provides "un espacio intermedio en el que el cuerpo no logra una trascendencia totalizadora, sino que se queda en ese lugar de negociación y agencia" (42) ["an intermediate space where the body fails to achieve a totalizing transcendence, but rather, remains in a space of negotiation and agency"].

We are reminded once again of Felski's two poles of postmodern philosophy, where the metaphors of transsexuality and transgenderism represent either the nostalgic pessimism of Jean Baudrillard, who sees nothing but the sign emptied of meaning, or the transgressive optimism of Donna Haraway (or Judith Butler). What if neither of these options are enough to explain the novel? Certainly, there is no room in *Sirena Selena* for nostalgia (other than the kind fabricated by the bolero) or pessimism. Martha, forever the impresario hoping for her next best deal, does not allow that kind of talk; for the characters who live in this book, looking back is equivalent to annihilation. They do not feel the loss of the transcendental signifier, since they were never its empowered (white, male, European, heterosexual) subject. They can only exist in the fluid, borderless, and postmodern present.

At the same time, following Hardt and Negri, we may no longer be able to locate transgression quite so easily in the multiple articulations of difference performed by *Sirena Selena*. Even Arroyo, who provides a very convincing reading of *Sirena Selena*, must, in a sense, put her own happy spin on the ending of the novel (Arroyo 2003, 50). While I would agree that *Sirena Selena* certainly opens a space for negotiation (42), I would argue that these acts of negotiation have much more to do with simple survival than with transgression. Perhaps the metaphor of transgenderism is deployed in the novel, not so much as transgression, but rather to describe the act of survival itself. As Martha tells Sirena, "Todas queríamos ser otra cosa, estar en otro lugar, el Studio 54, el Xennon, paseándonos por la Quinta avenida de Manhattan sin que se nos notaran en las piernas las ronchas negras de tanta picadura de mosquitos. El asunto siempre fue negar la cafre realidad" (Santos Febres 2000b, 31); "We all wanted to be something else, to be somewhere else, Studio 54, Xenon, walking down Fifth Avenue in Manhattan without anyone noticing the dark blotches from the mosquito bites on our legs. It was always about denying our miserable reality" (Santos Febres 2000a, 20). Martha is herself a survivor, "[una de las l]ocas viejas, como yo ahora, las que sobrevivimos al país, al SIDA, a los fracatanes de exilios que siempre ha tenido que echarse al cuerpo una para poder sobrevivir ..." (Santos Febres 2000b, 30); "[one of the] old *locas*, like me, the ones who outlived the country, AIDS, and all the ravages that a body in exile must suffer in order to survive ..." (Santos Febres 2000a, 19), as is Sirena, who, while she makes love to hotel owner Hugo Graube, wishes for a brief moment that she could allow herself to be loved as he promises to love her – before making off with his wallet and Cartier watch.

In an interview with Teresa Peña-Jordán included in the 2003 *Centro Journal* special issue, Mayra Santos Febres is asked whether she thinks that Hugo Graubel, as the only character who manages to overcome the repression and violence done to him as a closeted gay Dominican man, is the most transgressive character in the novel (121). If Graubel is transgressive, Santos Febres replies, it is only because transgression is a privilege of the powerful. One can only transgress when the limits and borders are clearly delineated. Transgression is much easier for the upper classes in the white, heterosexual First World. Sirena and Martha, more than transgressive themselves, play with the notions of transgression of others:

Desde Sirena y Martha, no hay tal transgresión, hay superviviencia.... También existe una valentía muy grande en tratar de sobrevivir. Yo no creo que ni Solange [la esposa de Graubel], ni Sirena, ni Martha estaban haciendo otra cosa que negociar con los deseos de los poderosos, tratar de hacer lo que se puede para no sucumbir.... (Peña-Jordán 2003, 121)

> [From the perspective of Sirena and Martha, there is no transgression, there is just survival.... There is also great courage in simply trying to survive. I don't think that Solange [Graubel's wife], nor Sirena, nor Martha are doing anything but negotiating with the desires of the powerful, trying to do what they can to stay alive....]

For Santos Febres, this is not a story of liberation, but rather of negotiation for survival.

Of course, this story of survival (in our globalized times) is quite sad. Many of its characters do not make it, and those who do remain locked in the present, with no discourse of resistance or liberation to point them towards the future, and no history to which they can return for sustenance, just the bolero. While as readers we might momentarily enjoy the show (the bright lights, the humour, the makeup, and the beautiful music), in the end we are left with a fairly brutal depiction, not just of contemporary society, but also of the philosophical cul-de-sac described by Brett Levinson in the Latin American context as well as more generally by the authors of *Empire. Sirena Selena* seems to say that the only "thought and praxis of the transition from transition" (Levinson 2001, 9) available to its characters is survival itself. Martha and Sirena are heroic because they stay alive. In this sense, the novel is actually far more distressing than the notions expressed by Antonio Negri and Michael Hardt (2000), who end up turning in circles, unable to move beyond their own expression of postmodern politics except to formulate a somewhat melodramatic notion of the "multitude," who will naturally and spontaneously rise up to fight empire, destroying "with its own productive force the parasitical order of postmodern command" (66), turning "resistance into counterpower," and making "rebellion into a project of love" (413). *Sirena Selena* does not permit this flight into fantasy. Here the critical/philosophical text becomes cheap fiction (another bolero) and the novel "tells it like it is." Surely this indicates something about the role of literature in globalized culture, and perhaps even that of writers and critics.

The newest generation of Latin American and Caribbean writers are fully reconciled to globalization. As Edmundo Paz-Soldán says (2002, 48) of Alberto Fuguet, they seem to recognize that the construction of fictions for mass consumption (and what is identity, if not a fiction constructed for mass consumption?) is best left to film and television (and popular music, computer games, and videos), leaving literature to concentrate on individuals whose only act of heroism seems to be survival, more so in peripheral economies. Nonetheless, because it has abandoned the "myth-making function," staying on the sidelines while still (necessarily) engaging (and yes, manipulating) with mass-media culture and the identitarian options it offers, this brand of Latin American realism may offer a slightly skewed view of that culture and therefore of its politics, which are the politics of global capital. *Sirena Selena* is constantly in dialogue with mass-media forms of cultural production and easily concedes their superiority. At the same time, however, *Sirena Selena* refuses to allow the reader to believe fully in the transformative properties of popular music, or show, or performance; yet, it offers no alternatives. This is very sad and very courageous.

Works Cited

Anderson, Benedict. 1983. *Imagined Communities. Reflections on the Origin and Spread of Nationalism*. London: Verso.

Appadurai, Arjun, ed. 2000. *Globalization: Public Culture* 12 (1).

Arroyo, Jossianna. 2003. Sirena canta boleros: travestismo y sujetos transcaribeños en *Sirena Selena vestida de pena. Centro Journal* 15 (2): 38–51.

Barradas, Efraín. 2003. *Sirena Selena vestida de pena* o el Caribe como travestí. *Centro Journal* 15 (2): 53–61.

Benítez-Rojo, Antonio. 1989. *La isla que se repite: El Caribe y la perspectiva posmoderna*. Hanover, NH: Ediciones del Norte.

Beynon, John and David Dunkerley, eds. 2000. *Globalization: The Reader*. New York: Routledge.

Bongie, Chris. 2003. Exiles on Main Stream: Valuing the Popularity of Postcolonial Literature. *Postmodern Culture* 14 (1). *Project Muse*. http://www.iath.virginia.edu/pmc/issue.903/14.1bongie.html (accessed 15 Nov. 2004).

Castro Gómez, Santiago. 2003. Apogeo y decadencia de la teoría tradicional: Una visión desde los intersticios. *Revista Iberoamericana* 69 (203): 343–53.

Caves, Richard E. 2000. *Creative Industries: Contracts between Art and Commerce*. Cambridge: Harvard Univ. Press.

Dash, J. Michael. 1998. *The Other America: Caribbean Literature in a New World Context*. Charlottesville, VA: Univ. Press of Virginia.

De la Campa, Román. 1999. *América Latina y sus comunidades discursivas: Literatura y cultura en la era global*. Caracas: Fundación Centro de Estudios Latinoamericanos Rómulo Gallegos, Universidad Andina Simón Bolívar, Sede Ecuador.

Delgado-Costa, José. 2000. Fredi Veláscues le mete mano a *Sirena Selena vestida de pena. Centro Journal* 15 (2): 66–77.

Den Tandt, Catherine. 1999. Caribbean 2000: Still Here, Still Waiting. *Journal of Caribbean Literature* 3 (1): 57–76.

———. 2003. Inversiones culturales: Literatura, cultura e identidad. Feria Internacional del Libro de Guadalajara. *Lengua, literatura e identidad: Puerto Rico y Québec.*

Díaz, Luis Felipe. 2003. La narrativa de Mayra Santos y el travestismo cultural. *Centro Journal* 15 (2): 25–36.

Esquivel, Laura. 2000. Front Cover Publicity. *Sirena Selena vestida de pena*, by Mayra Santos Febres. Barcelona: Mondadori.

Felski, Rita. 1996. Fin de siècle, Fin de sexe: Transsexuality, Postmodernism, and the Death of History. *New Literary History* 27 (2): 337–49.

Ferré, Rosario. 1995. *House on the Lagoon*. New York: Farrar.

———. 1998. *Eccentric Neighborhoods*. New York: Farrar.

Franco Ramos, Jorge. 2000. *Rosario Tijeras*. Barcelona: Mondadori.

Frank, Thomas. 2000. *One Market under God: Extreme Capitalism, Market Populism, and the End of Economic Democracy*. New York: First Anchor.

Fuguet, Alberto. 1999. *Por favor, rebobinar*. Santiago: Aguilar.

García Canclini, Néstor. 1995. *Consumidores y ciudadanos: Conflictos multiculturales de la globalización*. Mexico: Grijalbo.

———. 2001. *Consumers and Citizens: Globalization and Multicultural Conflicts*. Trans. George Yúdice. Minneapolis, MN: Univ. of Minnesota Press.

García Cuevas, Eugenio, and Vicens, M. 2000. Travesti nocturno. *El Nuevo Día* (21 May): 79.

Glissant, Edouard. 1981. *Le discours antillais*. Paris: du Seuil.

González, José Eduardo. 2001. Los nuevos letrados: posboom y posracionalismo. *Revista Iberoamericana* 67 (194–195): 175–90.

Grant, Peter S. and Chris Wood. 2004. *Blockbusters and Trade Wars: Popular Culture in a Globalized World*. Vancouver: Douglas.

Gutiérrez, Pedro Juan. 1999. *El Rey de La Habana*. Barcelona: Anagrama.

Hardt, Michael, and Antonio Negri. 2000. *Empire*. Cambridge: Harvard Univ. Press.

Irr, Caren. 2001. Literature as Proleptic Globalization, or a Prehistory of the New Intellectual Property. *South Atlantic Quarterly* 100 (3): 773–802.

Jameson, Fredric, and Masao Miyoshi, eds. 1998. *The Cultures of Globalization*. Durham: Duke Univ. Press.

Levinson, Brett. 2001. *The Ends of Literature: The Latin American "Boom" in the Neoliberal Marketplace*. Palo Alto, CA: Stanford Univ. Press.

Lowe, Lisa and David Lloyd, eds. 1997. *The Politics of Culture in the Shadow of Capital*. Durham: Duke Univ. Press.

Menchú, Rigoberta. 1985. *Me llamo Rigoberta Menchú y así me nació la conciencia*. Mexico: Siglo Veintiuno.

Monsiváis, Carlos. 1997. Bolero: A History. In *Mexican Postcards*. Trans. John Kraniauskas. London: Verso.

Paz Soldán, Edmundo. 2002. Escritura y cultura audiovisual en *Por favor, rebobinar* de Alberto Fuguet. *Latin American Literary Review* 30 (59): 43–54.

Paz-Soldán, Edmundo, and Debra Castillo, eds. 2001. *Latin American Literature and Mass Media*. New York: Garland.

Peña-Jordán, Teresa. 2003. Romper la verja, meterse por los poros, infectar: Una entrevista con Mayra Santos Febres. *Centro Journal* 15 (2): 116–25.

Rama, Angel. 1985. El boom en perspectiva. In *La crítica de la cultura en América Latina*, ed. Saúl Sosnowski and Tomás Eloy Martínez, 266–306. Caracas: Ayacucho.

Sánchez, Luis Rafael. 1976. *La guaracha del Macho Camacho*. Buenos Aires: de la Flor.

Sandoval Sánchez, Alberto. 2003. *Sirena Selena*: A Novel for the New Millenium and for New Critical Practices in Puerto Rican Cultural Studies. *Centro Journal* 15 (2): 4–23.

Santos Febres, Mayra, ed. 1997. *Mal(h)ab(l)ar: Antología de nueva literatura puertorriqueña*. San Juan, Puerto Rico: Yagunzo.

———. 2000a. *Sirena Selena*. Trans. Stephen A. Lytle. New York: Picador.

———. 2000b. *Sirena Selena vestida de pena*. Barcelona: Mondadori.

———. 2002. *Cualquier miércoles soy tuya*. Barcelona: Mondadori.

Sarlo, Beatriz. 1994. *Escenas de la vida posmoderna: Intelectuales, arte y videocultura en la Argentina*. Buenos Aires: Ariel.

Sommer, Doris. 1991. *Foundational Fictions: The National Romances of Latin America*. Berkeley: Univ. of California Press.

Tomlinson, John. 1999. *Globalization and Culture*. Chicago: Univ. of Chicago Press.

Valdez, Pedro Antonio. 2000. Los motivos del cuento. In *Los nuevos caníbales: Antología de la más reciente cuentística del Caribe Hispano*, 107–9. Havana: Unión.

Van Haesendonck, Kristian. 2003. *Sirena Selena vestida de pena* de Mayra Santos-Febres: ¿Transgresiones de espacio o espacio de transgresiones? *Centro Journal* 15 (2): 78–96.

Vega, Ana Lydia. 1981. Letra para salsa y tres soneos por encargo. In *Vírgenes y mártires*, ed. Ana Lydia Vega and Carmen Lugo Filippi, 81–88. Río Piedras: Antillana.

Velasco, Xavier. 2003. *Diablo Guardián*. México: Alfaguara.

Wilson, Rob and Wimal Dissanayake, eds. 1996. *Global/Local: Cultural Production and the Transnational Imaginary*. Durham: Duke Univ. Press.

Notes

1   All translations are mine unless reference is made to a published translation.

Teatro da Vertigem: Performing Resistance in an Era of Globalization

Paola S. Hernández, University of Wisconsin-Madison

As a result of the return of democracy in 1984 after an eighteen-year dictatorship, Brazil became a country of strong neo-liberal investments in the 1990s, converting the public space and a large part of the state into private marketing entities. By the beginning of the twenty-first century, globalization developed into a catchphrase in Brazil, just as it has in all of Latin America. Scholars such as José Joaquín Brunner, Nestor García Canclini, Edward Said, and Zygmunt Bauman have explored the effects of globalization in marginalized and underdeveloped countries. Common to their studies is a critical examination of the negative consequences of neo-liberal economies in developing nations like Brazil. These authors unveil a simple truth: with globalization there are both winners and losers, and the marginalized nations are, for the most part, on the losing end. Their studies also advocate that these societies do not benefit from globalization. Instead, they are impoverished, saddled with high foreign debt, and many are controlled economically by transnational companies. In addition to an economic restructuring, globalization has produced a culture of resistance and defiance. Edward Said (2001, 66), for example, sees globalization – a capitalist model that includes free commerce, transnational enterprises, international investments, deregulation, and privatization of state-owned industries – as a major fraud when it comes to marginalized societies, where large numbers of people do not enjoy the benefits and have become impoverished in the process. Many Latin Americans perceive globalization as an attempt to homogenize their cultures. This, in turn, has created a resistance, a new desire to relocalize and reappropriate their national identities. Roland Robertson's (1992) neologism of "glocalization" – where the global and the local can coexist peacefully – shows that it does not function in developing countries like Brazil. As a result, national identity and local interests collide with – and confront – the homogenizing forces of globalization.

Brazilian sociologist Marilena Chaui has explained: "Neo-liberalism transforms politics into a performance and a simulacrum and, as such, it simulates the theological liturgy of power" (1994, 29).[1] Chaui's reference to the performance-oriented politics at the end of the twentieth and the beginning of the twenty-first centuries illustrates how theatre can take advantage of a situation to postulate a socio-political message on a stage.

Theatre, in both its textual and performative modes, uses the stage as a platform to question, to resist, and to bring about, among other things, awareness of past and present socio-political issues. Indeed, theatre, due to the dialogical relationship that it establishes with its audience – different from media such as film and television – constructs a stage that confronts globalized cultural invasions. In a world where artifice, the mass media, and the Internet share the common side of everyday life, theatre, together with its stage, manifests from the periphery its natural resistance to globalization's virtual space, creating in contrast a local, usually small place for people to gather.

This article will shed light on how economic and cultural globalization has resonated in the urban theatre of São Paulo, Brazil, where society is shown to be struggling in a postmodern and fragmented world. Through the study of the theatre of Teatro da Vertigem, I intend to show that globalization has not benefited the majority of Brazilians. Instead, the plays expose the negative consequences of globalization in Brazil – high incidences of poverty, government corruption, and socio-political instability. I will also demonstrate that it is through the voices of a variety of underrepresented characters that Teatro da Vertigem unveils and rediscovers the hybrid identities that form the present-day nation.

In this context, the Brazilian theatre group Teatro da Vertigem first became known in 1992 with the premiere of its first play, *O Paraíso Perdido*. The group then premiered *O Livro de Jó* in 1995, and *Apocalipse 1, 11* in 1999. These three plays were later published in the trilogy, *Trilogia Bíblica* (2002), which received significant critical attention in newspaper reviews and literary journals. Through collective creation, Teatro da Vertigem depicts the human consequences of globalization in Brazil – a country peripheral to this phenomenon. Their work exposes the struggles, the loss, and the confusion confronting people in a city such as São Paulo. In an era when the government of Brazil has diminished economic subsidy to local theatre groups, Teatro da Vertigem literally takes on public space and sets the stage in abandoned and decrepit churches, hospitals, and prisons. For David George, Brazil's reaction to globalization is apparent in both the kinds of plays that are staged and those that are not. He argues that the "globalization of economic models (e.g., market economy) has led to the virtual elimination of government subsidy for the arts in Brazil and has given rise to the hegemony of the theatrical entrepreneur, the 'catador de recursos.' This influences what plays will be staged, [and] what space is available" (2003) [an unpaginated e-mail to the author]. Teatro da Vertigem addresses this dilemma as it pushes the public boundaries of national theatre. The group's motivation is to lure people into the center of the community. By doing this, they are exposed to national theatre rather than Broadway plays. In fact, Teatro da Vertigem has made an impact in the theatre movement of the 1990s not only by manipulating public spaces into performance stages of São Paulo, but also by reintroducing the audience to a theatre that questions the role of globalization in the center of a metropolitan, marginalized, and globalized city. Theatre critic Sílvia Fernandes (1998, 35) explains that the success of Teatro da Vertigem is due to a combination of artistic decisions that include: collective creation, the well-founded techniques of the theatre of the absurd,[2] the use of public space, and the treatment of current events in a dislocated fashion that questions the confusion and fragmentation of a postmodern and globalized society at the end of one era and the beginning of the next. Indeed, *Trilogia Bíblica* deals with the postmodern cultural phenomenon and performs the intricacies of the neo-liberal and globalized world in plays that attract not only audiences, but the attention of critics and awards.[3] As a consequence, the *Trilogia Bíblica* intertwines the economic and cultural aspect of globalization as it reinforces the social consequences of a marginalized society. Román de la Campa (1999, 149) has established that "globalization, postmodernism, and neo-liberalism – have come to occupy the same horizon. They respond to a logic that fuses marketing, culture, and politics into a performative doctrine." In this sense, the postmodern is seen as a cultural counterpart of economic globalization. Thus, de la Campa concludes, "in Latin America, the postmodern cultural logic is almost unavailable without a neo-liberal political sense, and both are increasingly absorbed by the engulfing rhetoric of globalization" (150). The idea of "engulfing" is a peculiar and debated rhetoric in Brazil where dependency on national and global entities is a vital part of the country's economic survival. Brazilian cultural critic Ivo Mesquita alludes to this phenomenon when he explains that:

The political and economic changes and the acute social crisis in Brazil in the last ten years have placed this country as a society founded under a colonial project and thus, dependent on others. We are "connected" to them, many times involuntarily, because of the technological advances, the information overload, urban cultural globalization and the markets' interdependency that are part of the transnational system. (2002, 302)

The involuntary "connection" and the economic "engulfing" of the Brazilian economy is portrayed by this theatre group through direct references to current social, economic, and political events.

Teatro da Vertigem makes use of the Bible to recreate and transform well-known stories with a contemporary twist. The group's performance of

O Paraíso Perdido in an old church is an ironic representation of paradise lost from the book of Genesis. As in Dante's *Divina Comedia*, *O Paraíso Perdido* takes the spectator on a search for redemption. With the expulsion of Adam and Eve, the audience accompanies these characters in mourning and takes an allegorical as well as literal journey through the corners of the church with the hope of finding human dignity and affection in contemporary society. The second play, *O livro de Jó*, is an adaptation of the Book of Job. On the stage of an old and abandoned hospital, Teatro da Vertigem brought to São Paulo a play that inquires into the consumer-driven aspects of today's world. Thus, the story of Job, a wealthy man who loses everything due to God's wrath, traps the audience and, once again, presents them with a well-known ancient story that features strong commentaries about consumer society, which values material wealth rather than human worth. As in *O Paraíso Perdido*, where the audience walks through a church, this play makes the audience wander around the hospital, where wealth does not necessarily buy health, questioning the role of money, and highlighting the need to search for a more humanistic experience.

The third play, *Apocalipse 1, 11*, was staged in an old prison in São Paulo. In this play, the group seemed to take more liberties, thus creating, in my opinion, the best play of the entire trilogy. Even though *Apocalipse 1,11* is an adaptation of the Book of Apocalypse, it differs from the previous two plays in that it distances itself more from the Bible. In this respect, *Apocalipse 1, 11* takes more risks and goes beyond presenting a mere interpretation of the Bible as it applies to today's world. The Book of Apocalypse (also known as the Book of Revelations) is Saint John the Revelator's "eyewitness report" of the end of the world. In it Saint John begins his pilgrimage towards the New Jerusalem, the city of gold and jewels where a wall prevents any evil from entering. Only those who are worthy can enter this New Jerusalem; all other sinners remain in eternal suffering.[4] In *Apocalipse 1, 11*, João enters the first scene in search of the New Jerusalem. Staged in a modern prison, João's journey presents the image of contemporary man dealing with the perverse and dark corners of present-day society. The image of the New Jerusalem, adorned with gold and jewels, is quickly altered and João becomes a silent pilgrim who guides the audience through the various labyrinths of the prison. In contrast to the biblical Saint John, who provides a written account of his experience, João will never be able to pass on a written history.

The play begins at the center of the prison when João closes the entry door and traps the audience inside for two full hours of torment and pilgrimages. The urban setting within a central São Paulo prison has a direct symbolism, playing with the actors' and the audience's perceptions.

Requiring the audience to walk through different scenes brings a special theatrical effect to the play. The creator, Luis Alberto de Abreu (2002, 315), explains that: "Walking or the displacement of scenes through the many prison labyrinths, forces the spectator to walk through an in-between space between the real and the fictional, thus, creating permanent tension by suspending the audience in this taboo-space." As such, the prison represents, and actually is, an enclosed center built to capture, punish, and judge prisoners. This space conveys a message of repression, emptiness, and corruption, leaving prisoners waiting for final judgment or death to take them away. The similarity between the prison's symbolism and São Paulo's recent history emphasizes the idea of collective urban memory. During a military dictatorship, people from different cities would use public gathering places such as churches, hospitals, parks, and even prisons to promote political changes in the government:

In these spaces of representation, negotiation, public representation, and public interlocution, workers, poor residents, homeless families, women, blacks, and marginalized minorities are the characters who have appeared on the Brazilian public stage in recent times ... in making themselves known on the political scene as subjects capable of public dialogue, these actors had the effect of destabilizing or even subverting symbolic hierarchies, which had held them in a subordinate position through a dense web of discrimination and exclusion. (Paoli 1998, 66)

As in these public gatherings, Teatro da Vertigem utilizes and reforms the stage into a location for the marginalized and underrepresented classes to meet and make their voices and histories heard. The use of a prison, a place of enclosure, rehabilitation, and sometimes torture, becomes a symbol of Brazil's tumultuous past, where both the private and the public aspects of human life becomes distorted and fragmented.[5] By utilizing the Book of Apocalypse in contemporary times, Teatro da Vertigem creates a subtle allegory of how Brazilian citizens, more specifically "Paulistas," live and react to the consequences of globalization. In his own words, director Antonio Araújo comments that this play "is a product that speaks about our anguishes due to our unhealthy situation in which this country finds itself and about the degradation of life in a city like São Paulo" (Abreu 2002, 315).

The subaltern class makes its presence felt in *Apocalipse 1, 11* through eccentric characters. João's pilgrimage with the audience is a tour of the various degraded characters of society who do not benefit from the new globalized world of consumerism. This is the case with a drug-addicted prostitute, a transvestite, a mulatto, and a mentally handicapped woman.

The play demonstrates through these characters how mainstream society demeans those who do not fit the standard prototype of economic success. The hypocrisy of today's society, blinded by wealth, consumerism, and the appropriation of imported goods facilitated by global markets, is a strong factor throughout the entire play.[6]

Within the biblical epistolary readings, a mailman comes out to the audience and introduces João to the stage:

CARTEIRO. Carta ao anjo da igreja em Éfeso! Os inteligentes serão transformados em burros. Aos burros se dará o mínimo necesario para que possa se portar em fila. Os pretos serão catastrados como morenos. Os mulatos serão catastrados como brancos. As mulheres maduras terão directo a plástica nos seios ou barriga depois dos sessenta e cinco anos de idade.... Traficantes pagarão impostor. P.S.: os incomodados que se mudem. (Teatro da Vertigem 2002, 193)

> [POSTMAN. Letter from an angel of the church in Ephesus! The intelligent ones will be transformed into asses. The asses will be given the bare minimum so that they can stay put. The blacks will be classified as browns. Mulattos will be classified as whites. Mature women will have the right to breast implants and tummy tucks after sixty-five years of age.... Drug lords will pay taxes. P.S. if you don't like it, move out.]

Without hidden meanings, this letter literally represents the realities of Brazilian's society. The combination of the epistolary biblical genre blended with contemporary social expressions demonstrates, in an abrupt and concise way, Brazil's mixed identity at the end of the twentieth century. The mixture of races and relations is established from within comments on the heterogeneous culture of the Brazilian society. Identity in Brazil is not just a question of race, but also of cultures and religions that coexist. In this respect, the scholar Fernando Arenas has defined Brazilian identity:

Brazil's "kaleidoscopic" reality in socioeconomic, racial, and cultural terms has led critics to define it as a "hybrid society" long before this term became common in debates around a possible Latin American postmodern condition; as a "space in between," emphasizing the fact that Brazilian culture cannot be defined in terms of "unity" or "purity" because it is neither entirely European nor African nor Amerindian. (2003, 24)

The hybrid mixture of colors, races, and religions are defined in this play by the contemporary perceptions of the "spaces in between," as Homi Bhabha

(2002) has stipulated.[7] This pushes the envelope on whose voices are going to be heard and how they are going to transmit their message. According to the director, the play opens with a letter in order to "question and reflect on the dialectic between hope and terror that is present in these last years of the end of a century" (Araújo 1998, D1). Indeed, Teatro da Vertigem's representation of contemporary Brazil not only questions and reflects on this dialectic between hope and terror, but it also expresses the agony of many marginalized characters that are barely ever heard.

After João enters the scene, he is welcomed by two rebellious angels. In contrast to the angels in the Book of Apocalypse, these two bring a sarcastic and pragmatic view of contemporary life, inviting João to forget about his search for the New Jerusalem. However, the true conflict of the play begins when João enters a nightclub ironically named New Jerusalem. Derived from the metatheatrical technique of a play within a play, João and the audience are spectators of a new show. As if in a real nightclub, the stage turns smoky. Big-screen TVs then alternate between images of the Bible and automobile accidents. The back of the stage is covered with "macumba" images, Catholic and non-Catholic virgins, and pornographic pictures. Within the juxtaposition of sacred and profane images, a new character, a transvestite dressed as the Beast, appears from the gloomy smoke and places him/herself at the center of this "mass-show." In a vulgar and dark-humoured way, this transvestite Beast embodies João's internal conflict: take the Bible literally or understand the fragmented segments left behind. The Beast twists the Commandments and blends that ideology with the figure of Satan in the contemporary world:

BESTA. Adorarás muitas imagens! Te prostrarás diante de vários deuses. Pronunciarás o nome dele em vão.... Matarás; cometerás o adultério; roubarás.... Apresentarás falsos testemunhos.... Cobiçarás casas, mulheres, computadores, automóveis, pós-graduação, dietas, relógios de pulso.... Me venerem ... me amem. (Teatro da Vertigem 2002, 206)

> [BEAST. You will worship many images! You will obey many gods. You will utter his name in vain. You will give false testimony.... You will buy houses, women, computers, automobiles, graduate degrees, diets, watches ... you will worship me.... You will adore me.]

The play's worship of consumerism is a fundamental thematic component that signifies the impact of economic and cultural globalization. Indeed, there is a mutual conspiracy between the two elements. According to José

Joaquín Brunner (2002, 152), "cultural globalization has much to do with the controlling capitalist system in the world." *Apocalipse 1, 11* exposes the pleasure that people find in acquiring material possessions. The transvestite-Beast is the sarcastic voice that invokes the sins of the world through the desecration of the Mass and its transformation into a production. The "macumba" images and the white and black virgins represent a religious syncretism of the general public.[8] Part of this syncretism is the foundation for the cultural diversity in Brazil's identity (Hess and DaMatta 1995, 2). This play appropriates this cultural, religious, and racial syncretism in a "mass-show" that exposes the many facets of Brazilian society and cultural identity.

Teatro da Vertigem also uses the technique of a "mass-show" as a way to capture and "educate" the audience with a contemporary view of the Apocalypse. The play satirizes the *autos* – a medieval form of allegorical religious drama used by Portuguese and Spanish priests to "educate" and convert the indigenous people to Christianity. With a few modifications, such as the Beast as the main educator, the "mass-show" parodies the traditional forms of religion and theatre, instructing the audience on how they should behave in a corrupt society.[9] Just as Hollywood utilized Carmen Miranda bearing fruit on her head as the symbol of a bountiful Brazil, Teatro da Vertigem exposes a postmodern ironic visualization of the true Brazil. After the Beast makes her/his speech, a second character, Babilônia, a prostitute – dressed in purple and with her chalice full of "impurities" – takes the stage. With graceful moves, she begins to undress and while signaling to her now naked feminine organ, she speaks: "Aqui está aberta a pátria. Aqui boceja o seio da família" (Teatro da Vertigem 2002, 207) ["Here our nation is open. Here the family's heart opens up"]. While still naked and with a black character next to her, the prostitute goes on to push the boundaries of Brazilian international ideology: "E agora ... un pouco de Brasil que vocês tanto gostam ... A alegria! A sensualidade ... A ginga! O nosso jeitinho ... a mistura de raças! Dá-lhe negão!!! (Negro dança) (207) ["And now ... a little bit of the Brazil you all like so much ... Happiness ... Sensuality ... A *ginga* ... and our *jeitinho* ... the mixture of races! Keep it up Negro! (Negro dances)"]. This performance of Brazilian identity has two important connotations. First, the prostitute plays with the international stereotype of Brazil as paradise, full of sensual men and women. Secondly, the play depicts the stereotype of the racial and social denigration of the lower classes. The *ginga* and the *jeitinho* are typical Brazilian expressions that indicate a type of corruption or method for taking shortcuts in order to avoid paperwork. *Jeitinho* can have both positive and negative connotations; it is the way society functions and how people live, ask favors, and take care of business.[10] *Jeitinho* is also manifested through corporal movements. In this scene, the "Negro" starts dancing while the prostitute makes direct references to his penis as "A malícia ... a força ... a vibração ... a potência" (207) ["the malice ... the force ... the vibration ... the potency"] coming from Africa. However, this brief sexual exposure comes to a halt when the prostitute accuses the "Negro" of stealing her purse:

BABILÔNIA. Roubou, sim. Tinha mais alguém lá atrás com a gente?! Tinha mais algum preto nojento, ladrão filho-da-puta por aqui?! Ahn? Tinha? É isso que dá lidar com esse tipo de gente.... (209)

> [BABILÔNIA. He stole it. Was there anybody else over there with us? Do we have a disgusting black, thief, son-of-a-bitch? Eh? Do we? That is what we have to live with when it comes to those people....]

This insulting rage shows the rough edges of Brazilian society, where lower-class blacks are thought to be thieves and criminals.[11]

This metatheatrical play within a play of a "mass-show" exposes Brazil as a collage or kaleidoscope of historical, political, cultural, and religious fragments. The kaleidoscope can be perceived as a consequence of a postmodern culture that, in turn, is impacted by global culture. In this regard, Terry Eagleton (2000, 30), who has studied the effects of postmodern society, stipulates: "In the postmodern world, culture and social life are once again closely allied, but now in the shape of the aesthetic of the commodity, the spectacularization of politics, the consumerism of lifestyle, the centrality of the image, and the final integration of culture into commodity production in general." In his postmodern perspective, Eagleton emphasizes how this image is central to a consumerist society, making superficiality a gleaming attribute of life. The term "aesthetics of commodity" makes reference to how society has come to associate consumerist behavior with a mundane style of living transmitted through advertising and media (30). On a similar note, García Canclini (2001) coins the term "world-culture" to describe the same postmodern effect. For him, forms of mass media such as television, Internet, radio, and film have devalued culture. The necessity to sell more at a lower price has promoted this new "world-culture," closely linked to the economic market. In this regard, culture becomes homogeneous, creating "well-known myths for all spectators" (49). According to Canclini, "world-culture" has wrongly portrayed Latin America as an idealistic natural preservation or a premodern landscape, making it impossible to see the gradations of difference between all countries (49).

Apocalipse 1, 11 confronts this idealistic and homogeneous vision of Latin America by exposing some innate Brazilian issues. For example, the prior scene where a black character is first revered for his African sexual potency and later blamed to be a thief puts an end to an oneiric vision of the "untouched" premodern Latin American culture. Marilena Chaui (1994, 24) notes that in the Brazilian national anthem, Brazil is represented as *país-jardim*, a country with natural beauty, similar to paradise. Teatro da Vertigem dismantles the oneiric vision of Brazil as *país-jardim*, unveiling a disturbing reality. In the play, the postman comes onstage one last time. This time his letter deconstructs this vision of paradise: "Ah Brasil! Toda essa pureza com sangue nos sorrisos. Todas essas gangues armadas até os dentes que não temos.... Todos esses sorrisos esburacados e esses bacanas, com suas vontades assassinas.... Ah, Brasil, país dos acertos ... pastando a grama rala de sua ingorância" (Teatro da Vertigem 2002, 219) ["Oh, Brazil! All that purity with bloody smiles. All those heavily-armed gangs that we don't have.... All these holy and nice smiles, with their murderous wishes.... Oh, Brazil, the country of all the right things ... chewing on the insipid grass of its own ignorance"]. The violent and unhopeful image of Brazil's present exhibits the real perspective of the contemporary "paradise," a much more gruesome picture than what the national anthem paints (Chaui 1994, 23).

In this play, the "world-culture" perspective is seen through the many different political and economic angles. Structured as a postmodern *auto* but using a "mass-show," many facets of Brazilian identity come to light. Eagleton explains that the "spectacularization of politics" and "the consumerism of life style" (2000, 30) determine central ideals of the neo-liberal movement of the later part of the twentieth century. The mass media have created a space for these "spectacularizations" to convene and thus invade people's everyday life. *Apocalipse 1, 11* parodies the effect of the mass media in popular culture and highlights the major roles of politics and consumerism in society. In one of the later scenes of the "mass-show," the Beast, together with Babilônia, thanks popular TV stars such as Xuxa, Angélica, and Eliana, as well as Miguel Falabella, a commercial theatre playwright (Teatro da Vertigem 2002, 204). Both the Beast and Babilônia adhere to Eagleton's "spectacularization of politics" and his idea of a consumerist lifestyle by making constant reference to popular TV stars. According to journalist Mariangela Alves de Lima (2002, 309), the Beast and Babilônia "are the blasphemous manifestations of two allegories; they have undisputable credibility of bad taste and mockery of the mass media."

Indeed, mockery is an allegorical way to represent some of the contemporary problems of Brazil. In the following scene, Babilônia introduces a new character, Pastor Alemão (German Priest), so that he can exorcize all wrongdoings from Brazil. Following a true religious syncretism, as stipulated by Hess and DeMatta, the Pastor Alemão invokes all "macumba" gods (Pombajira and Iemanjá) while clutching a Christian Bible:

P. ALEMÃO. Quem é que tá aí? O BID? O FMI ... Eu te exorcizo pelo dinheiro desviado, pelo caralho da dívida externa subindo sempre. Eu exorcizo a tua falta de futuro ... perdida do país dos aflitos ... Abram-se as portas do Inferno! Que Lucifer ... Getúlio Vargas, Roberto Campos, Jânio Cuadros, Trancredo Neves ... que você venha a minha presença. Eu te esconjuro MDB ... Bolsa de Valores, Alphaville ... AI-5 ... Filhos da puta! Em nome do Pai, do Filho, do Banco Central e do Espírito Santo. (Teatro da Vertigem 2002, 213)[12]

> [P. ALEMÃO. Who is there? The IBD? Or the IMF? I exorcize you of all the money laundering, of the damned, always-rising foreign debt. I exorcize your lack of future ... lost in the country of the afflicted. Let's open the doors of Hell! Satan ... Getúlio Vargas, Roberto Campos, Jânio Quadros, Tancredo Neves...all: come to me. I exorcize the MDB ... the Stock Exchange ... Alphaville ... AI-5 ... Sons of bitches! In the name of the Father, the Son, the Central Bank and the Holy Spirit.]

João's apocalyptic pilgrimage is an exorcism of the last fifty years of Brazilian history. In a sense, the pastor's "cleaning of sins" parallels a contemporary reading of the Apocalypse in Brazil. Among these sins, the Pastor emphasizes the economy, the intervention of the International Monetary Fund, the Central Bank, and the all-encompassing roles they play in contemporary Brazil. The voice of the pastor denounces this while expressing anger and resistance against these forces.

In one of the play's most ironic scenes, the Beast thanks contributors for this show: "Quero agradecer também aos patrocinadores da cultura deste país.... Essa gente boa, que, além de blindar as suas BMWs e abrir contas no Caribe, ainda acha tempo para investor em cultura" (Teatro da Vertigem 2002, page number) ["I would also like to thank our cultural sponsors.... Those good people, that, although they bulletproof their BMWs and open bank accounts in the Caribbean, still have time to invest in culture"]. The globalized economy's reality is an advertisement, thanking those with access to foreign bank accounts and foreign cars for making this play possible. Even though the exorcist Pastor denounces these people, who have "redirected moneys," and invested them abroad, the Beast introduces a fact of life: the need to obtain some of this money in order for cultural events to survive. It is only with sponsors – those whom the Pastor was exorcizing – that this play or "mass-show" can continue.

As the "mass-show" concludes, the audience is led to the next scene, the final judgment. In a disturbing and playful manner, the judge and two rebellious-looking angels throw eggs at a mentally retarded woman named Talidomida. Her character represents an aspect of Brazil's sorrowful past. During the fifties and sixties a sedative drug, talidomida, was known to cause mental and physical retardation in newborns.[13] In incongruous, fragmented sentences, Talidomida repeats part of Brazil's constitution: "(*Destrambelhada, gaguejante*) A República Federativa do Brasil tem como fundamentos ... a soberania; a cidadania; a dignidade da pessoa humana ..." (Teatro da Vertigem 2002, 236) ["(*scatterbrained, stuttering*) The Federated Republic of Brazil has as its foundation ... sovereignty; citizenship; human dignity ..."]. As she speaks these lines, ironically the judge and the two angels silence her with violence. This scene represents a strong allegory of the corrupted, handicapped, and underdeveloped nation of Brazil. Even the judge questions: "Somos o que somos será porque sejamos uma sub-raça, um país de mestiços, uma fusão de elementos étnicos inferiores? Ou porque sejamos uma nacionalidade em vias de formação, o que explica o estado de delinqüência social do povo brasileiro?" (241) ["Are we who we are because of being an underdeveloped race, a country of *mestizos*, a blend of inferior ethnical elements? Or is it because we are a developing nation that explains the social delinquency of Brazilian people?"]. Talidomida becomes the voice of national consciousness that exposes yet another side of Brazilian identity. The judge's questions represent a hypocritical and sarcastic comment on the formation of this identity. While committing the violent act against Talidomida, he points to the mixture of races and ethnic groups as the main contributors to Brazil's economic and political situation in the world.

When comparing the judge's behavior to that of the drug-addicted prostitute or the transvestite Beast, an ironic truth comes to light. It is through the eccentric and marginalized characters that the audience can see and hear the true problems of society, while a clean-cut judge hides behind his white-collar and social position and commits crimes. In the final judgment, all characters face this judge. As is expected, neither the Beast nor Babilônia apologize for what they have done. In fact, Babilônia exposes the hypocrisy of society while confessing that she is infected with AIDS: "Eu não me arrependo! Se é o que vocês querem saber ... Eu gostei de tudo o que eu fiz ... muito! Toda vez que eu me julguei, eu me absolvi.... E vocês? Pois pra mim o inferno foi sempre aqui" (Teatro da Vertigem 2002, 259) ["I don't repent. If you all want to know ... I liked everything I did ...

very much! Every time I judged myself, I absolved myself ... and all of you? Hell was always here for me"]. The Beast later suffocates Babilônia as a sign of redemption from this world and adds: "Eu não tenho pecados pra confesar a Deus ... Por que ele fez todo mundo tão fraco e tão cego? Vivem tomando no cu e agradecendo! E ainda se sentem culpados. E eu é que sou o mal!! Graças a Deus!!!" (260) ["I do not have sins to confess to God ... Why did he create such a weak and blind world? They all live kissing ass and thanking! And they still feel guilty. And I am bad!! Thank God!!!"]. These characters take pride in who they are and what they have done. Unlike Babilônia and the Beast, the judge takes pity on himself and his corrupted habits. He sits on a throne-like chair and confesses: "Eu peço desculpas por tudo que eu não fiz, por tudo-tudo-tudo que eu não fiz. Desculpa! ... Quem é que vai me salvar de mim? (266) ["I apologize for everything I have not done, for everything, everything, everything I have not done. I apologize! ... Who will save me from me?"]. He then hangs his head in mortification of his sins and corruption, leaving the stage in total silence.

At the conclusion of the play, João goes to the stage and separates himself from the audience. He claims that he now understands the meaning of life and is no longer frightened of the unknown. Opening the exit door, he looks at the audience one last time and says: "Eu não tenho medo de encontrar ou de não encontrar Nova Jerusalém. ... Não tenho mais medo de polícia, nem tenho mais medo de ladrão" (Teatro da Vertigem 2002, 274). ["I am not afraid of finding or not finding New Jerusalem. ... I am not afraid of the police, and I am not afraid of the thief"]. The search for New Jerusalem turns out to be an internal search of each individual's being. The mythical city of gold becomes an abstract image, making the journey more important than the destination. As João departs, he implores the audience to follow him outside in search of their own New Jerusalem.

Teatro da Vertigem shows the audience the many facets of Brazilian identity and society, while attempting to postulate a message of resistance against the homogenizing forces brought on by mass media and global culture. It is with their sarcastic, ironic, and even pornographic techniques that this group parodies tumultuous and painful historical times. *Apocalipse 1, 11* unveils a broad range of truths that are usually hidden or forgotten. This rediscovery brings out the gradation of identities that make the nation of Brazil known as "kaleidoscopic." With a direct and critical approach, Teatro da Vertigem expands the "kaleidoscopic" nature of Brazilian identity, and includes marginalized classes as part of the forgotten minority who do not fit in with today's illusory homogeneous society. In a postmodern, incongruous fashion, this group takes theatre to another level of performance and explores other avenues of creativity to produce an insightful two-hour play that captivates an audience and helps it to understand the many facets of Brazilian society.

Works Cited

Abreu, Luis Alberto de. 2002. O Coletivo Constructor. In *Trilogía Bíblica*, 59. São Paulo: Publifolha.

Alves de Lima, Mariangela. 2002. O Intrigante e Pungente Apocalipse 1,11. In *Trilogía Bíblica*, 318–19. São Paulo: Publifolha.

Araújo, Antonio. 1998. Fim do milênio mistura terror e utopia. *O Estado de São Paulo*. Caderno 2 (17 Feb. 1998): D1.

Arenas, Fernando. 2003. *Utopias of Otherness: Nationhood and Subjectivity in Portugal and Brazil*. Minneapolis: Minnesota Univ. Press.

Associação Brasileira dos Portadores da Síndrome de Talidomida. 20 Feb. 2004. <http://members.tripod.com/~abpstalidomida/historico.htm>

Bauman, Zygmunt. 1998. *Globalization: The Human Consequences*. New York: Columbia Univ. Press.

Bhabha, Homi K. 2002. *El lugar de la cultura*. Buenos Aires: Manantial.

Brunner, José Joaquín. 2002. *Globalización cultural y posmodernidad*. Santiago de Chile: Fondo de Cultura Económica.

Chaui, Marilena. 1994. Raízes Teológicas do Populismo. In *Os anos 90: Política e Sociedade no Brasil*, Evelina Dagnino, org, 19–30. São Paulo: Brasiliense.

Columbia University Press. 2004. *Columbia Encyclopedia*. 6th Ed. New York: Columbia Univ. Press.

De la Campa, Román. 1999. *Latin Americanism*. Minneapolis: Minnesota Univ. Press.

Eagleton, Terry. 2000. *The Idea of Culture*. Berlin: Blackwell.

Fernandes, Sílvia. 1998. Infidelidades brasileiras. *Bravo!* 1 (6): 123–26.

——. 2002. O Lugar da Vertigem. *Trilogía Bíblica*, 35–40. São Paulo: Publifolha.

García Canclini, Néstor. 2001. *Culturas híbridas: estrategias para entrar y salir de la modernidad*. 9th ed. Buenos Aires: Paidós.

H. Barbosa, Livia Neves de. 1995. The Brazilian *Jeitinho*. In *The Brazilian Puzzle: Culture on the Borderlands of the Western World*, ed. David Hess and Roberto DaMatta, 35–48. New York: Columbia Univ. Press.

Hess, David J. and Roberto A. DaMatta, eds. 1995. *The Brazilian Puzzle: Culture on the Borderlands of the Western World*. New York: Columbia Univ. Press.

Holy Bible: Revised Standard Version. 1953. New York: Nelson.

Ianni, Octavio. 1999. *La era del globalismo*. Mexico: Siglo Veintiuno.

Mesquita, Ivo. 2002. Panorama da Arte Brasileira 1996. *Trilogía Bíblica*, 302–3. São Paulo: Publifolha.

Paoli, Maria Celia and Vera da Silva Telles. 1998. Social Rights: Conflicts and Negotiations in Contemporary Brazil. In *Cultures of Politics, Politics of Culture: Re-Visioning Latin American Social Movements*, ed. Sonia E. Alvarez, Evelina Dagnino and Arturo Escobar, 64–92. Boulder, CO: Westview.

Robertson, Roland. 1992. *Globalization: Social Theory and Global Culture*. Newbury Park, CA: Sage.

Said, Edward W. 2001. Globilizing Literary Study. *PMLA* 116 (1): 64–68.

Teatro da Vertigem. 2002. *Trilogía Bíblica*. São Paulo: Publifolha.

Telles, Edward E. 1994. Segregação Racial e Crise Urbana. In *Globalização, Fragmentação e Reforma Urbana: O Futuro das Cidades Brasileiras na Crise*, Luiz

César de Queiroz Ribeiro and Orlando Alves Dos Santos Júnior, orgs,189–212. Rio de Janeiro: Civlização Brasileira.

Ulhôa Carvalho, Martha de. 1995. Tupi or Not Tupi MPB: Popular Music and Identity in Brazil. In *The Brazilian Puzzle: Culture on the Borderlands of the Western World*, ed. David Hess and Roberto DaMatta, 159–79. New York: Columbia Univ. Press.

Vernengo, Matias. 2003. Late Globalization and Maladjustment: The Brazilian Reform in Retrospective. *International Development Economics Associates*. www.networkideas.org/featart/jul2003/fa19_Late_Globalization.htm. (Accessed 4 Oct. 2004).

Notes

1 This and all subsequent translations are my own. I thank Professor Cacilda Rêgo for her help in this process.

2 According to Silvia Fernández in her 1988 article "Infidelidades brasileiras," Teatro da Vertigem is a group that knows how to write theatre in a collective manner and that also understands the complexities of Artaud's theatre by creating plays of profound psychological cruelty (124).

3 With the publication of *Trilogia Bíblica*, Teatro da Vertigem became the most controversial and award-winning group of the '90s. For a detailed description of their awards, see pages 328 and 329 of *Trilogia Bíblica*.

4 This summary and any other subsequent reference to the Bible come from the Book of Apocalypse, *The Holy Bible: Revised Standard Version*.

5 According to Silvana García, the prison, a place highly used during the military repression, also evokes memories of the massacre of the prisoners of Carandiru in 1992.

6 Indeed, poverty in Brazil worsened in the last decade of the twentieth century. In a recent article, professor of economics Matias Vernengo explores the high rates of unemployment brought by the liberation and privatization movement of the 1990s. According to his study, the unemployment rate increased from 10.3 per cent in 1990 to 19 per cent in 2002, leaving many more Brazilians, especially Paulistas, in greater poverty (2003, 22).

7 I am referring to Homi Bhabha's explanation of the marginalized voices of the "spaces in between" where there is a place for the subaltern and minority voices to be heard and to form part of a nation (2002, 195).

8 Martha de Ulhôa (1995) explains that a well-known attribute of Brazilian identity comes from the slaves who transformed African music. They also changed the figures of non-Catholic religions into Catholic virgins to disguise their true beliefs and religions.

9 Another example of a parody of the traditional genre of *auto* or *auto sacramental* is seen in the play "Auto da Compadacida" by Ariano Suassuna, where Lucifer is also the main character who tries to educate his audience.

10 Livia Neves de H. Barbosa describes this term as a true part of Brazilian identity. Barbosa explains that the *jeitnho*

> can be defined, in a very broad sense, as a fast, efficient, and last-minute way of accomplishing a goal by breaking a universalistic rule and using instead one's informal social or personal resources ... it is a way of identifying Brazil making this particular mechanism suitable for by-passing rules and getting things done. (1995, 36)

11 I base my analysis on studies done on segregation and the hidden racism that exists in Brazil. In one such study, the author points out that "[t]here is a lot more racial discrimi-

nation against blacks in this country than whites are willing to admit" (Telles 1994, 189).

12   BID represents the International Development Bank; Roberto Campos was secretary of economy during the military dictatorship; Jânio Quadros was president (1961–63); Tancredo Neves was the first civilian president to take over after the dictatorship; MDB stands for Brazilian Democratic Movement; Alphaville are private condominiums; and AI-5 was an amendment made to the constitution during 1968–86 that allowed for censorship and torture. It is also worth mentioning that in the globalization paradigm, many scholars have referred to the IMF or the Central Bank as "the Holy Trinity of global capitalism" (Ianni 1999, 93).

13   *Talidomida* refers to a sleep-inducing drug found to produce skeletal defects in developing fetuses. The drug was marketed in Europe, especially in West Germany and Britain, from 1957 to 1961, and was thought to be so safe that it was sold without prescription. In 1961 an extremely high incidence of European babies born with malformed, shortened limbs was correlated with use of thalidomide by women in their first trimester of pregnancy. Before it was recalled from use the drug had caused the malformation of about 8,000 children throughout the world. In 1961, the world market prohibited its sale, however it never disappeared. In 1998, after a complex safety monitoring system had been established to prevent further birth defects, thalidomide was approved for use in the United States for a complication of leprosy. The drug is also used to treat multiple myeloma, a cancer that affects the bone marrow (*Columbia Encyclopedia*). However, in Brazil it was not until 1965 the pill was officially taken off the market. Due to corruption, self-medication and lack of education, women kept taking this painkiller pill. Finally, in 1993, an official law prohibited its use by young women. Today there are about 800 *Talidomida* victims in fourteen states of Brazil. (See also http://members.tripod.com/~abpstalidomida/historico.htm)

To Bet or Not To Bet: Gambling Identities

Claudine Potvin, University of Alberta

From Dostoyevsky's *The Gambler* to Cristina Peri Rossi's *La última noche de Dostoievski*, and from Martin Scorsese's 1995 film *Casino* to Argentinean filmmaker Fabián Bielinsky's *Nueve reinas* (2000), the reader/spectator witnesses an almost identical scene belonging to gambling culture: the dream of a lucky moment. This fantasy of a kind wheel of fortune persists even though the movement of the wheel almost always brings down any adventurer daring to beat luck. The scene more often suggests how ephemeral, transitory, and illusory chance really is. This article will examine five diverse players. First among these is Alexei Ivanovich from *The Gambler*, ruined and waiting impatiently for his old grandmother to die so that he can get his hands on the inheritance. Jorge, the protagonist of *La última noche de Dostoievski*, is a successful journalist who works in a very popular but mediocre magazine and is obsessed by Dostoyevsky's gambler. Sam Rothstein (*Casino*) is a force in the Las Vegas underworld, particularly for a number of gangsters who have confided their fortune in his ability to never lose and to never reveal God's secrets. The two poor *diablos* in *Nueve reinas* who glance at the possibility of changing their life in one day through the dubious prospect of one lucky bet complete this set. These are four stories inscribed as quest narratives driven by the protagonists' desire to appropriate the other (money) and to thereby affirm themselves. Constructed around a triple obsession (the game itself, the money, and love or desire) these narratives install the character in a dialogic monologue between the "I" of the narrator/observer and the object of manipulation.

Quebec writer Hubert Aquin wrote in his *Journal* (1992, 208–9) that "le pari est déjà une obsession" ("to wager is already an obsession"), that every gambler "croit à la magie" ("believes in witchcraft"), and that, fundamentally, every gambler is "un joueur magique ensorcelé par une mélancolie de mort" ("a magical player haunted by a melancholy of death").[1] Considering the gravity of the exercise, as all gamblers will confirm, all games are susceptible to become far more than a pastime or entertainment. We bet at the horse track, at the theatre, at the casino, at poker, at the stock market, at the roulette table, in the sports arena, and in love. We risk it all because we are tempted and hopeful to substitute the illusion or the possibility of a reversal of fortune. Pascal proposed to always take a risk, that is, to bet on God's existence, as this passage shows:

When there is an equal risk of winning and of losing, if you had only two lives to win, you might still wager; but if there were three lives to win, you would still have to play (since you are under the necessity of playing).... But here there are a number of chances of losing, and what you stake is finite. That removes all infinity of chances of loss against the chance of winning, there are two ways about it; you must risk all. (1960, 343)

Pascal's principle of rational gambling as a basis for decision on matters of God and life goes against the attitude of today's gambler, who operates irrationally to risk fortune, family, reputation, and identity.

Does the gambler try to fool himself from the moment he bets on probability, since the identities re-enacted in the casino seem to proliferate only to vanish? In this context, this essay will explore the concept of identity through the representation of gaming culture in four texts separated in time, location, and genre (two novels and two films), but linked by a common motif – the addiction to or the familiar frequentation of games and money. My commentary on this theme (gambling), associated with some brief reflections on the (de)construction of identities, goes beyond a form of nationalistic identification to a "people" and a culture. Identities exist at an individual level as much as the collective one: they are flexible, multiple, always threatened, nomadic, and open.

As Nicholas Rescher (1997, 149) has noted, "When things go well it is all too often the result of happenstance – and the same when things go ill. Accordingly, life is in large measure a gamble – a game of chance, like roulette, rather than one of skill, like chess! The very words 'luck' and 'lot' link our condition to the theme of gambling." The gambling metaphor thus questions the possibility of a fixed identity and the construction of a multiple self (Latin American/other) through chance or luck. Gambling or word games, libidinal games, carny games, children's games, forbidden games, games of luck, political and/or war games: all of these are rule-governed practices that are at times licit or illicit, but always cultural. Real or imagined, games disturb, threaten, trouble, but nonetheless fascinate the participant and the spectator. Does the gambling economy, pure commodification, reside upon an exchange impossible to define? Is the ultimate wager the gain or loss of a meaning that could justify or alienate existence, identity and desire? Does the writer or the cineaste, like the gambler, inscribe himself/herself into a dynamic of lies about this essentially nomadic and fictional identity? If gaming supposes a set of rules, an absolute control and order, it equally suggests the trickery – a way of cheating oneself that is a form of illusion and chaos.

It is not possible here to define the identities of the heroes/protagonists/narrators from a unique spatial perspective of being from a nation or belonging to a land or country, or by their embrace of an ideology, a language, or history. Borrowing Graciela Montaldo's 1999 commentary about Latin America, the identities considered here refer to her book's title, *Ficciones culturales y fábulas de identidad* [*Cultural Fictions and Fables of Identity*]. In Régine Robin's words,

Une identité n'est supportable que lorsqu'elle constitue un espace souple, des jeux d'aller et retour, lorsqu'elle évite l'épinglage, l'assignation automatique, lorsqu'on peut s'en prendre et s'en déprendre, lorsque au-delà du donné on peut se construire des jeux d'identifications partielles multiples, lorsqu'on est capable d'un dedans/dehors créateur. (1994, 217).

> [An identity is bearable only when it constitutes an open space, games of going and coming, when it avoids the categorization, the spontaneous label, when we can adhere to it or leave it, when we can elaborate partial and multiple games of identifications, when we are capable of an inside/outside creativity.]

So, the notion of identity is from the very beginning shattered into pieces that reveal the absence of a fixed or static self. Pierre Ouellet wrote in *Identités narratives: Mémoire et perception* that

Les identités sociales et individuelles ne sont jamais fixées une fois pour toutes. Elles se transforment au gré de la mémoire et de la perception qu'on a de *soi* et de *l'autre* à travers les images et les traces mnésiques qui sous-tendent le discours social et les pratiques esthétiques, constitutives d'un état toujours transitoire d'une culture donnée (2002, 1; original emphasis)

> [Social and individual identities are never fixed once and for all. They transform themselves according to the memory and the perception we have of *ourselves* and *others* through the images and the traces that underline the social discourse and the aesthetic practices, which constitute a permanent transitory state of a given culture.]

In his movie *Casino*, Scorsese situates the drama in the city where the American capitalist dream becomes real each time a gambler throws the dice, plays a card, or inserts money into a slot machine. "It is little wonder," notes Rescher,

> that *casino* (diminutive Italian for *casa*, a house) became in the 17th century the name for a place of public amusement at pleasure resorts, where concerts, theatrical performances, and public balls were given, and where there was also usually a café-restaurant and – more relevantly to present purpose – a gaming saloon. (1997, 160)

If the word *casa* suggests initially a connotation of home and comfort, the gambling mania that will follow will recreate a rather false illusion of pleasure contained in Scorsese's movie. The cinematographic language reworks the typical clichés of the casino culture: lights, noise, mall effects, undefined or insipid music, excitement, hope, despair, anxiety, obsession and, above all, greed. In the last film of his trilogy on crime and corruption in America, Scorsese explores a world dominated by a few powerful Sicilian families who infiltrated Las Vegas in the 1970s. Sam, the protagonist in charge of a prestigious casino, the Tangiers, has the reputation of "betting like a brain surgeon." His precision, seriousness, and rigidity present him as the ideal man for the operation. He enters the casino like others enter a convent.

The apocalyptic opening scene offers an image of total destruction comprised of explosion, fire, flying bodies, and violent images. A church choir and a religious aria reinforce the biblical dimension of the fall and punishment. This repressive, religious atmosphere dominates the film. Sam himself looks like a colourful priest; dressed like a pope or a Grand Inquisitor, he is moralistic and incapable of enjoying himself because he denies his body and his emotions. On the one side Sam shows a tendency to keep everything inside; on the other, he encourages the release of forced confessions, punishments, begging, forgiveness, and money transfers "back home" (similar to the deliveries from Catholic churches to Rome). What is released or given is linked to the guilt, the fault, and what is withheld belongs to the pleasure and the recognition of his voice. His wife associates him with the figure of the serpent because of his double identity, his impenetrability in spite of his apparent open face, both characterized by his surveillance mania.

Sam is always on the other side of the table. He checks, looks, gazes, kills, or authorizes with only one look. He obviously bets on nonexistent reality, at least for thousands of dreamers with fluid identities; on capital and above all, on himself and on his identity. According to Sam, the others have no chance at all of winning since the whole apparatus locks them on their side of the table forever: The longer you play, the more you lose. For Sam, only the sign/gesture counts: the way one throws the dice, the way one piles the tokens, the posture of the croupier, the etiquette, the gaze, and the running of the machines. In reality, it does not matter who wins; the profit always seems to be elsewhere and to benefit the other. In this context, the transfer supposes a return to the self. However, if Sam Rothstein[2] always wins, he also loses because he rapidly hides what he "finds" or wins. If, by any chance, he feels lost, he will choose the camera eye, the television angle, or a show to recreate his image. However, this "finding" is precisely only a spectacle: it is like a coat, an empty body, or a "superficial" identity located in a nowhere. This nowhere of infinite luck is like utopia thought of in terms of an eternal present. Finally, *Casino* is not an introspective film, and the hero belongs to the long tradition of impenetrable men whose identity is that of a billboard.

However, everything happens in the casino as if there were nothing but false representations (or a simulacrum of the simulacrum, as Baudrillard sees it). In the casino/theatre/show, games are blocked because they are codified in advance, as if the repetition of a *mise en scène* of a unique event (losing) would not really allow chance to intervene. Swindlers susceptible to disturb the order are immediately and violently expelled. Ultimately, Sam's function is to maintain the fiction of luck, keeping the loser ignorant of who he is/was before the fall. Again, Rescher concludes that:

An instructive symbolism is at work in this conjunction of events. Indulgence in gaming and gambling paradigmatically illustrate the irrational side of human nature, since placing one's hard-gained resources at risk on the throw of a die or the draw of a card may be viscerally thrilling but may wittingly and deliberately hand one's fate over to circumstances wholly beyond one's control. (1997, 162)

Game and identity are framed very differently in Cristina Peri Rossi's novel, *La última noche de Dostoievski* [*Dostoyevsky's Last Night*]. Using *The Gambler* and the Russian writer as an intertext, Peri Rossi recreates the gambling fiction through a psychoanalytical setting that is parallel to intense sessions in game rooms (mainly bingo halls). In the novel, Peri Rossi links thirty-seven narrative fragments into seven intersecting dialogues or meetings between Jorge and the psychiatrist. The protagonist consults Lucía in order to get rid of his "solitary vice" or addiction, even though Jorge considers his visits as another game that is just as secret as the initial one that is asphyxiating him. In the therapeutic cure, the patient plays hide-and-seek with the psychoanalyst who intends to discover the drives that motivate Jorge to "erase" himself through his addiction. The fact that the doctor gets money for the "treatment" disturbs Jorge, who sees it as another loss.

Peri Rossi recalls in her novel that, in Freudian terms, the feeling of guilt represents an objective substitute under the form of debts/money. Dostoyevsky liked gambling *per se* not for the gain; he never left the table until totally destitute. Apparently, gambling offered him a new form of self-punishment. We could suggest that he might instead have surpassed or gone through hysteria using his body, his despair, and his writing. Jorge keeps punishing himself for Lucía because he continues to play even knowing that he is going to lose, freeing himself from his feelings of guilt. As we see, religious discourse is part of the game dynamic and is always likely to resurface: "el juego es una manifestación tardía y desplazada de las religiones" (Peri Rossi 1992, 42) ["to play/gamble is a late and displaced manifestation of religions"].

Jorge compares the casino to a temple or a bordello because of the illusions the place creates: between purification and damnation/ruin. The gambler hopes that tomorrow it will be over; it will be "the last night of Dostoyevsky." Peri Rossi repeats this last sentence of *The Gambler* twice in her novel. Inscribed in the title, these last words will become the initial syntagm of the book that Jorge projects to write. However, he will eliminate the future, transforming the hypothetical mode into an accomplished past. Jorge affirms, "Anoche, anoche dejé de jugar. Me parece un buen comienzo" (Peri Rossi 1992, 159) ["Last night, last night, I stopped gambling. I believe it is a good beginning"].

It is how we can talk about identity in the case of *La última noche de Dostoievski*, or can we talk about it at all? Jorge defines himself in a very brief and explicit manner:

Verdaderamente, soy un tipo adictivo. Tengo adicción al juego, al cigarillo, a las mujeres, a la lectura del periódico, a la ducha, y a la vida: detesto la certeza de ser mortal. Pero los otros – los que no juegan – tienen, también, sus adicciones: son adictos al trabajo, al dinero, al fútbol, al alcohol, a los medicamentos, a las hierbas, a la actualidad, o a la moda. (Peri Rossi 1992, 95)

> [Really, I am an addicted type of person. I am addicted to gambling, to tobacco, to women, to newspapers, to showers, and to life: I hate the certitude of mortality. The others, the ones that do not gamble, are equally addicted: to work, to money, to football, to alcohol, to medications, to herbs, to the present, or to fashion.]

Of course, the text presents a certain ambiguity. We could read the addiction at multiple levels: the protagonist's habits with various "substances," the women's desire or obsession for Jorge, even the psychoanalyst's closeness to her patient, reminiscent of the connection between the author and Dostoyevsky. Lucía, the psychoanalyst, recurs to Freud's approach about Dostoyevsky whom he qualified as a hysterical neurotic.

The list of possible addictions shared by everybody installs Jorge within a collective and uniform perception of his community. Despite belonging to a certain culture, Peri Rossi's novel proposes an individualistic view of identity. "Al pensar en identidad cultural," writes Magdalena García-Pinto (1986, 104), "ésta podría definirse entonces como permanencia en medio del cambio, o como unidad en medio de la diversidad, a la que se añade la necesidad de confirmación de la propia identidad tan sólo por intermedio de otros, de los cuales se demanda reconocimiento" ["In terms of cultural identity, we could define it as permanency within change, or as unity within diversity, to which we add the necessity to confirm individual identity, even if through the others from whom we ask recognition"]. This concept of identity is mainly based on unity. However, in Latin America and elsewhere, diversity is a major component of identity that has been too many times ignored. While he associates himself with the group, Jorge displaces his own subjectivity through therapy and game. If the identitarian discourse is often constructed on visions of culture and nation, history and politics, memory and language, race, class, gender, ethnicity, geography, borders, and daily life, the player's philosophy shows that identities are elaborated on fragmentations and separations.

Finally, writing appears to be the ultimate gain for Jorge, a gain signifying both the end (of his therapy, the victory over his addiction) and the beginning (of the book): Dostoyevsky's novel, *The Gambler*, is already given as a diary. In it Alexei Ivanovitch keeps writing some sporadic notes on his personal experiences. As he rereads these notes, Alexei realizes that, for him, money makes sense only through words. All he wants is that somebody would eventually write his story. First, Alexei sees casinos with a certain disdain. He will first gamble for a woman's love, but he will rapidly abandon this amorous preoccupation, one which takes away the seriousness of the practice.[3] So, if everything looks dirty, morally bad, pompous, false, and empty in the casino, he nonetheless signs a slave contract with the gambling practice. Actually, the gambler literally develops a relation of possession with the gaming spaces, essentially reminiscent of his person. Desire is linked to this obsession of possession, more so than to the fantasized object. The gambler will become, in many cases, aware of his own delirium only at the moment of his total dispossession and reversal of fortune.

As the gambler's identity cannot be seen as fixed, the movement seems to be one of simultaneous gain and loss. The text proposes a multiple identity defined by Régine Robin in these terms:

L'identité de soi est totalement pulvérisée. Tout est non-coïncidence entre la personne et son nom, la personne (le personage) et elle-même, sa langue et sa culture, ses actes, sa destinée. On ne sait jamais si l'on est dans le domaine de la copie ou de l'original, dans le réel (le réel supposé tel dans le texte de fiction) ou le fictif, au second ou au troisième degré. Tout se déploie sour le régime de l'dentité multiple. (1997, 89)

> [The identity of the self is totally shattered. All is non-coincidental between the person and his/her name, the person (the character) and herself, her language and her culture, her acts, her destiny. We never know if we are talking about the copy or the original, about the reality (what is seen as real within the fiction) or the fiction, at the second or third level. Everything belongs to the order of multiple identities.]

As far as Jorge and Alexei are concerned, it appears that one has to lose in order to gain. The link between gain and loss remits to the gambler/player's desire to give and hold simultaneously and to his relation to a possible *jouissance* and a concept of reality/identity. In parallel, this link, in turn, is contained in the gambler's fragmentation, between being, becoming multiple, and finding oneself one day while losing oneself the next.

Apparently unable to stop – but does he really want to? – unable to deny the circulation, the hand's movement, the gambler needs to reinvest the capital obtained almost immediately, creating in this way a form of permanent potlatch. If there is then a *perte/pérdida*, a loss of *jouissance* in the text, it is because in a world where usefulness is the only value, the *jouissance* is what is useless, and has no utility except that of *jouir/jouer*. The erotic dimension of the game is contained within the double process of ejaculation and replenishment. So, in these texts, to bet, though in an obsessive way, is possibly the quest for the ultimate orgasm, and the ultimate quest for recognizing and naming oneself. If it exists for Jorge, the erotic nature of the game disappears in the case of Alexei and Sam. Ivanovitch forgets his love and Rothstein becomes the patriarchal cold figure. In the casino, the object of desire is rapidly located outside the body.

All games displace the signifier to a point. To play, to fantasize and to phantasm, engages the player in the action of tripping more than falling while waiting for the good number and luck. Loss, ruin, and debt (and identities) reproduce an economy based on falseness first, and on desire and need second – the need to lose but, above all, to lose oneself, to *trans* (transfer) beyond the limits of the rational and beyond meaning. To believe in hazard, chance, and luck is to place oneself outside the divine order and the father's discourse. Alexei condemns vehemently the German tradition attached to the father figure, the family, and the accumulation of money:

[E]verywhere among these people every house has its *Vater*, dreadfully virtuous and exceedingly honest. So honest, in fact, that it's terrible to go near him. I can't stand people who are so honest it's terrible to go near them. Every one of those *Vaters* has a family, and in the evening they all read improving books aloud to one another.... They all work like slaves and they all scrape up money like Jews. (Dostoyevsky 1966, 41)

The accumulation of wealth is obviously problematic to the gambler who believes in risking it all. Sam and Alexei have neither past nor family: transplanted into the gaming culture, they become their own reference, one without meaning. What matters is that the vacuum to which they are exposed offers all the possible combinations.

The two protagonists of *Nueve reinas* [*Nine Queens*] explore all these possible combinations. In this wonderful film, the game takes place in the street, and the dealing or bargaining takes place in a very elegant hotel reminiscent of a casino. The director, Bielinsky, portrays two con artists engaged in a series of twists and turns to make a fortune by selling a forgery of nine Weimar-era stamps (the Nine Queens of the title) to a rich collector who must leave the country the next morning. It is "una oportunidad en un millón, una en la vida" ["one opportunity in a million, one in a life time"]. The stamps get stolen and, given the tense relation between the two thieves (Juan and Marcos), the spectator wonders who is really scamming whom. The conclusion shows that the one who controlled, in his mind, the whole game, the one who initiated the other, turns out to be the big loser. The whole coup is arranged from the very beginning, although the spectator is kept in the dark. As the film progresses, we start understanding that the movie sets up a number of games based on impressions, illusions, transfers, lies, and cheating. It is as if all that matters is to let the other believe that he really was on top of the game. The player's position appears to be a total illusion, partly because his position is not clearly defined and partly because the main player does not know that his partner knows more than him. As it turns out, everybody (the friend, the sister, the expert, and the partner) is involved and has been preparing the fall of Marcos, the main character.

Nueve reinas does not insist on a solitary gambler even if there is a tentative attempt by Marcos to control the scene. The film accentuates the elaboration of a game by a team. However, this group hides behind the camera, waiting to play the final hand of poker that will "freeze" the original gambler in an anxiety crisis. In a way, we learn that a collective effort manages to deconstruct the image of the great gambler, supposedly knowledgeable and sure of himself. Through the representation of a common medieval motif of the "engañador engañado" [betrayer betrayed], *Nueve reinas* enacts a vibrant switch of identities. Juan ends up with the money, the girl, the friends, the self-esteem, the pride, the laugh, and the future, while Marcos keeps yelling in front of the bank, not yet aware of his humiliating situation, buried in debts, stuck in his past, unable to transform himself into the image that he initially projected. Of course, both men have been lying to each other all along. Each partner has been playing a role (one the master and the other a pupil) that invents a never-ending story (one of teaching and learning). Each pose was from the beginning a fallacy. So, when they exchange identities, the spectator is faced with a new reality. In the end, it becomes obvious that this so-called reality was never anything but a gambling act and that identity (identities) is (are) forever interchangeable.

The first thing that every gambler/player puts on the table and risks losing is precisely his/her identity. As long as the player hangs onto his fixed self, he will keep losing. In *Nueve Reinas*, Marcos loses because he has been setting his own rules, unconscious of the rules of probability. Juan wins partly because he hides his strategy and partly because he plays with a team but, above all, he wins because he does not trust chance. He sets the rules of the game himself. The rules of all games challenge the laws of capitalism, logic, and semantics. Evidently, the text does not break or blow the bank, but money, as well as meaning, is displaced every day. Ultimately, it is on meaning and on personal identity, as well as on the power of money, work, life, desire, and dreams, that the player bets. To bet or not to bet: either prospect contains its share of fiction and reality. Every player's gesture is polysemic and promises the sliding of past and future, escapades, expectations, and long periods of waiting. Each spoken word is a Pascal's wager, a dialogue or an addiction.

If in *Nueve Reinas* the game is played on the basis of treachery, and in *Casino* it is played in the name of control, repression, and faith, gambling belongs to an obsessive quest for the self and a form of mental sickness (hysteria, schizophrenia, or psychosis) in Dostoyevsky and Peri Rossi's novels. Through the paradigm of gambling/play, a brief look at these four texts, which belong to different periods and genres (the two novels from the nineteenth and twentieth centuries, the two relatively recent films from Argentina and the United States), shows how impossible it is to reduce the concept of identity to fixed categories. This is why I choose to examine the concept of identity within the lens of a socio-cultural practice instead of concentrating exclusively on the political-cultural Latin American perspective.

Even though it is relatively easy to define the gambler prototype through a series of stereotypes or clichés, the texts examined in this essay reveal a perceptible movement and displacement of subjectivities, visible in the apparent pursuit of money or chance. In fact, all categories of identification (origin, nationality, language, race, class, culture, and gender) can be read in these narratives through the gambling practice itself. However, equally a border or edge narrative, gambling represents, to a degree, the ultimate challenge of relocating identities: every player bets on displacement, absolute (or total lack of) control, limits, pride, pleasure, indifference, escape, and, above all, territory that is the place of the subject. Gambling implies precisely a constant relocating of the dice, a permanent questioning of chances, possibilities and probabilities, a certainty about uncertainties and inabilities, to establish once and for all the name of the game or the name of the subject. For the gambler, there is no origin and there is no death; the identity resides in the rupture of all social codes and the continuity of the game.

Works Cited

Aquin, Hubert. 1992. *Journal*. Ed. Bernard Beugnot. Montreal: Leméac.

Dostoyevsky, Fyodor. 1966. *The Gambler Bobok: A Nasty Story*. London: Penguin.

García-Pinto, Margarita. 1986. La identidad cultural de la vanguardia en Latinoamérica. In *Identidad cultural de Iberoamérica en su literatura*, ed. S. Yurkievich, 102–10. Madrid: Alhambra.

Montaldo, Graciela. 1999. *Ficciones culturales y fábulas de identitad en América Latina*. Rosario, Argentina: Beatriz Viterbo.

Ouellet, Pierre. 2002. Preface. In *Identités narratives : Mémoire et Perception*, ed. P. Ouellet, S. Harel, J. Lupien, and A. Nouss, 1–4. Sainte-Foy: Les Presses de l'Université Laval.

Pascal, Blaise. 1960. *Les Pensées*. Trans. John Warrington. London: Dent.

Peri Rossi, Cristina. 1992. *La última noche de Dostoievski*. Madrid: Grijalbo Mondadori.

Rescher, Nicholas. 1997. The Philosophers of Gambling. In *Essays in the History of Philosophy*, ed. Nicholas Rescher, 149–66. Avebury, Aldershot, England: Ashgate.

Robin, Régine. 1994. Défaire les identités fétiches. In *La question identitaire au Canada francophone: Récits, parcours, enjeux, hors-lieux*, ed. J. Létourneau, 215–39. Sainte-Foy: Les Presses de l'Université Laval.

———. 1997. *Le Golem de l'écriture: De l'autofiction au Cybersoi*. Montreal: XYZ.

Films

Casino. Directed by Martin Scorcese. Universal, 1995.
Nueve reinas [*Nine Queens*]. Directed by Fabián Bielinsky. Sony, 2000.

Notes

1   All translations are mine.

2   Ironically, Sam's Jewish identity is totally erased, reaffirming the importance of eliminating any defining element that could reveal his personality.

3   Aside from "Dame Fortune" and "Lady Luck," women do not traditionally belong to the gambling culture unless serving as wives, lovers, counselors, artifacts, décor, and sex objects. Obviously, in the gambling economy, there are today as many women as men playing in Las Vegas casinos, but on the floor, the masculine/feminine is not a pertinent category. Men and women are kinds of neutral robots who have no gender. However, the feminine body is strongly validated in the context of attraction/seduction/incentive.

NOTES ON CONTRIBUTORS

NAYIBE BERMÚDEZ BARRIOS is an assistant professor of Spanish at the University of Calgary. She earned a B.A. in Translation and a Master of Arts in Education from the Moscow Linguistics University (formerly known as the Maurice Thorez Institute for Foreign Languages [1988]), a Master of Arts degree in Spanish from the University of Arkansas in Fayetteville (1996), and a Ph.D. in Spanish from the University of Kansas in Lawrence (2004). She currently teaches Latin American film and literature, translation, and culture classes. Bermúdez Barrios is now working on a project tentatively titled "Lesbian Representation in Latin American Film and Literature." She has published in *Caribe*, a U.S. publication, and in *Revista de Fuego* of Mexico. Her article *"Ilona llega con la lluvia* de Sergio Cabrera: representación, dialogismo y negociación" ["Sergio Cabrera's *Ilona llega con la lluvia*: representation, dialogism and negotiation"] will shortly appear in the Colombian *Revista de la Universidad de Antioquia*. Her article "Memorias y melodrama: la negociación en *Novia que te vea* de Rosa Nissán" has been accepted for publication in the *Revista Canadiense de Estudios Hispánicos*.

NORMAN CHEADLE is an associate professor of Hispanic Studies and chair of the Department of Modern Languages and Literatures at Laurentian University. His publications include *The Ironic Apocalypse in the Novels of Leopoldo Marechal* (Tamesis, 2000). He is currently working on a SSRHC-funded project to produce a critical edition of Leopoldo Marechal's *Adán Buenosayres* in English translation.

RITA DE GRANDIS is an associate professor of Spanish American Literature and Comparative Literature at the University of British Columbia. She teaches in the Department of French, Hispanic and Italian Studies and for the Latin American Studies program. Her areas of specialization include modern and contemporary Latin American literature, particularly narrative, literary theory, cultural and gender criticism. She is the author of *Polémica y estrategias narrativas en América Latina* (1993), and co-editor of *Questioning Hybridity in the Americas* (co-edited with Zilà Bernd Rodopi, 1999). She also was the invited editor of the special issue on the cinema of Argentinean filmmaker, María Luisa Bemberg, for *Revista Canadiense de Estudios Hispánicos* (2002). She similarly edited *Relaciones entre cine y literaturas hispánicas*, for ANCLAJES, *Revista del Instituto de Análisis Semiótico del Discurso* (2000), and the special issue on *Eva Perón: Variations on a Myth*, for *Journal of the Canadian Association of Latin American and Caribbean Studies* (1999). She has published numerous articles in refereed journals in Canada, Argentina, Chile, Brazil, Cuba, Peru, Puerto Rico, Spain, the United States, and Israel.

CATHERINE DEN TANDT is an independant scholar. She lives on a farm on the Niagara Escarpment near Georgian Bay and grows organic vegetables with her husband and two daughters. Her research focuses on the literature and cultures of the Hispanic Caribbean, specifically contemporary literary production in the context of globalization. She has written on the cultural politics of Québec and Puerto Rico, women's writing, race and identity in Puerto Rico, and popular music in the Caribbean. Research for this article was supported by the Social Sciences and Humanities Research Council of Canada.

PAOLA S. HERNÁNDEZ is an assistant professor in the Department of Spanish and Portuguese at the University of Wisconsin-Madison. Her field of research is Latin American theatre and performance, specializing on issues of identity, memory, nation building, gender and border crossings. Her teaching focuses on theatre as both a literary and performance art, bringing together the text, the stage and the representation. Her publications are forthcoming in specialized theatre journals. *Latin American Theatre Review* and *Gestos*. She is currently working on her manuscript titled: "Staging Historical Memory and Cultural Identity in the Southern Cone: Latin American Theatre in a Globalized Context."

ELIZABETH MONTES GARCÉS is an assistant professor in the Department of French, Italian and Spanish at the University of Calgary. She earned her M.A. and Ph.D. from the University of Kansas in 1993. She has held several teaching positions at the University of Texas at El Paso, the University of Lethbridge, and the University of Arkansas at Little Rock. She was hired at the University of Calgary in 2000. She is currently the secretary of the Canadian Association of Hispanists and has been very involved in organizing the 39th and 40th CAH congresses in Halifax, Nova Scotia, and Winnipeg, Manitoba. She also organized the conferences *State and Society in Latin America* (University of Calgary, 30 January 2003) and *Negotiating Identities in Latin American Cultures* (University of Calgary, 30–31 January 2004) with Professor Hendrik Kraay. She has read papers at several conferences in the United States, Canada, Europe, and Latin America. Her area of expertise is Latin American women's writing. Her book *El cuestionamiento de los mecanismos de representación en la novelística de Fanny Buitrago* was published by Peter Lang in 1997. She has published several articles on Fanny Buitrago, Rosario Sanmiguel, Minerva Margarita Villarreal, Soledad Acosta de Samper, and Carmen Boullosa in prestigious journals such as *Texto crítico, Letras femeninas*, and *Revista de Literatura Mexicana Contemporánea*. She is a dual citizen of Colombia and Canada.

MYRIAM OSORIO is an assistant professor of Spanish at Memorial University of Newfoundland. She was the recipient of a 2002 National Endowment for the Humanities Fellowships for the summer institute entitled "Gendering the Americas: Beyond Cultural and Geographical Boundaries" at Arizona State University. She has presented conference papers in the United States and Canada on the work of Albalucía Angel. Her current research focuses on photographs of women smoking and producing cigars and their depiction in Cuban literature.

CLAUDINE POTVIN is a professor in the Department of Modern Languages and Cultural Studies at the University of Alberta. She teaches the languages, cultures, and literatures of Quebec and Latin America, women's writings, feminist literary criticism, and gender theory, as well as visual arts. She has published a book on medieval Castilian poetry, two collections of short stories (*Détails* and *pornographies*), numerous articles and fiction in various journals, and edited two collections of essays (*Women's Writings and the Literary Institution* and *Angéline de Montbrun*). She has organized three conferences on literature and women's studies issues. Currently, she is preparing a book on Latin American women writers, a study on museum narratives in Quebec literature, and a novel.

MERCEDES ROWINSKY-GEURTS is an associate professor at Wilfrid Laurier University in Waterloo, Ontario. She has published, among others: *Imagen y discurso. El estudio de las imágenes en la obra de Cristina Peri Rossi* (Montevideo: Trilce, 1997), which was awarded a special mention by the Ministry of Education and Culture in Uruguay in 1998. In 2002, together with Angelo Borrás, she published a translation of Cristina Peri Rossi's *Indicios pánicos, Panic Signs* (Waterloo: Waterloo University Press, 2002). This translation was awarded the Gold Medal for Fiction in Translation by *ForeWord Magazine* in 2003. In the same year, she published an edition of Cristina Peri Rossi's articles entitled, *El pulso del mundo. Artículos periodísticos: 1978–2002* (Montevideo: Trilce, 2003). This book was among the best sellers in Uruguay for the first three weeks of August 2003. In 2000, she was awarded the Wilfrid Laurier University Outstanding Teacher Award and in 2005 she was awarded the Faculty Mentoring Award in recognition of outstanding mentorship and support to undergraduate students while students are completing independent research as part of their degree requirements. She has also published many articles in national and international journals. Currently, she is working on a monograph entitled, *The Price of Exile: Stepping Into a Writers' World. Cristina Peri Rossi's Letters to Her Mother, 1974–2004*, which will be published by Ediciones Trilce in Montevideo, Uruguay in 2007.

LUIS TORRES is an associate professor of Spanish in the Department of French, Italian and Spanish at the University of Calgary. He is originally from Chile and came to Canada as a political exile in 1977. He is the author of a number of articles on Latin-American literature and of the book *Discurso indeterminado/discurso obsceno: El obsceno pájaro de la noche de José Donoso* (Concepción, Chile: Literatura Americana Reunida, 2001). He is also the author of *El exilio y las ruinas* (Santiago, Chile: Red Internacional del Libro, 2002), a collection of poems that received an honorary mention at the annual literary competition held by the Cuban cultural institution Casa de las Américas in 2000.

RICHARD YOUNG is emeritus professor of Spanish and Latin American Studies at the University of Alberta. His publications include books on Lope de Vega, Agustín Yáñez, Alejo Carpentier, and Julio Cortázar, and numerous chapters and articles on Latin American (especially Argentinean) literature and culture. His most recent volume is *Contemporary Latin American Cultural Studies* (London: Arnold, 2003), co-edited with Stephen Hart (University of London). He is preparing a historical dictionary of Latin American literature in collaboration with Odile Cisneros and current projects also include work on urban cultures in Latin America and representations of Buenos Aires in recent Argentinean fiction.

INDEX

Clytemnestra, 5, 100–107, 111–12
Cohen, Anthony P., 85
Collect Call (Urbina), 57, 62, 67, 77
Colombia, 3, 172
Colombo, Juan Carlos, 156
Communauté Désoeuvrée, La (Carroll), 78
community, 55–79, 137, 218
    and localities, 2, 67–69, 71–72, 79
    loss of, 56, 59, 63, 72, 74
    of memory, 74–77, 79
    of the nation, 72–73
    and poetry, 4, 63, 74–76, 78
"Community after Devastation" (Carroll), 77
consumerism, 225–26, 223
Convivio (Catholic publication), 21
Cornell, Drucilla, 162
Corominas, Joan, 55
Correspondence with Ana María Moix (Peri Rossi), 88
Cortázar, Julio, 17–18, 43, 44, 86
Cortés, Hernán, 5–6, 110–11, 119–20, 122, 126–27
Creative Industries (Caves), 192
créolité, 6, 204
criollismo, criollos, 14, 17, 26–27
Crisol (magazine), 20
Crisol de tiempo (Torres-Recinos), 61
Criterio (Catholic publication), 20
Cualquier míercoles soy toya (Santos Febres), 202
Cuba, 186, n9, 195, 197
Cuban Revolution, 21, 186n9, 187n15
"Culpa es de los tlaxcaltecas, La" (Garro), 6, 117–18, 123, 124, 127, 130. See also Garro
culture, cultural industries, 1–8
    in Argentina, 14–20, 24, 29, 35–37
    and the Caribbean, 193, 201, 204
    and García Canclini, 170–71, 173–82, 225
    and globalization, 81n2, 176–77, 190n28, 191–98, 218, 224
    and identity, 63, 192–98, 201, 224
    and intellectuals, 168–70, 176–81, 193–95
    and Latin America, 167–83, 189n25, 194
    and literature, 191–98, 201, 208–9, 212
    and Marechal, 16–20
    mass, 7, 176–77, 179–81, 190nn28, 31, 194
    and modernity, 19, 181, 188n18, 200, 209
    and national identity, 193–96
    and neo-liberalism,178, 199, 201, 219
    and postmodernity, 178, 181, 198–204, 207–12, 219, 225
    and Rama, 16–20, 180, 193

and Scalbrini Ortiz, 14, 16–17, 24, 29
and Sirena Silena, 201, 204, 208–9
and the state, 171, 174
"world culture," 225–26
Culture Offers Work (Stolovich and Mourelle), 179
Cypess, Sandra Messinger, 117, 118
Czechoslovakia, 133, 137, 139, 151–52, 155

D

Damasio, Antonio R., 92–93
DaMatta, Roberto A., 224, 227
dance
    Ameroindian, 118
    Mesoamerican, 122–23, 128–29
Dante Alighieri, 220
Dash, Michael J., 193, 203, 220
De chácharas y largavistas (Etcheverry), 62, 67, 77, 82n8
De cuerpo entero (Rodríguez), 67
De Grandis, Rita, 8, 167
De la Campa, Román, 194, 219
De Lauretis, Teresa, 138–39, 165n5
Del Carrill, Hugo, 42
Delgado-Costa, José, 204
De Maetzú, Ramiro, 21
Den Tandt, Catherine, 6–7, 8, 191, 194
desarticulación/disarticulation, 85–87, 88–89, 97n1
devils of Ocumicho, 177, 188n23
Diablo Guardián (Velasco), 196
diaspora, 61, 64, 66–67, 71, 82n13, 173
Díaz del Castillo, Bernal, 110, 126–27
Díaz, Luciano A., 60
Díaz, Luis Felipe, 202, 204
Discépelo, Armando, 17, 39, 42
Discours antillais, Le (Glissant), 6, 203
displacement, 85, 86, 117, 131n1
    and community, 55–56, 59, 66–67, 73, 77, 79
    and exile, 55–56, 63, 66, 73, 77
    and identity, 2, 4, 7
    territorial, 55, 63, 73, 243
    and trauma, 56–57, 71, 73
Dissanayake, Wimal, 192
Divina Comedia (Dante), 220
Docherty, Thomas, 62
Dombasle, Arielle, 135, 164n1
Dominican Republic, 196, 202, 208
Dostoyevsky, Fyodor, 7, 233, 239, 241, 242
Dos veces Alicia/Alice Twice Over (Ángel), 99
Dujovne Ortiz, Alicia, 35–52
    and the city, 36–37, 48–49

Fernández Moreno, César, 8, 167, 168–70, 181, 184n1
Fernández Retamar, Roberto, 168
Ferré, Rosario, 7, 197, 202, 203
Ficciones culturales y fábulas de identidad (Montaldo), 235
fiction. *See* literature
Follari, Roberto A., 182
FORJA (Fuerza de Orientación Radical de la Joven Argentina), 22
Foster, David William, 23
Foundational Fictions (Sommers), 206
France
  and Buenos Aires, 4, 35–37, 40, 43–51
  Paris, 7, 35–49
  Toulouse, 37
Franceschi, Gustavo J., 20
Franco Ramos, Jorge, 196
Franco, Jean, 127
Frank, Thomas, 209
Freud, Sigmund, 15, 103, 115n9
Froula, Christine, 103
FTAA (Free Trade Agreement for the Americas), 172
Fuerza de Orientación Radical de la Joven Argentina. See FORJA
Fuguet, Alberto, 195, 200, 212

G

Galasso, Norberto, 22
Galeano, Eduardo, 86
Gambler, The (Dostoyevsky), 7, 233, 237–39
gambling, 7, 233–43
  and *Casino* (motion picture), 7, 233, 235–37, 242
  and Dostoyevsky, 233, 239, 241, 242
  The Gambler, 7, 233, 237–39
  and guilt, 236, 238
  and identity, 234–36, 238–43
  and Las Vegas, 233, 236, 244n3
  as metaphor, 234
  and *Nueve reinas* (motion picture), 7, 233, 241–43
  and Peri Rossi, 233, 237–39, 242
  and reality, 240, 242
  and Scorcese, 7, 233, 235–36
  and self, 234–35, 237, 240
  and *Última noche de Dostoievski, La* (Peri Rossi), 7, 233, 237–39
García Canclini, Néstor, 8, 167–83, 194, 217, 225
  and capitalism, 170–71
  and the cultural industry, 170–71, 176–80, 182, 225

and diasporas, 173
and the essay genre, 170–71, 173, 175–79, 182, 184n1
and *La globalización imaginada*, 171–72
and globalization, 170–78, 180–82, 217
and hybridity, 175, 186n12, 189n25, 190n32
and intellectuals, 167, 170–71, 173–82, 186n9
and Latin American identity, 170–75, 181–82, 185n3, 194
Latinoamericanos buscando lugar en este siglo, 8, 167, 170, 173, 176–78, 181–82
and mass culture, 176–77, 179–82, 190n31
and memory, 176, 178
and migration, 171
and neo-liberalism, 170–78
and populism, 174, 180, 186n9, 190n28
and the state, 171, 174, 179, 182
and the subaltern, 178, 189nn24, 25, 190n29
and a transnational community, 175, 177, 181, 186n11
García Cuevas, Eugenio, 200
García-Pinto, Magdalena, 239
Gardel, Carlos
  death of, 38, 40, 51
  lover of Mireille/Mireya, 35, 37, 49
  and "Tiempos viejos," 41–42
Garden of Eden, 5, 100, 108
Gardes, Berthe, 38, 40
Garro, Elena, 6, 117–30
  and Aztec mythology, 117–19, 121–24, 129–30
  "La culpa es de los tlaxcaltecas," 6, 117–30
  and displacement, 117, 131n1
  and gender, 6, 121, 130
  and male/female roles, 117–30
  and Malinche, 6, 117–20, 122–23, 126–29, 131n5
  and Mexican identity, 117–19, 121, 123–24, 127, 130
  La semana de colores, 117
  and Tenochtitlan, 117, 119–21, 125, 127, 130
  and time, 6, 117, 128, 131n1
gauchos, 3, 14, 182
Gavaldón, Roberto, 139, 140
gender, 2–9, 118, 165n5
  in Las Andariegas (Ángel), 99–112
  in *"La culpa es de los tlaxcaltecas"* (Garro), 6, 121, 130
  and Mireille/Mireya, 35, 37

Puerto Rican, 195, 203, 205, 208
and Rama, 15–17, 193, 200
and representation, 9, 52, 55, 63–70,
83n15, 193
and transition, 199, 201, 212
travel writing, 99–100, 117, 168
Lloyd, David, 192
Loaeza, Guadalupe, 6, 133–34, 136, 141–43,
164n1
localities, 2, 35, 66, 82n10
and community, 59, 63, 65, 68, 72, 79
and exile, 56, 62, 66, 70–71, 78–79
and spaces, 59, 62–63, 65–66, 70
López de Gómara, Francisco, 126
López Pacheco, Jesús, 61, 72, 74
Lost Rib, The, (Magnarelli), 106
Lowe, Lisa, 192
Lubezki, Emmanuel, 140–42, 144, 147–53,
156–60
Lugones, Leopoldo, 14, 17
Luis Cardoza y Aragón Foundation Essay
Prize, 170, 185n7
Lyotard, Jean-François, 77

M

"Madame Ivonne" (tango song), 43–44
Magnarelli, Sharon, 106
Malinche, La
in *Las Andariegas* (Ángel), 110
in *"La culpa es de los tlaxcaltecas,"* 5–6,
117–20, 122–23, 126–29, 131n5
in Díaz del Castillo, 116n28
and Max Harris, 114n6
*Malinche, La (*Núñez Becerra), 127
"Malinche Paradigm as Subject, The"
(Cypess), 117
Malkki, Liisa H, 4, 56, 64, 65, 71, 74
Marechal, Leopoldo, 3, 4, 13–29
and *Adán Buenosayres*, 3, 13, 17–19,
21–22, 25–29, 33n21
and Argentinian identity, 13–19, 26–29
and the "Buenos Aires Man,"13–14, 18,
29, 33n23
"Claves de Adán Buenosayres," 19
and Catholicism, 21–22, 28–29
and *criollismo*, 26–27
and cultural hegemony, 16–20
and "Espíritu de la Tierra," 26
and immigrants, 14, 26
and metaphysics, 19
and Peronism, 19
Rama on, 13–14, 17–18, 20, 32nn9, 10, 11
and Sarlo, 13

and Scalabrini Ortiz, 13–15, 25–29, 31n5,
33n23
and sexuality, 25
Mariátegui, José Carlos, 174
marginalization, 7, 17, 76–77, 208
and exile, 55, 62, 69, 82n8
and globalization, 217, 221, 228
Maritain, Jacques, 21
Martí, José, 178
Martínez, Erik, 60
Martínez Estrada, Ezequiel, 31n7
martinfierristas, 14, 22, 25
Marx, Karl, 180, 192
mass culture. *See also* populism
and cultural studies, 7, 176–77, 179–81,
190nn28, 31, 194
and the intellectual, 179–82, 188n22,
190nn28, 31
and literature, 7, 181, 190n31, 194
mass media
and culture, 212, 226
and globalization, 7, 9
and literature, 7, 11n3, 190n31, 205
Mastreta, Angeles, 11n3
*Me llamo Rigoberto Menchú y así me nació
la conciencia* (Menchú), 199
memory, 102, 117, 176, 178
communities of, 4, 74–79
and exile, 86–87, 92–94, 97n3
and *Mireya*, 37, 46
and *Miroslava*, 149–50
and self, 86–87, 92–94, 235
Menchú, Rigoberta, 185n5, 199
MERCOSUR, 172
Mesoamerican dances, 122–23, 128–29
Mesquita, Ivo, 219
metaphor, 19, 211, 234
dwelling, 67, 69, 78, 79
unhealable rift, 67–70, 78
uprooted tree, 63–65, 69–70, 82n12, 85
Mexico City, 117–18, 131n4
Mexico, Mexicans, 6, 117–20, 123–27, 130.
See also Aztecs; Spanish Conquest
cinema, 133, 161, 164n1, 165nn10, 12
Conquest, 101, 110, 126, 130
in *"La Culpa es de los tlaxcaltecas"*
(Garro), 6, 117–18, 123, 130
identity, 6, 109, 117–18, 141, 162, 165n10
Revolution, 127, 129
Mignolo, Walter D., 22
migration, 2–4, 171, 173, 174 (*see also*
immigration)
Miller, Nicola, 27
Miranda, Carmen, 224

TURNING POINTS

Occasional Papers in Latin American Studies Series

ISSN 1716-9429

Christon I. Archer, general editor

This series is a joint venture with the Latin American Research Centre at the University of Calgary (LARC), and is intended to reflect the wide range of issues with which the Centre is concerned. Since the signing of NAFTA, political and economic linkages between Canada and Latin America have increased greatly, a trend which has seen Alberta companies investing heavily in the new opportunities that have arisen. Turning Points will focus on such topics as Latin American economics, trade, and politics, as well history, literature, and anthropology. The publications will stem mainly from papers resulting from conferences and scholarly research.

Trade Negotiations in Agriculture: A Future Common Agenda for Brazil and Canada? · Edited by William Kerr and James Gaisford · No. 1

Relocating Identities in Latin American Cultures · Edited By Elizabeth Montes Garcés · No. 2